REKINDLING THE TORCH
THE STORY OF CANADIAN ZIONISM

David J. Azrieli

WITH THE COLLABORATION OF Joe King AND AN INTRODUCTION BY Gil Troy

KEY PORTER BOOKS

Library and Archives Canada Cataloguing in Publication

Azrieli, David J., 1922-
    Rekindling the torch : the story of Canadian Zionism / David J. Azrieli ; with the collaboration of Joe King and Gil Troy.

Includes index.
ISBN 978-1-55263-977-1

    1. Zionism—Canada—History. 2. Jews—Canada—History. 3. Jews, Canadian—Israel. I. King, Joe, 1923- II. Troy, Gil III. Title.

DS149.5.C3A97 2008   320.54095694'0971   C2007-904784-X

The publisher gratefully acknowledges the support of the Canada Council for the Arts and the Ontario Arts Council for its publishing program. We acknowledge the support of the Government of Ontario through the Ontario Media Development Corporation's Ontario Book Initiative.

We acknowledge the financial support of the Government of Canada through the Book Publishing Industry Development Program (BPIDP) for our publishing activities.

Every reasonable effort has been made to find ownership of copyrighted materials.

Frontispiece: An illuminated Israeli flag decorates the Azrieli Towers in the Mediterranean city of Tel Aviv on April 28, 2008 as part of celebrations marking the creation of Israel 60 years ago. Israel was founded on May 14, 1948, but independence is celebrated from sundown on May 7 to the following evening in accordance with the Hebrew lunar calendar. (JACK GUEZ/AFP/Getty Images)

Key Porter Books Limited
Six Adelaide Street East, Tenth Floor
Toronto, Ontario
Canada M5C 1H6

www.keyporter.com

Text design: Martin Gould
Electronic formatting: Jean Peters

Printed and bound in Canada

08 09 10 11 12 5 4 3 2 1

Contents

Preface

The great bulk of the Jewish people have, throughout their history, remained faithful to the dream of a restoration of their national life in Judea.

—Lucien Wolf, *Encyclopaedia Britanica*, 1910

THE STRUGGLE TO RE-ESTABLISH the Jewish homeland began twenty centuries ago when the Romans expelled most of the Jews from the Kingdom of Judea, the southern portion of the land now known as Israel. This is the story of the role that Canadians—Jews and non-Jews alike—have played in more than a century of dedicated efforts to re-create a Jewish state and ensure its survival in that embattled corner of the earth.

Even before Theodor Herzl inspired hundreds at the First Zionist Congress in Basel, Switzerland, in 1897, and crystallized the worldwide Zionist movement to restore the Jews to their homeland, many Canadians had already raised the banner of Jewish nationhood. In the early years of the twentieth century, Zionists created Canada's first national Jewish organization. Some thirty years later, two Canadians, Mr. Justice Ivan C. Rand and Prime Minister Lester Bowles Pearson, served on the UN Special Committee on Palestine and became godfathers to a nation yet unborn.

When Israel's return to the family of nations after the Second World War touched off a massive assault by five well-armed and highly trained Arab armies, Canadians were among those who shouldered weapons in defence of the nascent country. The story of Canadian Zionism that emerges in these pages also includes the names of hundreds of Canadians who have, since 1948, joined Machal, foreign volunteers in the Israeli armed forces—Canadians who have fought and given their lives for the survival of the Jewish nation.

The remarkable accomplishments of Canadian Zionists have been felt in many other ways throughout the tiny land of Israel: in the arts and sciences, business and education, on all seven university campuses, and in the forests lovingly planted on once-barren hills. Their extraordinary contributions to the Jewish state on an organizational and individual basis have inspired industrial development and influenced the way Israelis live.

More than a decade ago, when I served as president of the Canadian Zionist Federation, I promised myself that this exceptional story would be told, that the outstanding figures in Canadian Zionist history would be identified and their accomplishments described. I would like to thank Gil Troy who carefully reviewed the original manuscript and wrote an introducion. I am also grateful to Andrea Knight and Naomi Azrieli who edited and updated the manuscript in 2008. The indefatigable and talented Joe King added the photographs, captions, and anecdotal sidebars, and prepared the biographical snapshots in "The ABCs of Canadian Zionism." Joe's deep storehouse of knowledge, his keen eye, and his vivid style have enriched the project immeasurably. All of our work stands on the shoulders of many excellent scholars who have studied Canadian Jewry and who, in an academic work, would be properly credited in footnotes. We are especially indebted to Eugene Rothman, who added so much to an earlier draft, and to the others who have explained the rich history of Canadian Jewry to the rest of us, including Louis Rosenberg, Stuart E. Rosenberg, Arthur Daniel Hart, Irving Abella, Michael Brown, Gerald Tulchinsky, David J. Bercuson, Michael Marrus, Harold Troper, Harold Waller, and Morton Weinfeld, among others. For her invaluable help in preparing the materials for the manuscript in the early 1990s, I would like to thank Glenna Uline.

This project represents the deep passion that many Canadian Jews have for the Jewish state and Jewish nationalism. In researching and writing this book, we have delved into dusty archives and jogged the memories of many of the principals to ensure that this account is as thorough as possible. It is my hope that what follows provides a record of the unique and important ways in which Canadians have been partners in the historic reappearance of a Jewish state after an absence of two thousand years.

David J. Azrieli

Introduction

AS ISRAEL MARKS THE SIXTIETH anniversary of its founding, Canadian Zionists have much to celebrate. Throughout the nation-building process Canadian Jews and non-Jews have been instrumental in helping to fulfil Zionism's six main achievements:

- re-establishing Jewish sovereignty in the Jewish homeland;
- offering a welcoming Jewish home to Holocaust survivors, refugees from Arab lands, and other oppressed Jews;
- returning the Jews to history, transforming Jews' image from the world's victims to actors on history's stage, with rights and responsibilities;
- building a Western-style capitalist democracy with a strong Jewish flavour and a dynamic Jewish culture;
- reviving and modernizing Hebrew;
- making Israel a central force in revitalizing Jewish secular and religious life in the Jewish homeland and abroad.

Zionism, meaning Jewish nationalism, began as a European initiative in the nineteenth century that was focused on building Israel in the twentieth century. Yet the destruction of the European Jewish community in the 1940s, and the Jewish communities in the Arab lands shortly thereafter, shifted the historical focus of the Diaspora to North America. In this first decade of the twenty-first century, part of Zionism's proud past, and certainly the key to its future beyond Israel, lies with both American and Canadian Jewry.

Today, Canada may be the "Little Engine That Could" in the Zionist world. One of the most exciting Zionist-oriented initiatives of the last decade, birthright israel, was started in part by Canadian philanthropist Charles R. Bronfman. As of this writing, thanks to this wonderful program, 160,000 eighteen to twenty-six-year-olds have been given the opportunity to experience Israel in both peaceful and less-than-peaceful times. The most impressive Israeli office complex that dominates the Tel Aviv skyline, the Azrieli Towers, was designed and developed by the Canadian entrepreneur David Azrieli, who also coined the Hebrew word for malls—*kanyon*—when he opened the first mall in Israel in 1985.

In addition to these extraordinary endeavours, the Canadian Jewish community has consistently proved itself disproportionately generous and intensely engaged with Israel. Canada's Jewish day-school system is not only vibrant and popular, it continues to produce young educated Jews who are fluent in Hebrew and committed to Israel. In fact, through the Montreal-based Tal Am Tal Sela program, Canadian Jewish educators are setting the standard for teaching Hebrew throughout North America. It was the Canadian Jewish community that spearheaded the worldwide mobilization to support Israel after Palestinian terrorists murdered more than 130 Israelis in March 2002, including twenty-nine men, women, and children sitting down for a Passover seder. In downtown Montreal, an estimated 15,000 to 20,000 people gathered for a Yom Ha'atzmaut rally, raising in one night $10 million of the total $15 million in emergency funds the community collected. This outpouring from a community of less than 100,000 represented the highest ratio of participants-to-Jewish residents at any of the many rallies held around the world, as well as one of the most generous amounts of money raised per capita. The Jewish communities in Toronto, Ottawa, Winnipeg, Vancouver, and elsewhere also distinguished themselves that spring and throughout Arafat's war against the peace process.

A history of Canadian Zionism, however, provides more than a chronicle of one Diaspora community's love affair with Jewish nationalism, the Zionist idea, the Israeli reality, and the Jewish people's future. It illuminates the worldwide resonance of Theodor Herzl's Zionism more than a hundred years after he launched it at the First Zionist Congress, despite the movement's European orientation and the peculiar challenges of developing a North American Zionist language and ideology. It demonstrates the long-lasting tradition of Christian support for the Jewish national project and chronicles the nuanced position of Jewish Canadian Zionists who easily reconciled their enthusiasm for their adopted home with their passion for their people and the Jewish state. And whatever tensions there are today between some of the Left and Israel, this account shows that in Canada and in the United States progressives were often in the forefront of this movement, particularly with regard to early Zionism's contribution to modern communal living through the kibbutz and other collective endeavours.

In Canada, the centrality of multiculturalism as a concept has proved particularly hospitable to the Zionist idea. Canadian Zionists have been able to celebrate Jewish nationalism without sacrificing their Canadian identity, just as Greek Canadians and Italian Canadians freely and proudly celebrate their national origins and continuing ties. As scholars have noted, Canadian Zionism has been strengthened by operating in a bi-national context that has allowed Jews to unapologetically develop their own nationalism. In the past, Zionist fervour was often encouraged by anti-Semitism and the immigrant's sense of alienation and otherness. Today, Jewish communities that are more integrated into mainstream Canadian society nevertheless retain strong ties to the traditional Jewish homeland and to Jewish people throughout the world. Many of those national feelings are rooted in and routed through Israel.

This project came to fruition thanks to the wisdom, commitment, patience, research, perseverance, and vision of David Azrieli. Just as his sleek, gleaming Tel Aviv skyscrapers are a testament to his remarkable ability to synthesize old and new, defying sceptics to build a profitable modern business complex in the ancient Middle East, this enterprise demonstrates his commitment to learning from the past as a way of enhancing our present and building toward a future that makes relevant the very best of yesterday for use today and tomorrow.

Gil Troy

Acknowledgements

T HIS BOOK IS DEDICATED to my parents, my brother, and my sister who perished in the Shoah and to the builders of the State of Israel.

We are most grateful for the co-operation provided in the preparation of this book by the following persons and organizations: Janice Rosen and Helene Vallee, Canadian Jewish Congress National Archives, Montreal; Shannon Hodge and Eiran Harris, Jewish Public Library, Montreal; Ellen Scheinberg and Donna Bernardo-Ceriz, Ontario Jewish Archives, Toronto; Mordechai Ben-Dat and Janice Arnold, *Canadian Jewish News*, Toronto; John Jakobson, Canadiana Department, Toronto Public Library; the Jewish Heritage Centre of Western Canada, Winnipeg; Debby Shoctor, Jewish Archives and Historical Society of Edmonton and Northern Alberta; Wayne Murdoch, Provincial Archives of Alberta, Edmonton; the Jewish Historical Society of Southern Alberta, Calgary; Diane M. Rodgers, Jewish Historical Society of British Columbia, Vancouver; Library and Archives Canada, Ottawa; Brian Oickle, Ottawa; Jon Goldberg, Halifax; Sara Yablon, Sydney; Evelyn Davis, Sydney; Robin McGrath, Portugal Cove, Newfoundland; Jerry Rosenberg, Toronto; the American Veterans of Israel records maintained by Ralph Lowenstein, University of Florida, Gainesville.

PART I:

A History
of Canadian Zionism

I

Beginnings

WHAT CONSTITUTES THE BEGINNING of a movement? People love to find the one defining moment, such as Theodor Herzl's founding of the World Zionist Organization in Basel, Switzerland after the Dreyfus trial in the 1890s. Perhaps, in the case of Canadian Zionism, people could point to the emergence of a visionary leader such as Clarence de Sola. Or was it that moment in 1887 when Alexander Harkavy, Hyam Bernstein, and Lazarus Cohen established the Canadian branch of Hovevei Zion in Montreal? Or was it the formal founding of a Canadian Zionist organization, Agudath Zion, in 1898?

In the end, as with most movements that resonate widely, none of these events alone likely marked the birth of Canadian Zionism. With the benefit of more than a century of hindsight, we can see rather that it was the coming together of many beginnings a hundred or so years ago that launched the Canadian Zionist movement as an expression of Jewish national identity in Canada. But such an exercise may not be all that important. What is clearly of far greater significance is the fact that the movement made its rich and varied century-long journey parallel with the growth of the Canadian Jewish community, with the rise of the Zionist movement in Europe and in the United States, and with the evolution of Canada itself.

Jews in Canada

There were a few Jews in Canada in the eighteenth century, but Jews began to settle in Canada in appreciable numbers only in the middle of the nineteenth century. German and Central European Jews started arriving in the 1840s and 1850s, becoming the basis of the Montreal Jewish community. Spanish-Portuguese, or Sephardi, Jews joined a few decades later. By 1881, the Canadian Jewish community numbered 2,456.

The real beginnings of a Jewish community in Canada and the various expressions of its identity can be traced to Eastern Europe and the events of the 1880s. The anti-Semitic May Laws of 1882 enacted by the czarist government in Russia banned Jews from living outside the territory designated for Jews—beyond the Pale—and restricted their educational opportunities; vicious riots and pogroms accompanied the legislation. As a result, hundreds of thousands of Jews fled and sought refuge in North America, a great migration that revolutionized the Jewish world and brought many more people across the Atlantic.

Some of the immigrants found haven in the newly independent part of British North America—Canada. By 1891, the Jewish community there had more than doubled in size to 6,586. With the passing of another decade, the number had increased more than two and a half times, to nearly 17,000. In addition to Quebec, where they had originally settled, Jews had spread throughout Canada to put down roots in British Columbia, Manitoba, Ontario, and the Maritimes.

The increase in members made community life more diverse and complex, particularly in communal, social, and philanthropic activities. The first Hebrew Sick Benefit Society was established in Montreal in 1892. Jewish communal organizations soon appeared in Toronto, Winnipeg, Hamilton, and London. Montreal, the heartland of Canadian Jewry, became the seat of new national organizations.

The changes went beyond organizations, however; they touched the very core of the Canadian Jewish community's identity. Earlier Jewish settlers in Canada had come from Western or Central Europe and their origins were reflected in their culture and outlook. They were Europeans as much as they were Jews and, having adapted to European patterns of life, they often assimilated and rejected their Jewish identities.

The later arrivals were mostly poor, Yiddish-speaking Jews from Eastern Europe; of the 3,000 Jews who arrived on Canadian shores in 1899, for example, more than 2,600 were from Romania and Russia. The newcomers, generally Orthodox in their religious outlook and always exuberant in their cultural expression, transformed Canadian Jewry. Emerging from a culturally rich Eastern European existence that emphasized religion and community, they were also refugees from persecution and a social structure that exaggerated their otherness, their alienation. Together, these factors shaped a national identity and the expression of that identity—the Jewish national movement known as Zionism.

A Jewish National Identity

The idea of Jews as a people—and their connection to the land of Israel—goes back to Abraham. Throughout the five thousand years of Jewish history, "Eretz Yisrael," the land of Israel, has been central to the Jewish people. Even when all the Jews were not living on the land, they defined themselves by that land, considering themselves to be in exile from their homeland.

By the eighteenth century, Jews found themselves disillusioned with the unfulfilled promises of European liberalism. The Enlightenment had promised them freedom, order, and reason, yet had unleashed against them forces of authoritarianism, prejudice, and chauvinism. Many Jews realized that, at best, the goods the Enlightenment peddled only served individuals. "The Jews must be granted everything as individuals—but nothing as a nation," Count Clermont-Tonnerre famously told the French National Assembly of 1789. Sobered, many Jews turned instead to the Jewish Enlightenment that emerged through the eighteenth and nineteenth centuries, the Haskalah. The Maskilim, the intellectuals of the Haskalah, looked to their collective Jewish past for signposts to a better future and relief from the troubles facing European Jews.

The Jewish national movement that emerged in Europe in the mid-nineteenth century and culminated in the 1880s—the concept of the distinctiveness of Jews as a people and a nation—developed in an atmosphere of nationalist idealism that had been spreading throughout Europe since 1848. These expressions of European nationalism—which manifested in such phenomena as the unification of Germany under Otto von Bismarck, the reunification of Italy (the Resorgimento) under Giuseppe Garibaldi, and the rise of Slavic nationalism—stressed the unity of peoples and nations and the uniqueness of their cultural identities. The elements that distinguished one people from another had become more important than the elements that united them as human beings.

In Eastern Europe, language, dress, dietary restrictions, religion, and culture had long separated Jews from their neighbours. In the latter part of the nineteenth century, new nationalist ideas and expressions of Jewish uniqueness began to take hold in the cities of Eastern Europe and then trickled down to the Jewish *shtelach*, or villages, in the countryside. As the rise of anti-Semitism further alienated Jews from their surroundings, the new nationalist ideals renewed their sense of belonging to an ancient community and Jewish intellectuals sought a foundation for a Jewish national identity. While the Orthodox Jews of Eastern Europe turned to the past for a Messiah who would lead them to the perfect Jewish world, secular Jewish intellectuals looked to the rebirth of Hebrew, the re-engagement with Jewish history, and the revival of Jewish culture as vehicles for improving the Jewish condition. In the end, even if intellectuals and traditionalists did not share piety and prayer, they did have a common belief in a better world for Jews.

Early Zionism

The Jews of Eastern Europe and, to some extent, other parts of the world began to consider a return to their ancient homeland. The idea of the centrality of Zion and a new beginning in Jerusalem took hold and became an important force in the Jewish world. Pioneers from the 1830s and through the 1860s—people such as Mordecai Manuel Noah in the United States, Rabbis Zvi Hirsch Kalischer of Prussia and Yehudah Alkalai of Serbia, and the German Jewish socialist Moses Hess—became advocates for return. Hess articulated the concept in his book, *Rome and Jerusalem*, and the message spread among Jewish intellectuals throughout Europe in such journals as *Hashahar* (The Dawn) and *Hamaggid* (The Speaker).

One of the most important vehicles for expressing the ideals of early Zionism was the Hibbat Zion (Love of Zion) movement, established in the early 1880s under the leadership of Moses Leib Lillienblum and Dr. Leon Pinsker in Russia. Many Russian Jewish intellectuals felt excluded from Russian society after the introduction of the anti-Semitic May Laws

When the secret Zionist order B'nei Moshe was founded in 1889, Lazarus Cohen was the lone member from North America.

(Canadian Jewish Congress National Archives)

in 1882. Turning their focus toward their own community and the cultural traditions of the Jews of Europe, Hibbat Zion stressed the view that there was no solution for anti-Semitism or Jewish alienation in Europe. The only answer was the return of the Jews to Zion. The Bilu movement, founded by high school and university students in Kharkov in 1881, was guided by the same convictions and sent young Jewish pioneers to Palestine throughtout the 1880s. The name Bilu comes from a passage in Isaih—"*Beth Ya'aqov l'khu ve-neylkha*" (Children of Jacob, come let us go!).

Eastern European thinkers, such as Dr. Leon Pinsker, author of *Auto-Emancipation*, and Asher Ginsberg—who used the pen name Ahad Ha-Am, meaning "one of the people—lent rich and varied ideas that supported the growth of Zionism in Eastern Europe. The roots of Zionism were thus founded in the rejection experienced by Russian Jewish intellectuals and in the *shtetl* experience of Eastern Europe. It is somewhat ironic then, that the Zionist movement found its greatest leader in secular Austro-Hungarian journalist Theodor Herzl.

Theodor Herzl could hardly have started out as a less likely torch bearer for Zionism. Born in Pest in 1860, at eighteen he moved to Vienna, where he studied law and took up journalism as a profession. At one time, he even considered the possibility of mass conversion to Christianity as the solution to the Jewish problem.

However, his experiences in Paris as a journalist covering the treason trial of Alfred Dreyfus turned the assimilated Herzl into a secular Jewish prophet of near-biblical proportions. Dreyfus was a French army captain who was falsely accused and convicted of betraying his country. It is widely accepted by historians that he was both suspect and extremely unpopular because he was Jewish. When Herzl heard crowds yelling, "Death to the Jews," his vision of a secular, sophisticated, welcoming Europe

Hovevei Zion 1892

Lazarus Cohen, a Montrealer, was an important figure in the early years of Zionism. When Ahad Ha-Am founded the secret order B'nai Moshe in 1889 (in Odessa), Cohen was its only member in North America. In 1892, when a branch of Hovevei Zion (Lovers of Zion), one of European Jewry's first and most effective Zionist organizations, was formed in Montreal under the name Shavei Zion (Returnees to Zion), he was elected treasurer.

In 1894, the society delegated him to visit Palestine and look into possibilities for settlement of Canadian Jews in the Holy Land. His son, Lyon, wrote of that trip: "The visit of my father to Palestine was the first direct contact by Canadian Jews with their homeland.... He felt that the land was very suitable for plantations and that the future was very promising."

On his way home, Lazarus Cohen met in Paris with Barons Rothschild and de Hirsch and "reported favorably on colonization work in Palestine." When he returned to Canada, he reported that "the country was only awaiting its long-banished children to become again a land flowing with milk and honey."

Theodor Herzl (1860–1904), the Austra-Hungarion journalist who founded the Zionist movement in angry reaction to European anti-Semitism. Engraving by Hermann Struck, 1897.

(World Zionist Organization Archives, Jerusalem)

was shattered. So profound was the effect of the Dreyfus affair that Herzl became convinced that the Jewish people would never be fully accepted in Europe and spent the last years of his life in pursuit of what he saw as the only possible solution to the "Jewish Question"—a national homeland for the Jewish people.

The vicious anti-Semitism unleashed by the Dreyfus trial inspired Herzl to write his historic pamphlet *Der Judenstaat* (The Jewish State), which called for a meeting of the First Zionist Congress in Basel, Switzerland, in 1897. It was at that gathering that the World Zionist Organization first came into being.

Herzl's elegant European bearing gave Zionism a modern sophisticated facade that would be essential in garnering support for the movement in North America. While North American Jews were occasionally plagued with anti-Semitic outbursts, they did not experience Europe's systemic, deeply entrenched, often government-sponsored or establishment-approved anti-Semitism as a defining motivating force. Although Jews on both sides of the Atlantic usually found more motivation to organize and act when they were under attack rather than feeling comfortable, North American Zionism nevertheless achieved the greatest support—and resonated most widely—as a progressive force rather than a defensive reaction.

Judaism and Zionism

Although many members of the Orthodox Jewish community opposed Zionism in the late nineteenth and early twentieth centuries, it was not because Orthodox leaders were averse to the idea of a return to a Jewish national home centred on Zion. Instead, the disagreement arose from the Orthodox belief that the return to Zion should come "at the end of days," when the Messiah would lead the Jews from the "four corners of the earth" back to their home. In this early period, Zionism was seen to be anticipating the end of days and usurping the role of the Messiah.

20

These views were not shared by all members of the Orthodox community. Indeed, some leading members of the Orthodox community played significant roles in the birth of Zionism and the early growth of its religious stream. The Ashkenazi rabbi Zvi Kalischer of Prussia and the Sephardi rabbi Yehudah Alkalai of Serbia recognized the centrality of the idea of Israel and the need for the Jewish people to take their fate into their own hands and precipitate the Messianic Age by returning to their homeland. Moreover, the great rabbi Avraham Kook, chief Ashkenazi rabbi of Palestine in the 1920s and 1930s, became a symbol of the union of Judaism and Zionism.

Belief in such a union was also expressed by the great religious political leader Rabbi Jacob Reines in Lithuania. He played an instrumental role in the establishment of the Mizrachi (Eastern) Party, a modern Orthodox Zionist movement with educational, youth, and political arms. The link between religion and Zionism was inherent in the force behind Ha-Poel Ha-Mizrachi, founded in 1922, an Orthodox labour organization that developed religious kibbutzim. Similarly, it would be a principle of the MAFDAL—the Miflaga Datit Leumit, or National Religious Party, founded in 1956 in Israel's parliament, the Knesset. Clearly, religion and national identity were integrally linked in the minds of many leaders in Palestine and later in Israel itself. In fact, Zionism can be seen as yet another stage in the evolution of Jewish civilization based on Jewish faith, Jewish community, and the Jewish people. Zionism is the national expression of the beliefs of a people wishing to return to their home and live an autonomous and sovereign life.

The relationship between religion and Zionism in Canada was similar, where the Orthodox community was the first to accept Zionism and provide leaders for the movement, and Canadian adherents to Conservative Judaism, the branch that allowed only minor departures from traditional ritual, unquestioningly accepted the centrality of Israel to Jewish life. The same principle was subsequently adopted by the Reform movement, particularly after the Second World War. Today, all three branches of Judaism are represented in the official Canadian Zionist movement by organizations such as Mizrachi, Merkaz-Canada, and Kadima.

Alexander Harkavy, a renowned lexicographer, organized the first Zionist society in Canada in 1887, ten years before the birth of the world Zionist movement in Basel. The organization was Hovevei Zion (Lovers of Zion). Harkavy is seen here in 1920 (seated in the centre).

Early Zionism in Canada

The events that led to the emergence of Zionism in Europe also resonated in Canada, intensified by the arrival of thousands of Jewish refugees fleeing from czarist pogroms and other forms of persecution. In 1887, the famous Russian-born Jewish linguist and lexicographer Alexander Harkavy spearheaded the first organized effort to create a Zionist presence in Canada, establishing a Canadian branch of Hovevei Zion in Montreal. Some fifty men joined the group and Hyam Bernstein was elected president. Despite their enthusiasm, however, early efforts sputtered and the organization languished.

In 1892, the American Zionist community helped found a new branch of Hovevei Zion in Montreal. The new society enlisted approximately fifty members of the Montreal Jewish community, including Lazarus Cohen who became its treasurer. One of the most important leaders of Canada's early Zionist movement, Cohen quickly moved beyond organizing activities in Montreal. A year later, he led a delegation to New York to investigate the possibility of assisting Jewish settlement in Palestine. The difficulties discouraged many of his associates, but Cohen persisted, helping to raise 24,000 francs to send to Hovevei Zion members in Paris for the purchase of land in Palestine and support for Jewish settlement there.

Financial support and aliyah (immigration to Israel) were early hallmarks of Zionist activity in Canada. In 1895, two Jewish families from Canada settled in Palestine with community assistance, although the harsh conditions they encountered and the restrictions of the hostile Turkish government led them to return to Canada much discouraged. In the meantime, the funds remitted to Paris were returned to Montreal, thereby ending this early chapter in the history of the Canadian Zionist movement.

The Founding of the *Jewish Times*

In the same year that the First Zionist Congress gathered in Switzerland, the fallout from the Dreyfus affair led two Montrealers—Samuel William Jacobs and Lyon Cohen—to decide that the time had come for a Jewish periodical. The *Jewish Times* rolled off the presses on December 10, 1897, and, as Cohen related a few years later,

> The continuous growth of the community in size and importance made the need for a periodical urgent. It was imperative that a medium be created whereby the community should be brought into closer contact with the rest of Jewry....
>
> We felt that such a record of current events would be of great historical value and the achievements of prominent Jewish leaders throughout the world would inspire youth to greater ambition and effort....
>
> We were spurred to action by the Dreyfus affair. Ugly anti-Semitic articles appeared in certain local papers in commenting upon the matter and had created a certain animosity toward local Jews. We could no longer remain silent. We felt that these articles must be answered. The truth must be presented, and, although not being journalists, nor having any thought of making it a business venture, we decided to embark on the enterprise.

Lyon Cohen served as president of the Zionist Organization of Canada and Canadian Jewish Congress and co-founded (with S.W. Jacobs) the *Jewish Times* —the first Anglo-Jewish publication in Canada.

(Canadian Jewish Congress National Archives, Montreal)

From its earliest days, the *Jewish Times* was the Zionist voice of all Canadian Jewry. It was also the voice of Canadian Jewish education, social work, philanthropy, and religion.

Interestingly, the editor of the *Jewish Times* from 1897–1909 was an Irish Catholic veteran of the Crimean War, William Thomas Carroll Ryan. Ryan's articles and poetry in American Jewish periodicals give him a prominent place in the literature of Zionism and the Jewish people. He worked zealously in the interests of the Jewish community and infused his editorials and articles with the very soul of Jewish thought, gained by his many years of contact with the Jewish community. The poem "Rosh Hashanah, 5660 [September 1899]" written by this Irish Catholic journalist, is worth recalling:

Samuel W. Jacobs (circa 1920), one of the greatest figures in Canadian Jewish history. He was first elected to Parliament as a Liberal in 1917 and sat as an MP until his death in 1938. For much of this time, he was the only Jewish MP. Sir Wilfrid Laurier, stepping down as prime minister of Canada, recommended Jacobs as one of two possible successors. The other candidate, William Lyon Mackenzie King, became prime minister, and Jacobs did not even make it into the Cabinet. Nevertheless, even from the back benches, he was an eloquent voice for Canadian and world Jewry.

(Canadian Jewish Congress National Archives, Montreal)

When chaos lay beneath God's hand,
    And there was neither eve nor morn,
The heavens answered His command,
    Broke into light, and day was born!

Together stand the stars, and all
    The host of heaven chorus'd clear;
Then deep to deep was heard to call
    A greeting to the first New Year.

It was the Malchioth they sang,
    Proclaiming God the sovereign King:
Through all the host of space it rang,
    And it will never cease to ring.

Then send your voices from the shore
    Of time until all things are done:-
'The Lord will reign forevermore!
    O! Israel, your God is One!'

Remember, in this day of life,
    The thrilling memories of the past;
He led you safe thro' fear and strife,
    And He will lead you to the last.

From slavery He led you free,
    You children of His word and will,
O'er desert waste and stormy sea
    He led you, and He leads you still.

The blast of Shophar – hear it swell?
    O! Israel awake, arise!
Remember, O! Remember well!
    'Remember!' soul to soul replies.

O, hear the call! Eternity
    May touch your feet ere it be morn;
Another year and you may be
    Beyond the sound of Shophar horn.

The work of life unfinished lies:
    You ask a blessing – have you blest
The bleeding heart, the weeping eyes,
    And to the weary given rest?

Have you through this departed year
    The path of duty firmly trod,
Not faltering, with doubt and fear,
    But trusting in the word of God?

Behold, advancing from afar,
    An army terrible and fierce;
Its banners blazoned for the war,
    Its spears aligned your hearts to pierce.

Up! Up! and face the dreadful foe,
    For you have arms to make them flee?
God-given arms to overthrow
    The sinful host and set you free!

The pardon, peace, and joy, and love,
    With happiness will fill your days,
And God, who watches from above,
    Will bless you in your works and ways.

In the early years of the twentieth century, the Canadian Jewish community benefited from many publications, periodicals, and newspapers chronicling events in Jewish life. Along with the *Jewish Times*, the *Keneder Adler* (The Jewish Daily Eagle) founded in Montreal in 1907; the *Canadian Jewish Chronicle*, which first appeared in 1914; and the Zionist *Jewish Standard*, established in Toronto in 1929, provided news, analysis, and reports on community events, as well as being the vehicles for the expression of Zionist thought and for transmitting news about the Jewish home.

Some Early Canadian Zionists

Influential Jewish individuals such as Alexander Harkavy and Lazarus Cohen helped nourish the growth of Canadian Zionism, but other early supporters were Christians such as the Reverend J. W. Beaumont, an Anglican clergyman who ardently supported the Jews' return to their ancient homeland. In 1876 he wrote a letter of advocacy to Benjamin Disraeli, a convert from Judaism and then prime minister of Great Britain. Decades before the Balfour Declaration of 1917, which expressed British government support for a Jewish national home in Palestine, Beaumont endorsed "Judea for the Jews under a Joint Protectorate of the Great Powers of Europe."

More broadly, scholar Michael Brown has noted how central biblical imagery was to the British Protestantism that flourished in Canada, and specifically the imagery of Eretz

Jewish Times, 1900

"On January 30, 1898, a great mass meeting was held in Montreal for the purpose of founding a Zionist Society. The B'nai Jacob Synagogue was filled to overflowing and the enthusiastic audience listened appreciatively to the addresses of Rabbi Aaron M. Ashinsky, Rabbi Meldola de Sola, and others. In an oration lasting two hours, Rabbi Ashinsky analyzed the age-old plight of the Jews, the sufferings, pogroms, and persecutions that were their constant lot and pointed to Zionism as the movement that would restore them to their ancient home – Palestine."
—B. G. Sack, *History of the Jews in Canada*, 1964

PROPOSED BANK OF ISRAEL.

CAPITAL £10,000,000.

ONE MILLION SHARES OF TEN POUNDS EACH.

WHEREAS all other means have hitherto failed to supply the urgent needs of the millions of distressed Jews in the East, it is now proposed to establish a Joint Stock Bank (Limited) for this special purpose. A Million Shares of Ten Pounds each. Ten per cent. to be paid on application, and Ten per cent. every subsequent month (if required) until the whole amount is paid up.

The Shareholders to appoint two managing committees, one of which will be responsible for the disposal of one half the amount of all paid up capital to the best advantage for the benefit of the distressed Jews generally, and the other managing committee to be responsible for the disposal of the remaining half of all paid up capital to the best advantage for profit, that large half-yearly dividends may be secured to the shareholders.

It is presumed that if a few of the ablest financiers in the world should thus have half-a-million pounds at command every month, for several months in succession (if so required); they could scarcely fail to turn it to such good account that the bank stock would probably be at a premium before half the amount should be paid up ; and that consequently the Shareholders might thus easily perhaps actually secure large profits for themselves, as well as benefit, enormously, millions of distressed people.

Should this project be viewed favourably by any capitalists, it is to be hoped that they will lose no time in declaring (in the Jewish Press or otherwise) the number of shares, hundreds or thousands of shares of such stock they are each prepared to take, that the Joint Stock Bank of Israel may soon be established and be hereafter recognised as one of the most efficient and beneficent institutions of our time.

HENRY WENTWORTH MONK.

16, Sydney-street, Fulham-road, London, S.W.
24th May, 1882.

Henry Wentworth Monk (1827–1910) was a Canadian Christian Zionist who, among his other efforts, pressed U.S. President Abraham Lincoln, shortly after the Emancipation Proclamation (1863), to do what he could to assist in the rebirth of Israel. "There can be no permanent peace in the world until the civilized nations…atone…for their two thousand years of persecution [of the Jews] by restoring them to their national home in Palestine," declared Monk. In his book, *Power, Faith and Fantasy*, the historian Michael Oren writes that Lincoln called the idea a "noble dream."

(advertisement run by Henry Wentworth Monk in the *Jewish World* in 1882)

Yisrael, the Land of Israel. In his essay "Zionism in the Pre-Statehood Years: The Canadian Response," in *From Immigration to Integration: The Canadian Jewish Experience*, edited by Ruth Klein and Frank Dimant (Institute for International Affairs, 2001), Brown notes that "in Ontario, for example, there are two Salems and a Mount Salem, a Jaffa, a Sharon, and a Bethany. There is another Bethany in Manitoba, as well as a Bethel, and an Eden. In Nova Scotia, there are towns named Hebron, Goshen, Jordan Falls, Jordan Bay, and East Jordan, and there is a River Jordan in British Columbia." Moreover, a love of Hebrew and a longing for Israel's restoration in order to shift the Christian centre of gravity back to Jerusalem from the Vatican and bring about the Christian millennial shaped generations of what we might call Christian philo-Zionists.

Henry Wentworth Monk, a Christian mystic and messianist in Ontario who was active in the proto-Zionist cause from the 1850s until his death in 1896, prominently devoted himself to the pursuit of a Jewish return to Zion. Influenced by proponents of the British Israel sect, he believed that European Christians, and especially Anglo-Saxons, constituted the Ten Lost Tribes of Israel. Seeking to right historical wrongs, he advocated the reinstatement of the Jews in the land of Israel as a prelude to the second coming of Jesus Christ and wanted Anglo-Saxons and all Western Christians to embrace their biblical—and messianic—legacy. Along with many Protestants from Europe and North America, best exemplified by Mark Twain's well-documented pilgrimage, Monk travelled to Palestine as a pilgrim in 1854 and 1863. As early as 1854, he proposed the establishment of a Bank of Israel as an important step in the restoration of the Jews to their homeland. He would eventually lobby British Foreign Secretary Arthur Balfour and even Queen Victoria herself. Monk's messianic fervour inspired him to propose that an international tribunal of the world's leading nations that would work to end war and conflict be established—with its headquarters in Jerusalem, the capital of a Jewish state.

At the end of his life, Monk issued his final manifesto, capturing the Protestantism and late-nineteenth-century Utopianism peppered with realpolitik that shaped his world view. Appearing in 1896, the manifesto titled *Stand Up, O Jerusalem, that the Land of Israel may soon become like the Garden of Eden, "The Joy of the Whole Earth," now that the "Federation of the World" and "Parliament of Man" has at last become an Imperative Necessity* called on the British Empire to assist persecuted Russian Jews and resettle them in their homland. Monk was not alone in his vision. In "Zionism in the Pre-State Years," Professor Brown notes that "at the turn of the century, it was estimated that there were some two million adherents of British Israel in North America and Great Britain, and the movement seemed to be on the way to becoming part of the mainstream of Protestant Christianity."

European proto-Zionists such as Dr. Leon Pinsker articulated the need for Jewish independence and self-reliance. In his book

Auto-Emancipation (1882), Dr. Pinsker argued that Jews would never be the social equals of Gentiles unless and until they had a state of their own. Beaumont and Monk, however strange their zeal seemed to some, represented the potential for non-Jewish involvement in rebuilding the Jewish home. These two themes came together most clearly in the life and work of one of the essential figures in early Canadian Zionism—Clarence de Sola.

Clarence de Sola and Zionism

In 1899, the Federation of Zionist Societies of Canada was formed and Clarence de Sola was chosen as its first president. He held this position until June 1919, championing the future of Zionism both inside and outside Canada. In 1900, de Sola travelled to London to attend the Fourth Zionist Congress as Canada's delegate. The *Jewish Times* of October 26 records that he reported from the Congress, "Words cannot paint the scene. Only those who have been to a Zionist Congress can realize the strength of the movement and the absolutely overwhelming enthusiasm that is at the back of it." In December of the same year, Canada's newly formed Federation of Zionist Societies held its first convention in Montreal. Total membership in the Federation was 828.

After 1900, Zionism began to spread quickly in Canada, extending outside the traditional centres of Jewish activity—Montreal, Toronto, Winnipeg, and Vancouver. By the 1903 convention, delegates attended from Saint John, Glace Bay, Yarmouth, Ottawa, Kingston, Hamilton, Dundas, London, and Brandon. The idea of a movement that actualized traditional Jewish yearnings for an expression of national Jewish identity spread throughout the country. Zionist conventions met annually and symbolized the growing strength and acceptance of organizations promoting Zionism in Canada. From the beginning, in Canada, as in America, the emphasis was on supporting the Jews who were already living in Palestine or were now choosing to move to Palestine. Zionists in

Clarence de Sola (1858–1922) was elected president of the Federation of Zionist Societies of Canada at the first Canadian Zionist Convention, and continued to provide leadership until his death. De Sola, third son of the renowned Montreal rabbi Abraham de Sola of the Shearith Israel Congregation, was a contractor and also served in the consular service. In his years as president, he was a pioneer architect of the Canadian Zionist movement. De Sola, in 1899, had a private meeting with Herzl in Vienna.

(Canadian Jewish Congress National Archives, Montreal)

The Herzl Girls' Zionist Society in Toronto in 1906— one of the earliest Canadian Jewish women's groups.

(Ontario Jewish Archives, Betty Goldstick Lindgren fonds, # 6641)

Canada did not want their ideals to clash with the ideals of modern liberal and pluralist democracies that emphasized integration rather than segregation.

Under de Sola, even American Zionists would envy Canadian Zionism for both its infrastructure and its ideology. Canadian Jews were appreciably less ambivalent and defensive about Zionism than were American Jews. In his essay "The Canadian Jewish Experience: A Distinct Personality Emerges" in *From Immigration to Integration*, Canadian historian Gerald Tulchinsky writes that

> Jews in Canada did not understand that there were any tests of Canadian nationalism they had to meet. In Montreal, insofar as both French and English were concerned, Jews were pariahs, and barely tolerated. But the predominant strain of pre-1914 Canadian-nationalist thought, that of the imperial federationists, though expressing a narrowly British view of history, national character, and Canada's mission, also indirectly implied an integration into British imperialism, a toleration, an openness, a liberality towards racial

The Canadian Women of Zion

Canadian women picked up the Zionist cause with dedication and enthusiasm. The first women's group, the Daughters of Zion, was formed in Toronto in 1900. The Jewish Women's League for Cultural Work in Palestine followed, with its members focused on providing hospital care in Palestine.

In 1916, Anna Selick of Toronto formed what was to become the Canadian Hadassah organization. Henrietta Szold, president of American Hadassah, visited Toronto and encouraged Selick to build a Canadian counterpart to her U.S. organization. Chapters quickly sprang up in five Ontario communities—Toronto, Hamilton, Brantford, London, and Windsor—and then growth exploded. Soon almost every Jewish community in Canada had its Hadassah chapter. The organization's initial projects were the Helping Hand Fund, a Girls' Domestic and Agricultural Science School at Nahalal, a nurses' training school in Jerusalem, a convalescent home, and a hospital for tubercular patients.

The Pioneer Women and Mizrachi Women followed as Canadian Jewish women sought to provide help to their sisters in Palestine.

and cultural diversity, and a grudging acceptance in this polity in which freedom is said to wear a crown.

Canadian Zionism could stand proudly under the British imperial umbrella—especially once the British mandate in Palestine began—while also feeling comfortable as a solid, shining tile in what would eventually be known as the Canadian mosaic.

Zionist Activity 1900–1910

Throughout the years of his leadership, Clarence de Sola remained loyal to Theodor Herzl's Basel program that emphasized diplomacy and pragmatism. De Sola negotiated with Canadian federal cabinet ministers, as Herzl did with the Turkish sultan, the kaiser of Germany, and Emperor Franz Joseph of Austria. De Sola shared Herzl's view that cautious exploration and constructive engagement with leaders would secure recognition of Palestine as the national Jewish homeland.

In addition to diplomacy, de Sola also promoted education and fundraising. Both the Jewish Colonial Trust shares and the Jewish National Fund proved to be successful vehicles for fundraising and identity building. In May 1909, de Sola proposed raising $10,000 in Canada to purchase land in Palestine over the coming two years. That

November, the Zionist convention in Montreal endorsed the resolution, despite widespread scepticism. Achieving the objective by 1912 marked a clear triumph for de Sola.

In 1907, a Talmud Torah (Jewish day school) was established in Edmonton for the handful of Jews who lived there which by the 1930s would evolve into Canada's first Hebrew Day School. With the support of Zionist organizations, Jewish schools soon opened

An early poster for Keren Hayesod, 1906.

throughout Canada and would prove to be strong and effective partners in building Canadian Zionist identity.

The Federation of Zionist Societies of Canada held its tenth
anniversary convention in Montreal in 1909. Thirty-seven branches of
the organization were represented at the meeting of some 1,500 delegates. By 1910, the number of active Zionists organizations and
societies had exploded, with branches across the country in Montreal,
Toronto, Winnipeg, Ottawa, Glace Bay, Saint John, Kingston,
Hamilton, Dundas, London, Brandon, Edmonton, Calgary, Quebec
City, Yarmouth, Vancouver, and Brantford. The Zionist Institute had
opened in Toronto in March 1908.

One of the first Canadian Jewish poets, Isidore Gordon Ascher,
along with others, such as Hyman Edelstein and Rabbi B. M. Kaplan,
helped build a vibrant Canadian Jewish publishing scene. The growth
of Jewish publications during these decades furthered the Zionist
movement's educational thrust. Ascher recorded his own vision in
"The Zionist's Dream":

> And I see a radiant multitude, God's race,
> > that is my own,
> Who are singing at their eager tasks,
> > deep joy in every tone,
> As the land did yield its treasures,
> > like the Bible for all time,
> Gave the world a golden harvest in the truths
> > that are sublime!
> And the earth will pour its richness and the
> > skies shed joys in rain,
> And the happy land of promise shall become
> > Divine again!
> Then as I gazed in wonder, in my dream's
> > ecstatic thrall,
> There rose to charm the silences, as solemn.

As these Zionist societies, Hebrew schools, and Jewish publications flourished, many people outside the Jewish community noticed
and became more sympathetic to the Jewish community.

Jewish National Fund

In 1908, the council of the Federation of Zionist Societies of Canada appointed the first national chairman of Keren Kayemet Le-Israel, or Jewish National Fund, in Canada. JNF Canada passed resolutions in 1909 and 1910 calling for raising a land fund of $10,000 over a two-year period. By 1912, the objective had been met and the money was expended in 1913 to purchase eight hundred dunams in the Negev. A "dunam" was equivalent to 919.3 square metres at the time.

1913—An ad for a mass meeting of the Ottawa Men's Zionist Society.

Respectability and Support

During his presidency de Sola aimed to build general good will toward the Zionist cause, reaching out to prominent non-Jews for moral, if not financial, support for the movement. At a mass meeting in Ottawa in 1906, Prime Minister Sir Wilfred Laurier expressed his hope for the realization of the Zionst ideal and in 1907, two ministers of the Canadian government, Justice Minister A. B. Aylesworth and Customs Minister W. Patterson, spoke very sympathetically about Zionism. Aylesworth emphasized that the Canadian government fully approved of the work done by the Zionists, and indeed appreciated the importance of their aim to build a national home for the Jewish people. Patterson gave these statements his unqualified endorsement and made it clear that they voiced the sentiments of the Canadian government.

Acting Prime Minister George Perley repeated these sentiments in 1912, as did then-Solicitor General Arthur Meighen in 1915. It seemed that the movement had achieved hitherto unknown respectability and support in the non-Jewish world. The movement became a darling of progressives committed to righting a classic wrong. Amid growing respect for nationalism and national sovereignty, Zionism meant the end of the exile, dispersion, and homelessness of a long-oppressed people.

The Labour Zionist Alliance

Labour Zionism, as distinct from the political Zionism of Theodor Herzl, arose out of the Jewish workers' movements of Central and Eastern Europe. Where political Zionism focused on appeals to the international community to support the creation of a Jewish state, Labour Zionists argued that the Jewish homeland could only emerge out of the efforts of a Jewish working class settling in

Palestine and building the new state from the ground up. In North America, the Jewish National Workers' Alliance, or Farband, operated largely as mutual-aid societies alongside the political party Poale Zion (Workers of Zion) founded in 1905. The two Organizations later merged to become the Labour Zionist Alliance, which in turn became Ameinu in 2003.

The first Canadian branch of the Labour Zionist Alliance was established in Montreal in 1909. Although the Poale Zion movement already existed, the Canadian leadership decided they had to expand their orbit and formed a fraternal organization that expressed Zionist ideals but also emphasized the more immediate needs of the Jewish worker.

Zionist and Social Society Meeting, Vancouver, ca 1914. The JNF granted a charter to the Vancouver organization on December 10, 1913. Meyer Reifman was the first president.

(British Columbia Jewish Historical Society # 375)

On June 6, 1910, the movement defined its core principles. Members committed themselves to rendering mutual aid to one another in times of distress, sickness, or death. They undertook to educate Jewish workers to a full consciousness of their national and social interests. They promised to support activities leading to the national emancipation and regeneration of the Jewish people while vowing to join in activities to strengthen the working class.

In keeping with these principles, provision was made to provide medical, sickness, and death benefits to the membership of the Labour Zionist Alliance. Efforts were also made to establish progressive Jewish schools and to become active in all aspects of communal life.

The Jewish National Fund

In 1901, the Fifth World Zionist Congress created the Jewish National Fund to buy and develop land in Palestine for Jewish settlement. From that point on, the Jewish National Fund became one of the mainstays of the Zionist movement.

In 1913, the JNF used Canadian Zionists' contribution to purchase eight hundred dunams in the Castinia (B'er Tuvia) area in the Negev, south of Hebron, where Jews had lived relatively peacefully among their Arab neighbours for centuries. Following the First World War, the efforts of the JNF were also channelled into raising money for relief and emergency supplies for the many homeless and suffering Jews of Europe and the pogrom-plagued Jews of Ukraine.

Once again, in the early days, many people contributed their time, organizing abilities, and resources to ensure that the JNF functioned effectively. Among them were Menachem M. Ussishkin, A. J. and Lillian Freiman, Albert I. Silverman, Reverend J. K. Goldbloom, Michael Garber, Rabbi Charles Bender, and Anna Raginsky. Funds were raised initially through coin collection boxes (what would become the famous JNF blue boxes), the selling of JNF stamps and "tags," and the Golden Book inscriptions. Such forms of fundraising continued for many years, and new approaches were also added to help increase the level of awareness of Israel and its needs.

2

The First World War
Upheaval and Hope

AUGUST 1914 UNLEASHED THE TERRORS of twentieth-century warfare on the world. For the Jewish populations of the Middle East and Europe, the war initially stalled their search for a Zionist state. As the Ottoman Empire declined and the number of foreign settlements in the region increased, most of the tens of thousands of Jews who had arrived since 1882 and begun to develop the land remained despite intense hardship. Ultimately, however, the diplomatic negotiations and formation of the League of Nations that followed the war helped the Jews progress in their quest to rebuild their national home.

The Canadian Jewish Community's Reaction

With the outbreak of the war, Canadian Jews who had recently arrived from Europe were suddenly cut off from their immediate past as almost all communication with relatives ceased. Nevertheless, information about the upheaval and horror caused by the war filtered into Canada, eliciting a swift response on the part of Canadian Jews. The majority of the approximately 100,000 Jews who lived in Canada by 1914 were Eastern European immigrants who had arrived after 1900. They were ambivalent in their support for the war. On one hand, Canadian Jews were faced with a civic obligation to support the cause of the Allies and the Empire. On the other, it was difficult to fulfill this obligation wholeheartedly because the Allies included the hated Russian Empire.

The situation was further clouded by Germany's role as an enemy power. Most Jews cherished Germany as the seat of Western culture and the freedoms underpinning modern Jewish culture and

אם אשכחך ירושלים תשכח ימין

Toronto's Zion Benevolent Association, 1915. The Hebrew epigraph at the bottom of this picture reads, "If I forget you, O Jerusalem, let my right arm lose its cunning." (Psalm 137:5)

(Ontario Jewish Archives, # 1911)

the Western European Jewish Enlightenment. Germany was the country of origin for important movements such as Reform and Conservative Judaism.

Despite these conflicts, the Canadian Zionism movement allied itself with the British Empire. The Zionist Federation decided to call a conference of all Jewish organizations in Canada with a membership of more than twenty-five to discuss issues raised by the war. The First Canadian Jewish Conference, which took place in Montreal on November 14, 1915, as part of the Federation's fourteenth convention, called for the formation of an organization that would ensure that Jewish interests were represented at the peace table and would support the efforts of the U.S. Provisional Committee founded in August 1915 to provide relief to the Jews of Palestine. The *landsmanshaften*—Jewish fraternal organizations based on their members' European cities and towns of origin—were particularly concerned for the welfare of their Jewish brothers and sisters in the old country. It was at this meeting that Canadian Secretary of State Arthur Meighen expressed the sympathies of the Canadian government and his conviction that the British government would see that justice was rendered to the Jewish people.

The fourteenth Zionist Federation convention that was held in Montreal on the following day, November 15, 1915, was attended by two hundred delegates from sixty synagogues, organizations, and societies. A joint campaign to raise funds, for both overseas and local causes, emerged from the meeting. Eventually the campaign raised more than $24,000, but unfortunately, due to high overhead and gross inefficiency, only $6,000 ended up overseas. This episode generated bitterness that lingered for decades, particularly since Toronto's Jews did not participate in the Montreal joint campaign. All the money raised in a separate Toronto effort was sent directly overseas.

Prominent businessman and philanthropist Sir Mortimer B. Davis set up the Canadian Jewish Committee for the Relief of War Sufferers in October 1915. The committee raised $150,000 between October 15, 1915, and January 15, 1917, and a further $90,000 by January 1918, most of which was transferred to London. In all, Canadian Jews contributed hundreds of thousands of dollars toward alleviating the plight of Jews overseas.

In addition to the financial contributions from Canadian Jews, in 1918 the Jewish Legion (part of the British Army's 40th Royal Fusiliers) recruited five hundred volunteers from Montreal, Toronto, Hamilton, Winnipeg, and points west. Together with American volunteers, one of whom was David Ben-Gurion, they received military

In 1916, Army Capt. Isidore Freedman of Montreal recruited several hundred Jewish men for service overseas in the First World War. The five lieutenants of the Jewish Draft Company were Alex Solomon (killed in action), Herbert Vineberg, Charles Lesser, Albert Freedman, and Sol Rubin.

(Canadian Jewish Congress National Archives, Montreal)

training at Windsor, Ontario, and York Redoubt in Halifax, Nova Scotia. This commitment foreshadowed later contributions during Israel's War of Independence.

The Canadian Jewish Congress

Only months after the end of the First World War, the Canadian Jewish Congress held its inaugural convention in Montreal from March 16 to 19, 1919. Dr. Yehudah Kaufman of Montreal had been lobbying furiously to establish a body to defend political, economic, and other interests common to all Canadian Jews. One resolution that he initiated at the organization's first plenary argued the need for Jews to formulate united demands and speak with one voice:

The Balfour Declaration, issued by Great Britain in 1917, stated that the government "view[ed] with favour the establishment in Palestine of a national home for the Jewish people."

(World Zionist Organization Archives, Jerusalem)

...the condition of the Jews in the countries at war and their fate after the war is the most urgent phase of the present Jewish reality, and its fundamental and lasting resolution are the sacred duty of the entire Jewish people. Our entire history of our nation testifies to the bankruptcy of the practice of intercessionism. The proper resolution of the Jewish question can be dictated only by the will of the people....

The voice of the entire Jewish people is a factor that the great powers will need to take into consideration. This voice is already powerful if only because it is founded upon the right of each people to self-determination.

The Jewish people therefore needs to formulate its demands. Such possibilities can be created only by a people's tribune who comes with the directives of the people, to deal with the common Jewish interests. Such tribunes can be created only by the purposeful organization, the union of all classes and parties of all tendencies and colorations—in the interest of the present great moment.... This people's representation must be formed out of the existing religious, political, economic, cultural, welfare and mutual aid organizations.

Foreign Office,
November 2nd, 1917.

Dear Lord Rothschild,

I have much pleasure in conveying to you, on behalf of His Majesty's Government, the following declaration of sympathy with Jewish Zionist aspirations which has been submitted to, and approved by, the Cabinet

"His Majesty's Government view with favour the establishment in Palestine of a national home for the Jewish people, and will use their best endeavours to facilitate the achievement of this object, it being clearly understood that nothing shall be done which may prejudice the civil and religious rights of existing non-Jewish communities in Palestine, or the rights and political status enjoyed by Jews in any other country"

I should be grateful if you would bring this declaration to the knowledge of the Zionist Federation.

The Canadian Jewish Congress soon became the voice of Canadian Jewish democracy. Yehudah Kaufman believed the Congress could unite Jews of various perspectives and backgrounds—orthodox and radical, employers and workers, liberals and socialists, intellectuals and artisans, religious and secular, materialists and idealists—around three central ideas: helping their fellow Jews in lands afflicted by war immediately and effectively; representing the interests of all Canadian Jews; and galvanizing Jews across the political, economic, religious, and social spectrum to work for a common cause. The concept of the Jewish people as a dynamic entity able to resolve problems and shape its fate guided Kaufmann to his belief in the Congress. In fact, he saw the creation of the Canadian Jewish Congress as the first step toward organizing a World Jewish Congress.

In lobbying for the creation of the Canadian Jewish Congress Kaufman raised Canadian awareness of an important and far-reaching problem that was enraging millions of Europeans: the suffering of national minorities in states dominated by majority ethnic and cultural groups. To many, the conclusion of the war seemed to herald an opportunity for embedding a promise in the peace settlement of international and constitutional protection of the rights of minority groups.

David Ben-Gurion in the Jewish Legion uniform. He enlisted in Canada in 1918, but the First World War ended before he could see action.

(Ben-Gurion House, Tel Aviv)

The Balfour Declaration

November 2, 1917, marked a turning point in Zionist history and in the struggle to establish a Jewish homeland. On that day, British Foreign Minister Arthur Balfour issued a formal statement of British government policy of support for the establishment of a national home for the Jews in Palestine. Although Zionists around the world initially received the Declaration enthusiastically as the fullfillment of

Private David Ben-Gurion

David Ben-Gurion, the future founding prime minister of Israel, enlisted in the Jewish Legion in Montreal in 1918. He trained at a camp in Windsor, Nova Scotia, and then shipped out with other members of the Jewish Legion to Palestine—arriving too late to see action.

Although the Jewish Legion was attached to the British Army, the idea of a Canadian dimension to the legion came from Montreal. The Yiddish daily *Keneder Adler*, in the wake of the Balfour Declaration in 1917, called on young people to enlist: "The great moment has arrived! After a thousand years of persecution and oppression we are now recognized as a nation, as a people equal to other peoples. This momentous occasion has entrusted us with great responsibilities. With our blood we must seal our alliance with England and the other nations which granted us recognition. The Jewish Legion is the first manifestation of our redemption. Young and old, rise up to do battle for your people! To Arms! For the freedom of people and country!"

The Canadian military authorities, at the request of Member of Parliament Sam W. Jacobs from Montreal, granted permission for Canadians to enlist in the legion and a military base was established in Windsor.

The legion recruiting commission in Montreal included Joseph and Moses Brainin, Gershon Agronsky, and Louis Fisher. For a time Bernard (Dov) Joseph (the future military governor of Jerusalem) was in charge of the Montreal recruiting office, and he himself enlisted. More than fifty young men from Montreal alone served in the legion, training in Windsor, and then continuing on to Eretz Israel.

Vladimir Jabotinsky, Russian-born writer and Zionist leader, mentions 300 Canadian legionnaires in a letter. Historian Simon Belkin estimated that 350 to 400 Jewish Canadians served in the legion and, further, that 150 to 200 Jewish soldiers transferred to the legion from Canadian forces. A separate Jewish unit for Canadian military service had been organized by Captain I. Freedman of Toronto in the summer of 1916 as an integral part of Canada's overseas forces.

The Canadian Jewish Congress's Louis Rosenberg (a legendary figure in the accumulation of information on Canadian Jewry) estimated that 100 Jewish officers and 4,600 of other ranks served in the Canadian Army during the First World War.

The Labour Zionists, encouraged by Ben-Gurion and Yitzhak Ben Zvi (a future president of Israel), undertook to recruit the distinctive Jewish Legion under the broader auspices of the British to encourage Jewish pride in Jewish heroism. The Labour Zionists operated recruiting offices in Montreal, Toronto, and Winnipeg. The Canadian Department of Militia and Defence accepted this group of Jewish volunteers as the "Jewish units of the British Army for service in Palestine."

their goals, controversy with British government itself, as well as among the British public and Arab nations, almost immediately watered down its promise.

Arthur Balfour had informed Clarence de Sola of the British cabinet's intentions during the spring of 1917, when the two men discussed the plans for a Jewish homeland in Palestine in a three-hour meeting at Government House in Ottawa on May 29. De Sola, along with the Canadian minister of the interior, Arthur Meighen, supported the Declaration.

The Balfour Declaration is often regarded as the point of convergence of two historic currents. The first is the Jewish people's ancient yearning to restore their nationhood and their national home, a sentiment that had arisen after the destruction of the Jewish state in the first century of the Common Era and had persisted through more than eighteen centuries of dispersion and persecution. The second current is the profound sympathy for Jewish aspirations, nourished by both biblical prophecy and considerations of practical policy, that moved leaders in Britain to support a Jewish homeland.

The Balfour Declaration would become part of the Palestine Mandate, which the League of Nations entrusted to Britain to administer in a process started at the Paris Peace Conference—which

Legionnaires who stayed (1918)

Eight Canadians who served in the Jewish Legion in the First World War remained in Palestine. They have been identified as A. Aisenstadt, Leon Cheifetz, M. Epstein, A. Feldman, A. H. Friedgut, Saul Glazer, Philip Joseph, and S. C. Kernerman.

The Zionists of Regina, 1918.
(Jewish Public Library Archives, Montreal)

Soldiers of the Jewish Legion at the Western Wall, in Jerusalem, after fighting alongside British forces to free Palestine from the Ottoman Turks. The legion included volunteers from the United States, Canada, and Argentina.

was attended by many Jewish delegations—and fleshed out at the San Remo Conference of 1920. A special Committee on New States and for the Protection of Minorities was established at the Paris conference on May 1, 1920. As a result of its deliberations, the peace treaties contained clauses protecting minorities and granting minority rights to autonomy in education and religion. These aspects of the treaties nevertheless proved worthless as they specified no procedures for supervising the implementation of their terms or punishing those who violated them.

De Sola believed that the British would assume the task of setting up the Jewish homeland. Unfortunately, this optimism for the establishment of a national homeland and equal rights for Jews within their countries of residence was short-lived. Canadian Protestants also hoped that their British cousins would now help make the world right by bringing the Jews home. At Hebrew University's 1925 dedication in Jerusalem, Opposition Leader Arthur Meighen reflected on the Great War, remarking, "Of all the results…none is more important and more fertile in human history than the re-conquest of Palestine and the rededication of that country to the Jewish people." He hoped that "Jews in Canada [would] take a proper pride in this great event and that the sons of generations to come may go back to the land of their destiny."

In Palestine, the British military administration's attitude toward Zionist aspirations was cautious and even hostile. Given this lack of commitment and the ultimate ineffectiveness of the treaties drawn up during the Paris Peace Conference, hopes were dashed for the quick establishment of a Jewish homeland.

Local British officials charged with carrying out colonial policy and administering Palestine endeavoured to weaken the Balfour Declaration. They saw their main task as maintaining the status quo—the official languages in Palestine remained English and Arabic, Jews were prohibited from making land purchases and Jewish immigration curtailed.

Recruiting for the Jewish Battalion in Winnipeg in 1917.

Hope that the intent of the Balfour Declaration would be implemented arose when British prime minister David Lloyd George asked British statesman and philosopher Herbert Samuel to become the first British high commissioner to Palestine. The British government submitted the draft formula for its mandate to the League of Nations in the following December, and the league approved it on July 24, 1922. The preamble to the mandate stated:

> [T]he Principal Allied Powers have...agreed that the Mandatory should be responsible for putting into effect the declaration originally made on November 2nd, 1917 by the Government of His Britannic Majesty, and adopted by the said Powers, in favour of the establishment in Palestine of a national home for the Jewish people...and recognition has thereby been given to the historical connection of the Jewish people with Palestine....

The Mandatory authority also undertook to create "conditions as will secure the establishment of the Jewish national home" (article 2); to recognize "an appropriate Jewish Agency" that would co-operate with the Administration of Palestine in all "matters as may affect the establishment of the Jewish national home and the interests of the Jewish population in Palestine" (article 4). Finally, article 6 stated,

> The Administration of Palestine, while ensuring that the rights and position of other sections of the population are not prejudiced, shall facilitate Jewish immigration under suitable conditions; and shall

The delegates to the Zionist Convention of 1919, in Montreal. Presumably the children were members of the Zionist youth group, the Young Judaeans.

(*The Jewish Standard*)

encourage, in cooperation with the Jewish Agency...close settlement by Jews on the land, including State lands and waste lands.

Samuel did not implement the mandate however. Instead, he tried to appease the Arabs in Palestine by appointing an extreme Arab nationalist as mufti of Jerusalem and slowing down Jewish immigration. He also expected the Zionist organizations to raise funds to pay for nationwide development projects without any British aid.

Although he came to the post of high commissioner of Palestine as an avowed Zionist, Samuel's efforts to demonstrate his neutrality and mediate between the Jews and Arabs in the Mandate ultimately dashed Jewish hopes for the realization of a Jewish state. There was some progress made in creating infrastructure in the region through the 1920s, but the time for a true Jewish homeland had not yet arrived.

3

Building the Yishuv

THE FOUR MAJOR WAVES OF JEWISH immigration to
Palestine from the 1880s to 1930 are commonly known as
the First, Second, Third, and Fourth Aliyah. About 35,000
Jews—mostly Eastern European immigrants fleeing the Russian
pogroms—arrived during the First Aliyah (1882–1903), but almost
half of them left within a few years because of difficult conditions.
Again, nearly half of the roughly 40,000 immi-
grants who came during the Second Aliyah
(1904–1914) did not stay. Although settlers of
the Second Aliyah had also been driven out of
czarist Russia by anti-Semitic violence, they
differed from the immigrants of the First
Aliyah in that they were primarily young people who laid the groundwork for the early rural
settlement movement and some of the later
political organizations.

Following the end of the First World War,
the Third Aliyah (1919–1923), which brought
another 40,000 immigrants to Palestine, was
prompted by a complex set of events that
included the October Revolution in Russia,
continuing pogroms in Russia, Hungary,
Lithuania, and Poland, and—even more
importantly—the Balfour Declaration and the
institution of the British Mandate in Palestine.
Even though the British had imposed quotas on
immigration, by 1924 the *yishuv*—the Hebrew

Helping Hand Fund

In 1917, Canadian Zionists reacted to the
British takeover of Palestine by creating
the Helping Hand Fund and the Palestine
Restoration Fund. In less than a year, the
Helping Hand Fund raised nearly
$160,000. This was more money than
Canadian Zionists had raised in all their
previous campaigns since 1899.

The major figure in the campaign was
Lillian Freiman, wife of A. J. Freiman,
founder of a popular department store in
Ottawa. At her own expense, Mrs. Freiman
journeyed from coast to coast speaking to
Jewish groups, describing the destitution
of Palestinian Jews. In addition to cash, she
gathered $40,000 in gifts of medicine,
food, and clothing.

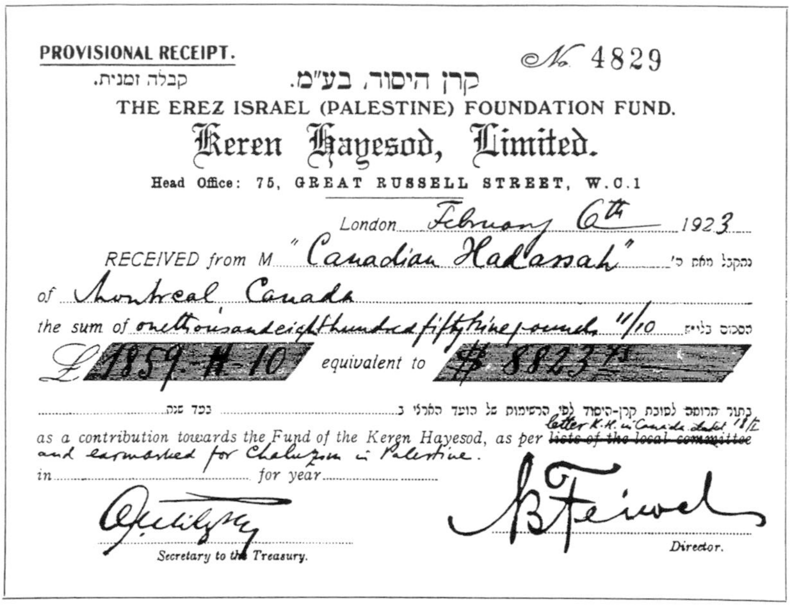

Receipt for the gift by
Canadian Hadassah to Keren
Hayesod in 1923 of £1,859s11
(at the time about $5,600
Canadian). Keren Hayesod
(Hebrew for "The Foundation
Fund") was a key component
in the Jewish diaspora's effort
to support the nascent Jewish
state.

(Canadian Hadassah-WIZO Archives)

term used to refer to the Jewish inhabitants of Palestine before the establishment of the Jewish state—numbered about 90,000.

The character of the Fourth Aliyah (1924–1928) differed markedly from the three previous waves of immigration to Palestine. Unlike the majority of their predecessors, the approximately 80,000 Jews who made up the Fourth Aliyah were not driven by socialist ideology and the working-class Labour Zionism of David Ben-Gurion. They were primarily middle-class business people and artisans much more drawn to the militant nationalist Revisionist Zionism of Zeev Jabotinsky that emphasized self-defence and laissez-faire economic policy. These new immigrants flocked to cities, especially to Tel Aviv, where they invested in the trades, small business, and light industry, laying the foundations of an urban industrialized economy in the *yishuv*. Most of the newcomers of the Fourth Aliyah came from Eastern Europe—about half from Poland and the rest from the U.S.S.R., Romania, Lithuania. This wave of immigration was catalyzed by the combination of a political and economic crisis in Poland that was accompanied by increasing anti-Semitism and the passage in 1924 of the American *Johnson-Lodge Immigration Act* that severely curtailed mass immigration to the U.S.

A major economic crisis in Palestine from 1926 to 1927—despite significant recovery from 1928 to 1929—prompted about 23,000 of the immigrants from the Fourth Aliyah to leave Palestine permanently. However, most of the immigrants who came to Palestine during the 1920s—both the young *chalutzim*, or pioneers, of the Third Aliyah and the urban business and trades people of the Fourth Aliyah—stayed and began to develop many of the institutions that would create the infrastructure of the Jewish state. Throughout the decade, the average annual increment of immigrants to the *yishuv* was approximately 8,000. By 1930, the population had grown to 160,000.

Some of the institutions that formed the beginnings of *yishuv* self-rule were integrated into the British Mandate government's legal and administrative frameworks, while others were secret or semi-underground bodies. There were Zionists in the West who believed that the British Mandate authorities would take over the task of implementing Zionist aims, but the local Zionists of the *yishuv* distrusted the British and supported the more clandestine organizations. Three representative bodies were established under the leadership of Zionist organizations during this period to oversee issues such as political affairs, education, health, and social welfare. At the local level was the Kehillah Ivrit, a secular variation on the traditional Jewish community council, and at the national level, created in 1920, were the central elected assembly —predecessor of the Knesset— the Asefat Hanivharim, and its executive council, the Va'ad Le'umi. The *yishuv* entrusted jurisdiction over religion and matrimonial law to the Chief Rabbinate and the rabbinical courts.

Alongside the development of self rule institutions, this period also saw the further evolution of Jewish political organizations in Palestine. The immigrants of the Second Aliyah had formed two labour parties in 1905—the nationalist anti-socialist Hapo'el Hatza'ir (Young Workers) party and the socialist Paole Zion (Workers of Zion). In 1919–1920, Paole Zion split into left and right factions; the anti-Marxist right-wing faction emerged as the Achdut Ha'avoda (Labour Unity) party founded by David Ben-Gurion. In 1930, Achdut Ha'avoda merged with Hapo'el Hatza'ir to become the mainstream labour Zionist party Mapai, which would later become today's Israeli Labour Party.

Ben-Gurion's vision went beyond the formation of a political party. To create an economic infrastructure to parallel the self-rule organizations, in 1920 he formed the Histadrut, a national organized Jewish labour movement that would include both agricultural and urban industrial workers. At the beginning of the 1920s there were fifty agricultural settlements in Palestine; as Jewish agriculture progressed, the number rose to 110 by the end of the decade. The Jewish National Fund raised money to purchase land in the Jezreel Valley and advances in irrigation made it possible to develop some 15,000 acres of orange groves. The majority of farmers still lived in colonies, but the number of *kibbutzim* (communal settlements) and settlements of co-operative small-holders increased rapidly. During this same period, there were 2,500 Jewish industrial enterprises with approximately 11,000 workers.

Another piece of critical infrastructure concerned matters of defence. Riots in Jerusalem in 1920 forced the *yishuv* to acknowledge that they could no longer rely on the British to protect Jewish lives and property, and that Ha-Shomer, the small group founded in 1907 to guard settlements, was no longer sufficient. Achdut Ha'avoda formalized the local defence committees started by activists after the riots into the Haganah (The Defence), a loosely organized defence network. After renewed riots in 1929, the Haganah became a much more formal paramilitary organization, the forerunner of the Israel Defense Forces.

In addition to building institutions to administer political affairs, settlement, agriculture, industry, and defence, the *yishuv* also established educational and medical services. The Technion in Haifa opened its doors as the *yishuv*'s first modern university in 1924, with faculties of architecture and civil engineering. In 1929–1930, approximately

Lillian Freiman and her husband, Archibald Jacob Freiman, were influential, dedicated Zionist leaders for decades. Mrs. Freiman (1885–1940) was president of Canadian Hadassah from 1921 to 1940, while Archie Freiman (1880–1944) was president of the Zionist Organization of Canada from 1920 to 1944. The Ottawa couple was also active in many other Jewish and non-Jewish causes.

(Canadian Jewish Congress National Archives, Montreal)

21,000 pupils attended 230 schools, and 200 students were enrolled in the Hebrew University in Jerusalem. Meanwhile, the Hadassah organization supplied a range of medical services that resulted in the *yishuv* having one of the world's lowest death rates (11.66 per 1,000 between 1926 and 1930).

The Freiman Era

On January 19, 1919, thirty-six-year-old Archibald Jacob Freiman was chosen president of the Federation of Zionist Societies of Canada after elderly founding president Clarence de Sola stepped down. During his tenure as president, in 1925, the Federation changed its name to the

A portrait of Chaim Weizmann, the future first president of Israel, taken during his 1921 visit to Montreal to confer with Zionist leaders. Weizmann worked tirelessly to bring about a Jewish state, taking his fervent message to governments, organizations, and individuals.

(Jewish Public Library Archives, Montreal)

The Mandate

The Jewish world exploded with joy in April 1920, when the San Remo Conference of the Supreme Allied Council assigned the Mandate for Palestine to Great Britain. The Mandate document incorporated the Balfour Declaration as an obligation for the Mandate administration. Zionist leader Archibald Freiman reflected the feelings of Canadian Jews when he proclaimed, "No longer are we a race without a country; no longer can we be regarded as wanderers on the face of the earth. We are now a nation with a national home; that goal towards which our hearts have always yearned has been reached, and we Jews of this generation ought to count ourselves doubly blessed that we have lived to see this great day."

Zionist Organization of Canada; in 1944 the name would finally change again to the Canadian Zionist Federation. Freiman's wife, Lillian, thirty-three, was named president of the Hadassah Organization of Canada the following year. The Freimans, married on August 18, 1903, were committed to their community, respected in government circles, and had excellent political and philanthropic connections.

Archibald Jacob Freiman had arrived in Canada in 1893. At the tender age of twenty-one, he represented the Kingston Jewish community as a delegate at the second convention of the Federation of Zionist Societies of Canada. At this convention, he secured election as a member of the Zionist National Council.

Just before becoming president of the Federation, Freiman had been chosen to head the Million Dollar Campaign for the Relief of Jewry in Eastern Europe. He realized the tasks ahead of him were formidable, but was always able to put his work in perspective. In a 1922 address, he said, "We have obstacles to overcome, but how can they be compared to the gigantic task the founders of our cause were faced with?"

Lillian Freiman also had a deep love for the Jewish people and respect for the young *chalutzim* building the Jewish homeland in Palestine. In a March 1921 address to Hadassah members, she said,

> In that far-off land that is to be ours, Jewish maidens are working side by side with Jewish men, in the real work of construction, digging, shovelling building roads, working in fields and elsewhere.
>
> These young women, many of whom have been reared as gently as our own daughters, are forgetting self in the idealism that is driving them to give up youth and life itself to the work of building up Palestine.
>
> These young *chalutzim* (pioneers) are not thinking of good times and pleasures! They are not concerned with the new dances or the new styles. They are working far beyond their strength to help in a task, the fruit of which they may never live to enjoy.

Let us try to pattern our own daughters after these young Jewish daughters. We are very anxious to give our girls all the advantages of easy living and a pleasurable existence. Sometimes we forget to inspire them with that steadfast idealism that has given us our most beautiful memories of our mothers—of all mothers of Israel.

Fostered by the commitment of individuals like the Freimans, the Canadian Jewish community flourished. The Freimans' deep attachment to the Jewish people, to the Jewish communities in Canada and Palestine, to the building of a Jewish homeland, and to their belief in a better future was inspirational. Canadian Jews were galvanized to mobilize around a common cause, to raise money for Palestine, and to see themselves as a part of history and their organizations as important instruments for education and for spiritual and national renewal.

Canadian Jewish Congress of 1919

By 1919, momentum had grown among the many separate and varied local and national Jewish organizations across Canada to support the calling of an assembly of the democratically elected representatives of Canadian Jewry. The Canadian Jewish Congress, at its first meeting on March 16–19, 1919, put support for Zionism on the agenda for the coming decade. The first point on Congress's agenda affirmed its recognition of the threat Communism posed to Jewish survival. The second addressed the need to keep Jewish immigration moving by organizing the Jewish Immigrant Aid Society and lobbying the federal government. The third declared Congress's support for the establishment of a Jewish state. The fourth point on the agenda echoed the Jewish delegations at Versailles who were seeking to enshrine in the constitutions of the new European states the fullest rights for their Jewish minorities.

Even the anti-Zionist socialist delegates at

Sir Mortimer B. Davis, seen here in 1925, was the president of Imperial Tobacco and the first Canadian Jew to be knighted (1917). He provided leadership to the community on issues ranging from helping pioneer settlers in Palestine to the establishment of the Mount Sinai Sanitorium. He was knighted in recognition for his contribution to the war effort by paying for the equipment of an entire Canadian division in the First World War.

(Canadian Jewish Congress National Archives, Montreal)

Lillian Freiman Honoured

In the January 1, 1934, New Year's List of
Honours, His Majesty King George V
conferred on Lillian Freiman "the rank
and decoration of Officer of the Order of
the British Empire, Civil Division," for
"community work; Service to returned
soldiers; Leadership in Jewish charitable
Organizations." There was widespread
approval of the honour. The *Canadian
Jewish Chronicle* wrote, "As the first member
of the Jewish race in Canada to receive the
coveted O.B.E. she has written a lustrous
chapter in the history of Canadian Jewry."
The *Jewish Standard* commented, "Her
influence has enriched Canadian Jewish
life beyond measure…"

The *Ottawa Evening Citizen* noted,
"Crowning a career unselfishly devoted to
philanthropic endeavour and charitable
effort in the interests of the needy and
unfortunate, the honour according Mrs.
Archibald Freiman, O.B.E., by His Majesty
the King will be welcomed by Jews and
non-Jews alike throughout the Dominion
as recognition of one of the most outstanding women in Canada."

the 1919 meeting of the Canadian Jewish
Congress voted in favour of the resolution urging that

the peace conference recognize the aspirations and historic claims of the Jewish people
in regard to Palestine, and that there be
established such political, administrative, and
economic conditions in Palestine as will
assure the development of Palestine into a
Jewish commonwealth, it being clearly understood that nothing shall be done which shall
prejudice the civil, national, and religious
rights of existing non-Jewish communities in
Palestine or the rights and political status
enjoyed by Jews in any other country.

The New Organizations

Inspired by the Zionist *chalutziut* (pioneering)
of the Third Aliyah and North American
progressivism, several Labour Zionist organizations flourished in Canada. The Canadian
branch of Achdut Ha'avoda (David Ben-
Gurion's Labour Unity party) was established
in Toronto in 1921, and by 1922 it had
branches in Montreal, Windsor, Hamilton,
Winnipeg, and Calgary. In 1924, the
Canadian Histadrut Campaign (the Canadian
Association for Labour Israel Collection) was
inaugurated as an affiliate of the American Histadrut Campaign.
Mo'etzet Hapoalot (Council for Working Women) was founded in
1921 and in 1925 became the Pioneer Women's Organization of
North America. Forty-six years later, in 1966, the organization
divided into two autonomous national groups in Canada and the
U.S., and the Canadian organization still thrives today as Na'amat
Canada.

Lillian Freiman's leadership helped organize many new Hadassah chapters across the country. Hadassah, the Women's Zionist Organization of America, was founded in New York City in 1912 by Henrietta Szold and the first Canadian chapter was established in Toronto in 1917 by Anna Selick (later Raginsky). At the organization's first national Canadian convention in 1921, Hadassah affiliated with the Women's International Zionist Organization (WIZO), founded in 1920 as a volunteer organization to provide community services in Mandate Palestine, and officially became the Hadassah-WIZO Organization of Canada. The 1921 convention elected Lillian Freiman to the national presidency of the new merged organization, an office she held until her death in 1940.

In September 1924, Archibald Freiman founded the Canadian Keren Hayesod Campaign, an educational campaign that would revolutionize Zionist fundraising in Canada. Jewish citizens from Vancouver to Saint John met the Freimans during the annual Keren

A. M. Klein and Zionism

Zionism was in the blood of Abraham Moses Klein, one of Canada's greatest poets. His family came from Ratno, a small Russian town in Ukraine. Family members, along with some four million Eastern European Jews, fled persecution and pogroms. In 1910, the Kleins arrived in Montreal.

A portrait of Theodor Herzl hung in the Klein family home. While studying at McGill University, Klein joined Young Judaea and, in 1928, became editor of the organization's publication *The Judaean*.

In 1929, when Arabs rioted in Jerusalem, Klein wrote "Greeting on this day":

> The white doves flutter
> From the roofs
> Where stones did utter
> Dark reproofs.

That these pale pigeons
Be alarmed
Guerilla legions
Have been armed.
Effendi, Mufti,
Holy Ones—
They are not thrifty
With their stones.
This is the manner
Doves take flight:
The sky a banner
Blue and white.

In 1934, Klein became national president of Young Judaea. In 1949, the Canadian Jewish Congress sent him to Israel on a fact-finding mission. The result was the novella *The Second Scroll*, published in 1951. He laid down his pen in the mid-1950s, when he became mentally ill. Klein died in 1972, after two decades of literary silence.

A. M. Klein (right), one of Canada's greatest poets, celebrates the launching of his book *The Second Scroll*, with Canadian Jewish Congress leaders Munroe Abbey (left) and Saul Hayes.

Hayesod visits. The campaign was to help build the foundation of the promised homeland. The *chalutzim* streaming into Palestine had nothing. They needed an infrastructure of houses, industries, hospitals, and schools, and the Keren Hayesod campaign helped to provide it. The campaign also became one of the most intense educational programs in Canadian history. It helped hundreds of thousands of Canadian Jews identify their own experience as that of a people long in exile and participate in current events and in the re-creation of a Jewish state.

Relief to Jews in Russia and the Ukraine

Following the abdication of Czar Nicholas II and the setting up of a provisional government in February 1917, Russia had been plunged into a civil war that pitted an informal alliance of anti-Bolshevik (White) forces against the Bolshevik (Red) forces from 1918 to 1920. The Allied countries conducted a military intervention in the civil war in an attempt to stop the Bolsheviks from seizing control of the country and to shore up defences against the German armies. At the same time, the fall of the czar prompted a strong independence movement in Ukraine and, in 1919, struggles over national boundaries between Russia and Poland triggered the Polish-Soviet War that continued until 1921.

This general instability in the region brought on a new wave of attacks from all sides against the Jewish population. In Russia, Jews were simultaneously vilified by the White forces who, in addition to their historical anti-Semitic attitudes, now identified the Jews with the Bolsheviks, and by the Bolsheviks who saw Jewish religious practices and separate labour organizations as a threat to their communist ideals. Throughout the 1920s the Bolsheviks seized Jewish properties, including synagogues, dispersed many of the Jewish communities, and forced rabbis and other religious officials to resign.

In Ukraine, the Jews were seen not only as obstacles to Ukrainian nationalist aspirations, but again, as identified with the Soviet Russian Bolsheviks. Horrific pogroms against Jewish communities began in November 1918 and persisted until 1920, exacerbated by the outbreak of the Polish-Soviet War. Red Cross estimates put the number of Ukrainian Jewish deaths at 120,000, with another 600,000 people suffering material losses.

Canadian Jews first heard about these terrible events in the summer of 1920 and, in particular, were galvanized by stories of the terrible conditions suffered by the Jewish children of Ukraine. There were reports that more than 137,000 Ukrainian Jewish children had been orphaned by the war, many of them left without homes or any means of obtaining sustenance. Aid for these children was imperative, and Lillian Freiman led an undertaking to provide it. In his 1925 article titled "The Jews of Canada," Martin Woolf describes Lillian Freiman's rescue mission as follows:

> ...permission was obtained [from the Canadian government] to bring in 200 Ukrainian orphans for adoption in selected Jewish homes. For this

The Jewish Press

From its earliest days, the Jewish press supported and encouraged Canadian Zionism. Hirsch Wolofsky's *Keneder Adler*, the Montreal Yiddish daily, was the first off the mark in 1907. Some other important Canadian papers are:

- *Der Idisher Zshurnal* (Daily Hebrew Journal) (Yiddish and English), started in Toronto, 1912
- *Der Yiddishe Worte* (Israelite Press) (Yiddish and English), Winnipeg, 1911
- *Canadian Jewish Chronicle* (English), Montreal, 1912
- *Canadian Jewish Review* (English), Montreal, 1921
- *Jewish Post* (English), Winnipeg, 1925
- *Western Jewish News* (English), Winnipeg, 1926
- *Jewish Western Bulletin* (English), Vancouver, 1930
- *Jewish Standard* (English), Toronto, 1930

purpose the Jewish War Orphans Committee was formed under the presidency of Mrs. A. J. Freiman, of Ottawa. The Committee sent a unit to Ukrainia to select the children fit to be brought in, and also to succour as far as possible those unfortunate orphans who were obliged to remain behind. This unit consisted of H. Hershman, of Montreal, as general director, Dr. J. Levitt, of Montreal, as medical advisor, and W. Farrar, of Hamilton, as financial administrator. The last-named was not a Jew but a great-hearted Gentile who volunteered his services gratuitously for this enterprise. Mrs. Freiman personally toured Canada from Halifax to Vancouver, forming sub-committees and securing suitable homes, which should be ready to receive the children upon their arrival. Having completed the organization on this side of the water, this philanthropic woman felt that her duty would only be accomplished by proceeding to Antwerp to meet the little ones in each one of whom she felt such a deep interest, and by crossing the ocean with them she became personally known to each one of her wards. On the arrival of the party at Quebec was witnessed a beautiful scene of true human charity as the children were overwhelmed with affectionate attention by the members of the Reception Committee…. Mrs. Freiman herself adopted one of the children and the others all found happy homes.

Lillian Freiman's hands-on approach to the work demonstrated her dedication to the task. She would examine each child and offer an assessment, such as, "This little girl has dark

Advertisement for "Palestine products for Passover" in the *Jewish Times*, 1926.

hair and dark complexion and needs this kind of dress and coat; this one has blond hair and rosy complexion…" and so on for each one, trying to capture the individuality of the children rather than just processing them as an anonymous collective. It is little wonder that she acquired the title of Mamma Freiman.

In September 1921, in addition to her work with the war orphans, Lillian Freiman championed the cause of would be immigrants who had been detained after their arrival on the ships *Megantic* and *Corsican*. These people, who had fled the pogroms of war-torn Eastern Europe, had been refused landed status as a result of minor immigration technicalities, and were going to be sent back to the lands that had abused them. Freiman, with the tireless assistance of Canadian Jewish philanthropists, the American Joint Distribution Committee, and the Jewish Colonization Association, prevented all but a few of the newcomers from being deported.

Leaders of the Canadian Zionist movement in Montreal in 1920: (front, left to right) Lillian Freiman; Louis Fitch; Camillien Houde, Quebec MLA and Montreal mayor; Victor Cavendish, the Duke of Devonshire, Governor General of Canada from 1916 to 1921; A. J. Freiman; and A. A. Levin.

(Jewish Public Library Archives, Montreal)

Canadian Moshavs, 1927

It was July 1927, and the president of the Zionist Organization of Canada, Archibald (Aharon, his Hebrew name) Freiman of Ottawa, was obviously tense and excited as he laid an immense proposal before members of his organization.

At this time, Canadian Jewry was contributing $25,000 a year to the Jewish National Fund, and Freiman was proposing that—somehow—they raise US$ 1 million to buy a stretch of land between Netanya and Hadera in the valley region known as Emek Hefer to provide land for settlers.

The enormous proposal touched off a fierce debate, but the project was adopted by unanimous vote. It was one of the most emotional moments in the history of Canadian Zionism as delegates embraced one another, tears streaming from their eyes, shouting "Mazel tov!" After a few excited moments, the delegates spontaneously began to sing the Zionist anthem, "Hatikvah."

Among the settlements dotting the area are Moshav Bitan Aharon, named after Freiman, and Moshav Havatzelet Hasharon, named after Freiman's wife, Lillian (Havatzelet in Hebrew).

One of the settlers, Pnina Sapir, remembers the earliest days of Moshav Bitan Aharon in 1933: "There were no roads, no electricity or phones. Cars would sink in the mud, so we had to use horses and carriages." Sapir was among those who stood guard in defence of neighbouring Jewish settlements.

Sam Bronfman and Abraham M. Klein

The Freimans were only one of a number of Jewish families and individuals who began to shape Canadian Jewish history in the 1920s. Sam Bronfman, whose family name is synonymous with the brands of liquor sold under the Scottish name Seagram, was another important member of the Montreal Jewish community. Although much of his most heroic work took place during the Second World War, he began carving a place for himself among prominent Canadian Jews more than a decade earlier, leading to his being elected president of the Canadian Jewish Congress in 1939.

Another person active in the 1920s Zionist movement, and whose involvement continued for more than thirty years, was one of Canada's greatest poets, Abraham M. Klein. Klein grew up in an immigrant home in Montreal. In the mid-1920s, he became the head of Young Judaea and the editor of Zionist publications. This marked the beginning of his career as a journalist and, in a broad sense, a popular educator.

Klein editorialized and commented on events pertaining to the Jewish scene in the *Judaean* and later, for a brief period, in the *Canadian Zionist*. From the early 1930s on, he contributed articles and reviews to the *Canadian Jewish Chronicle* and prepared outlines for study groups in Young Judaea on such topics as the history of the Jews in Poland and the treatment of the Jew in English literature. He was also a longtime speechwriter and public relations consultant for Samuel Bronfman.

For more than thirty years, Klein communicated with the Jews all around the world through his poetry, his declarations, and his

Convention of the Zionist Order Habonim in Ste-Marguerite, Quebec, in 1928.

(*The Jewish Standard*)

editorial columns. He also became known as one of the leading members of the Canadian literary world at large.

Disturbances in Palestine

The leadership that the Freimans provided from 1919 to 1933, a period of relative tranquility in Canada, made this a time of achievement for the Zionist movement, highlighted by the rescue of Jews in peril and growing respect for the Jewish community. In Palestine, however, tranquility for the Jews proved elusive as the alliance between the Jewish community and British administrators began to fray in the 1920s. In 1922, the colonial secretary, Winston Churchill, chose to interpret the League's mandate as allowing unfettered immigration into Palestine of those Jewish immigrants who could show that they could create or sustain their own livelihood. But Herbert Samuel, High Commissioner of the British Mandate in Palestine, faced growing sentiments from his own government that too much support had been shown to the Jews in the region at the expense of the Arab communities. In one of many efforts to show his neutrality, he had appointed Arab nationalist leader Haj Amin al-Husseini as the grand mufti of Jerusalem. The Arab nationalists completely rejected the idea of any compromise with the Jews and increasingly relied on violence as the main tactic in their struggle.

On August 23, 1929, riots broke out in Jerusalem over a dispute concerning the right of Jews to pray at the Western Wall. These riots quickly spread to Motza, Huldah, Hebron, Be'er Tuvyah, Tel Aviv, and Haifa.

In the aftermath of the riots the British appointed a commission to investigate their cause. Although the commission report found that the immediate cause was Arab "racial animosity" toward the Jews, the Arab hostility to the Jews arose out of "[t]he claims and demands which from the Zionist side have been advanced in regard to the future of Jewish immigration which have been such as to arouse among Arabs the apprehension that they will in time be deprived of their livelihood and put under the political domination of the Jews."

The report reassured the Arabs and disappointed the *yishuv*, and, on the basis of it, the British government halted Jewish immigration to Palestine in May 1930. To justify their actions, the British sent an investigator, Sir John Hope-Simpson, to examine conditions and economic opportunities in Palestine. In his October 1930 report, Hope-Simpson argued that there was not enough land to ensure a reasonable livelihood for Arab farmers and proposed the introduction of strictly supervised immigration to reduce Arab unemployment.

At the same time as the Hope-Simpson report, the British government issued a White Paper on its Palestinian policy that reinterpreted the country's "economic absorptive capacity." According to the Passfield White Paper, the frame of reference was not to the absorptive capacity of the Jewish *yishuv* alone, but to that of the entire country. From this perspective, Jewish immigration should not be permitted because as long as there was Arab unemployment, the entry of additional Jews would worsen the Arab predicament. Although British Prime Minister Ramsay MacDonald later distanced himself from these recommendations, immigration remained restricted.

4

In the Shadow of the Holocaust

CONDITIONS FOR THE JEWISH PEOPLE in Europe began to deteriorate in the years after the First World War. Post-war inflation and social and economic disarray overwhelmed liberal ideas and institutions, which became less and less capable of dealing with Europe's economic problems.

The Depression provided the opportunity for the rise of fascism, most prominently in Italy and Germany. Mussolini had created a fascist state in Italy shortly after the First World War, and over the next decade, against the backdrop of the growing economic crisis, authoritarian

Members of the Zionist Organization of Canada protest the 1929 Hebron Massacre.

(Jewish Public Library Archives, Montreal)

21ˢᵀ ZIONIST CONVENT[ION]

H. M. Caiserman spent his entire adult life working to strengthen the Jewish community in Canada and to bring about the re-establishment of a Jewish state in Palestine. In the 1929 postcard below, Caiserman is seated on the left next to Hirsch Wolofsky, publisher of Montreal's Yiddish daily newspaper *Keneder Adler*, which strongly supported the Zionist cause.

(Canadian Jewish Congress Archives, Montreal)

regimes took power in Hungary, Spain, Portugal, Poland, Yugoslavia, Albania, Romania, Bulgaria, the Baltic states, and Greece. Liberal political and economic institutions quickly collapsed, and the limited protection afforded to ethnic minorities in these countries in prior periods now disappeared. Anti-Semitism increased and spread. For European Jews, the precarious and deteriorating situation of the 1930s was a harbinger of the even greater evil that was about to befall them.

In Germany, the Nazis swept to power in March 1933, and soon afterward their reign of terror began. The following month, a boycott of Jewish stores was decreed and laws banning Jews from public office

Caiserman in Palestine

"As we approached by train from Egypt, we could see some railway cars marked with Hebrew letters. A Jewish conductor asked us for our tickets in Hebrew. Only a poet could describe our deep emotion. These were the first signs of a Jewish authority being born. An hour or two before Jerusalem, the passengers donned their best clothes, and a chant arose spontaneously in every car. It was as if the songs of all religions united into a magnificent hymn of gratitude for the privilege of approaching eternal Jerusalem."

—Canadian Jewish community leader H. M. Caiserman's description of his 1929 arrival in Palestine. He was accompanied by Hirsch Wolofsky, publisher of *Keneder Adler*.

WINNIPEG. MAN   JULY 10 TH. 11 TB AND 12 TH 1927.

and forbidding them to practice as lawyers and physicians (except for Jewish clients and patients) took effect shortly thereafter. Attacks on Jews became more frequent and more brazen. In Germany, new laws and regulations were enacted that singled out Jews for particular disqualification and discrimination. The Nuremburg Laws—which excluded Jews from German citizenship and prohibited marriages between Jewish and non-Jewish Germans—and successive legislation eventually placed German Jews outside German law and excluded them from economic life. Jewish ownership of businesses was at first restricted and later banned. Jews could not become lawyers or

Delegates to the 21st Zionist Convention, Winnipeg, 1927.

(Canadian Jewish Congress National Archives, Montreal)

The executive of the Vancouver Young Judaea, 1933–1934.

(British Columbia Jewish Historical Society)

Jewish Farmers 1939

"Jewish colonists in Palestine have made that country a garden and the products of Jewish farms are being widely distributed throughout the world."

—*Windsor Times*, January 27, 1939, commenting on the Canadian government's refusal to admit Jewish farmers, despite the growing danger from Nazi Germany.

accountants or doctors or professors, then finally, could not attend university at all.

Against this background, many Jews in Germany and elsewhere realized the urgency of leaving Europe. Tragically for them, countries all over the world began to shut their doors to immigration in this period. Canada, shamefully, was among them.

Anti-Semitism in Canada

The onset of the Depression brought anti-Semitism to the surface in Canada. Canadian immigration policy had always been ethnically selective and deeply prejudicial. During times of economic recession, immigrants were seen as competitors for scarce jobs who further depressed wages; recent immigrants who became unemployed were deported on the slightest pretext. Canadian policy was not only aimed at Jewish immigrants: Asians, blacks, and Jews were all grouped together as relative undesirables. By the mid-1930s, Canadian immigration officials preferred to permit the entry of people from Britain or the U.S., or those with enough capital to immediately start farming in Canada, ahead of Jews. Moreover, Canada, like all other countries at this time, did not have a separate policy for refugees.

The Zionist Order of Habonim Lodge, Vancouver, 1938.

(British Columbia Jewish Historical Society)

The Ontario Young Judaea Convention in London, Ontario, 1938.

(Ontario Jewish Archives # 6067)

As Irving Abella and Harold Troper have shown in their study *None is Too Many: Canada and the Jews of Europe, 1933–1948*, Canada's immigration policy in the 1930s was not only influenced by economic concerns but also reflected the nativism and anti-Semitism of Canadian public opinion. "Jewish quotas existed in various professions, universities, medical schools and industries. Jews were restricted from buying property in some areas, from holidaying at some resorts, from joining many private clubs or using their recreational facilities and even from sitting on the boards of various charitable, educational, financial and business organizations. Anti-Jewish sentiments were being voiced regularly—and with impunity—by many respectable newspapers, politicians, businessmen and clergymen…"

In Quebec, latent anti-Semitism fuelled francophone suspicion of federal immigration policy that had, for years, channelled English-speaking immigrants into Quebec, threatening a francophone identity. Apprehensive of immigrants who would both undermine the influence of the Roman Catholic Church and the unity of the francophone community, the rhetoric of French-Canadian identity in the 1930s became specifically anti-Jewish. Editorials in the newspaper *Le Devoir* attacked Quebec Jewish merchants and refugees who sought entry into Canada from Austria, Germany, and Poland; in one example the author asked, "Why allow in Jewish refugees?...The Jewish shopkeeper on St. Lawrence Boulevard does nothing to increase our natural resources." Other papers, such as *La Nation*, *L'Action catholique* (the official organ of the Roman Catholic Church in Quebec), and *L'Action nationale* issued similar attacks. Adrien Arcand, the leader of a small, but vocal group of Quebec fascists, used the economic climate and Quebec fears of Jewish immigration as a launching pad for his attacks on Jews in Canada. Anti-Semitism even lurked within the ranks of the Catholic Church, which took a strong stand against the Jewish schools that were legislated into existence by the Quebec government. Priests were heard preaching anti-Semitic sermons.

Members of Parliament from Quebec, most notably Ernest Lapointe, who was Minister of Justice in several successive governments under Prime Minister Mackenzie King in the 1920s and 1930s, as well as Wilfrid Lacroix, C. H. Leclerc, and H. E. Brunelle, spoke in favour of the restricted immigration policy. Their views were widely shared among anglophone Canadians, and for many of the same reasons. Frederick Charles Blair, the director of the Immigration Branch of the Department of Mines and Resources from 1936 to 1944 was the man most responsible for creating the immigration policies that reflected these widespread views and upholding the restrictions that kept Canada's doors shut to Jewish immigrants.

Liberal Prime Minister Mackenzie King, who came back to power in October 1935 after a five-year hiatus, listened carefully to these voices. On several occasions he pleaded for his cabinet to take a more liberal attitude and act with conscience regarding refugees from Europe, but he was always careful not to stray far from public opinion. Wishing to avoid a divisive issue, and acknowledging his need for French-Canadian support, Mackenzie King acquiesced in an illiberal

Golda Meyerson (centre, third row from the back) visiting Pioneer Women in Montreal, 1929. The future prime minister of Israel paid many visits to Canada and the United States, seeking support for Jews in Palestine.

(Jewish Public Library Archives, Montreal)

Oneg Shabbat at the National Young Judaea Convention, Toronto, 1935.

(Ontario Jewish Archives # 3872)

immigration policy to serve the basic Liberal objective of national unity.

Support for Jews diminished across Canada in the 1930s. Jewish businessmen saw their businesses suffer. Jews in many parts of Canada became increasingly isolated from the rest of society. The courts failed to protect Canadian Jews from attacks in print or from rising hooliganism. Legislatures were ineffectual in prohibiting the dissemination of racist hate propaganda. One result of these trends is that there were fewer contacts between Jews and Canadian leaders than there had been in prior periods, especially in Quebec, and the relations there were became increasingly strained. Some attempts were made by Canadian leaders to bridge this gap, and several prominent Christian Canadians attempted to persuade the Canadian government to open the country's doors to Jewish refugees. For example, Conservative Prime Minister R. B. Bennett, in power from 1930 to 1935, joined the prominent Ottawa businessman A. J. Freiman in April 1934 in a nationwide radio address to launch the Keren Hayesod–United Palestine Appeal. In his speech, Bennett stated, "When the promises of God, speaking through His prophets, are that the home will be restored in the homeland of their forefathers, and that despite defeat and persecution, sorrow and separation, the broken home will sometime be rebuilt: the historic and ancient homeland some time again settled by the descendants of dispersed and conquered people, faith triumphs over doubt, hope over despair, with confident belief that the promises will surely be fulfilled. Such is the story of the Jews."

Another important voice heard in opposition to government policy was Liberal Senator Cairine Wilson, appointed Canada's first female senator in 1930. Tirelessly fighting for the admittance of Jewish refugees and for a liberalization of Canada's immigration policy, Senator Wilson found herself among a small group of like-minded influential Canadians that included the Protestant Reverend Claris Silcox (who in 1940 became director of the Canadian Conference of Christians and Jews, but later became a vehement anti-Zionist); the journalist and editor B. K. Sandwell (editor of the magazine *Saturday Night* from 1932 to 1951); and Ellsworth Flavelle (son of the famous financier Sir Joseph Flavelle and chairman of the Canadian Palestine Committee, a group of non-Jewish leaders favourable to Zionism). The efforts of these people nonetheless failed as a result of the solid opposition within successive governments, especially from Quebec ministers, that largely reflected the sentiments of Canadians across the country.

The Yishuv under the British Mandate in the 1930s

With the threat to the Jews of Europe palpable by the 1930s, the demand for immigration to British Mandate Palestine had never been higher. In the wake of the Nazi rise to power, immigration increased from 4,075 in 1931; to 37,337 in 1933; to a record 66,472 in 1935. By 1939, there were approximately 400,000 Jews living in the *yishuv*. Yet just at the time when the Jewish search for refuge was most desperate, the British imposed onerous restrictions to entry.

Among the competing voices and views in London, there were many that supported Jewish aspirations in Palestine. Both the 1917 Balfour Declaration and the text establishing the British Mandate in 1920 clearly supported the establishment of a Jewish national home and the facilitation of Jewish immigration to Palestine. However, predominant and traditional colonial concerns—which viewed the Arabs in British middle-eastern holdings as the best allies for ensuring British commercial interests, access to oil, and control over the Suez Canal—largely drowned out these voices,

"In all the history of colonization, you will not find such signal achievements as have been attained by the Jewish pioneers in Palestine. Our young men and young women there are covering themselves with no end of glory. They are draining swamps, building roads, constructing colonies, converting a pest-ridden country into a wholesome paradise. The call of the ancient homeland has revealed hidden heroisms and unsuspected capacity for sacrifice in the Jewish people such as we ourselves had never dreamed of."
—Rabbi Dr. Herman Abramowitz, introducing Lord Tweedsmuir, governor general of Canada, at a banquet launching the United Palestine Appeal on April 20, 1936, in Montreal.

and the British commitment to Zionism was watered down from the start. Through the 1920s and especially the 1930s, British policy evolved through a series of "plans," "commissions," and "papers" that increasingly restricted Jewish immigration.

The first major reexamination of British policy on immigration to Palestine had come following the Arab riots of 1929 when the Shaw Commission (leading to the Hope-Simpson report and the Passfield White paper) recommended strictly limiting immigration or halting it altogether. These recommendations were not fully implemented and some immigration was allowed to continue—including that of 50,000 Jews who emigrated to Palestine over the course of 1933–1935 under the Ha'avara, or Transfer Agreement. This was an agreement signed in August 1933 between the Jewish Agency and the Nazi regime that allowed German Jews to leave and retain some of their assets by transferring them to Palestine as German export goods.

In 1936, an Arab national general strike broke out and sparked another Arab revolt against the British. The halting of Jewish immigration was one of the Arabs' key demands. The general strike also gave rise to the formation of the Arab High Committee headed by the Grand Mufti Haj Amin el-Husseini (who took a pro-Nazi stance and moved to Germany during the Second World War where he broadcast anti-British and anti-Jewish commentary for the Nazis). The Arab High Committee coordinated wholesale attacks and riots directed toward Jews over the next three years. During the first wave of this revolt, which lasted from April to October 1936, thousands of Jewish farms and properties were destroyed, and Jews were attacked and killed.

In response to the unrest, the British sent the Peel Commission to investigate and make recommendations. The Peel proposals of July 1937 were essentially two-fold: freeze Jewish immigration at 12,000 per year for five years, and partition the Mandate into a small Jewish state whose Arab population would be transferred, and a larger Arab state to be attached to Jordan. The proposal was rejected by the Arabs and eventually by the British themselves and many Zionists. The World Zionist Congress seriously debated the proposal, however, and many Zionists accepted that partition would be an acceptable realization of the dream of Jewish statehood and the basis of negotiations with the British for a future state.

The failure of the Peel proposals did not mean that immigration was allowed to continue as before. The highpoint of immigration to

John Buchan, 1st Baron Tweedsmuir, governor general of Canada, 1935–1940, was an outspoken Christian Zionist. As he noted on one occasion in Montreal, "Zionism has never been more important than at this moment…Is it not right and fitting that the Jew, after long wanderings, should again find his homeland?" While a member of the British Parliament from 1927 to 1935, he served for a term as chairman of the Pre Palestine Committee.

16th Annual Conference of Zionist Order Habonim

Montreal, November 3rd, 1940

AGENDA:

FIRST SESSION — 9.30 A.M. — 12.30 P.M. — Zionist Headquaters.
1. Opening of Conference — Chairman, Dr. S. H. Bernstein.
2. Minutes of XVth Conention — Hon. Secretary, J. N. Frank.
3. Presidential Report — President, Bernard L. Cohen.
4. Financial Report — Treasurer, N. Veinish.
5. Appointment of Nominations and Resolutions Committee.
6. Reports of Lodges.
7. Greetings by Mrs. A. Raginsky, Sr., for the Hadassah Organization of Canada and Dr. Mark Zimmerman for Canadian Young Judaea.

SECOND SESSION — 2.00 P.M. — 5.00 P.M. — Zionist Headquarters.
1. Report of Resolutions Committee.
   General Debate.
   Report of Nominations Committee.
   Election of Supreme Council.
   Symposium: *"The War and the Zionist Movement."*
   Participants: REV. J. K. GOLDBLOOM,
            Chairman, Executive Board, Zionist Federation of Great Britain.
         S. E. SCHWISBERG,
            Eastern Vice-President, Zionist Organization of Canada.
         RABBI JESSE SCHWARTZ,
            Executive Director, Zionist Organization of Canada.
         ALBERT J. SILVERMAN,
            Director, Jewish National Fund Bureau for Canada.

MASS MEETING: Mount Royal Hotel, at 8.30 P.M.
         PROGRAMME:
   Guest Speaker: RABBI MAURICE L. PERLZWEIG of London, England, *Member of the Executive Committee of the Jewish Agency for Palestine.*
   Musicale: PALESTINIAN SONGS—CANTOR NATHAN MENDELSON. BERNARD L. COHEN.
   Chairman: *President, Zionist Order Habonim.*
HATIKVAH   GOD SAVE THE KING
   The mass meeting will be open to the general public.

Shekel Registration Completed

The Central Shekel Board for Canada, through its chairman, Mr. Louis Miller, announces that the Shekel Registration for the year 5700 is closed and that the Shekel reports from all communities and Shekel money on hand must be forwarded to Montreal Headquarters, 527 Sherbrooke Street West, by this Monday. October 28th.

Zionist Convention January 19 and 20

The National Council of the Zionist Organization of Canada announces that the 26th Convention of the Organization will be held in Montreal on Sunday and Monday. January 19th and 20th. The sessions of the Convention will take place at the Mount Royal Hotel.

RABBI JESSE SCHWARTZ
Executive Director, Zionist
Organization of Canada

REV. J. K. GOLDBLOOM
Chairman, Executive Board.
Zionist Federation of
Great Britain

A. J. SILVERMAN
Executive Director. Jewish National
Fund Bureau for Canada

BERNARD L. COHEN
President, Zionist Order Habonim

S. E. SCHWISBERG
Vice-President, Zionist
Organization of Canada

DR. S. H. BERNSTEIN
Chairman, Conference Committee

RABBI M. L. PERLZWEIG
Member, Executive, Jewish
Agency for Palestine

CANTOR NATHAN MENDELSON
of Shaar Hashomayim Congregation
in a recital of Palestinian songs

the *yishuv* in the 1930s came in 1935. The 66,472 immigrants allowed in legally that year were viewed as far too many by the British, especially against the backdrop of the unfolding unrest in the Mandate, and they severely restricted quotas in the years that followed—to approximately 29,000 in 1936; 10,000 in 1937; and 14,000 in 1938.

The Jewish immigrants of the 1930s are known as the Fifth Aliyah. Coming mainly from Eastern Europe, this group also included many professionals, doctors, lawyers, and academics from Germany, as well as a high concentration of artists and musicians. This Aliyah gave rise to the vibrant Bauhaus movement in Tel Aviv (which today has the highest concentration of Bauhaus architecture in the world) and led to the founding of the Palestine Philharmonic Orchestra. During the 1930s, industrial enterprises increased in the *yishuv*, helped along by the completion of the port of Haifa and the construction of oil refineries there. While economies were suffering in the United States, France, and Britian, the economy in Palestine actually flourished, with Jews investing in new industrial and agricultural enterprises and urban development.

Increasing restrictions on immigration by the British especially after 1935, gave rise to a wave of clandestine and illegal immigration, called Ha'apala or Aliyah Bet. Occuring mostly by sea, and to a smaller extent by land through Syria and Iraq, Aliyah Bet would become the main form of Jewish immigration to Palestine during

A page from the November 1940 program of the sixteenth Annual Conference of the Zionist Order Habonim (opposite page).

(Canadian Jewish Congress National Archives, Montreal)

The Pioneer Women of Northern Alberta, circa 1930.

(The Jewish Archives and Historical Society of Edmonton and Northern Alberta)

The executive of Young Judaea in Saint John, New Brunswick, circa 1930.

(Saint John Jewish Historical Museum)

the Second World War and in the years leading to independence in 1948.

More violence flared in the wake of the Peel proposals and continued on and off until 1939. During this period the British lost control of Jerusalem, Nablus, and Hebron and began attempts to suppress the revolt by force. The continuing unrest and violence in Mandate Palestine led the British to establish the Woodhouse Commission in 1938 (which once again examined the possibility of partition but deemed it impracticable), and eventually the St. James Conference of 1939 that produced the McDonald White Paper.

The 1939 White Paper repudiated prior British statements that Palestine (in part or in whole) should become a national home for the Jews. It also sharply limited land transfers from Palestinian Arabs to non-Arabs, and called for the permanent limitation of Jewish immigration to Palestine. Only 75,000 Jewish immigrants would be allowed to enter over the next five-year period, and any subsequent requests for immigration would require the approval of local Arab authorities.

The McDonald White Paper policy represented the final evolution of British policy toward Mandate Palestine before the Second World War. Repudiating the principles enshrined in the Balfour Declaration and walking away from their commitments under the League of Nations Mandate system, the British now calculated that, with the world on the brink of war, mollifying the Arab population in their middle-eastern holdings was to their greatest advantage. They even put pressure on the German, Greek, Yugoslav, Bulgarian, and Turkish governments not to allow illegal immigrants into Palestine at this time. The great tragedy of this policy was precisely the timing: in 1939 the Jewish need for sanctuary could not have been greater. The issue at hand now was not only or even mainly that of Jewish national aspiration, it was the desperate search for refuge in the face of looming certain death in Europe.

New Priorities, Old Indifference

With Jews threatened all over the world in the late 1930s, Canadian Jews began to focus their energy toward a new priority—changing Canadian immigration policy. The Canadian Jewish Congress pinned its hopes in this regard on the efforts of three *shtadlonim*— or men of influence: Samuel Jacobs, a Liberal MP from Montreal and for many

A meeting of the Zionist Cadet Corps Reunion, Montreal, 1933. Rabbi Charles Bender is at the centre of the group.

(Jewish Public Library Archives, Montreal)

years the only Jewish member of the House of Commons; Samuel Factor, a Liberal MP from Toronto; and Abraham Heaps, a founder of the Cooperative Commonwealth Federation (CCF) and MP from Winnipeg. These three men functioned as an ad hoc Jewish lobby on Parliament Hill, plying their skills in backroom diplomacy toward the goal of liberalizing immigration policy and pressuring the government to allow Jewish refugees from the Nazis into Canada. Unfortunately, their influence in leading government circles was minimal and the roots of opposition to any change in Canada's immigration policy ran too deep. Canada's doors remained firmly shut.

Kristallnacht—the so-called Night of the Broken Glass pogrom against German Jews that took place on November 9, 1938—was a

Members of the Montreal Young Judaea, in the late 1930s, in front of the offices of the Zionist Organization of Canada at 527 Sherbrooke Street West.

(Canadian Jewish Congress National Archives, Montreal)

The 1931 Executive of Young Judaea in Ottawa.
Front row: Thelma Rivers, Norman Kilenowsky, Annie Goldman, Max Bookman (president), Ruth Epstein, Max Epstein. Centre row: Joe Lieff, Elsie Bendly, Charles Silverman, Annie Bookman, Nap Tapinsky. Back row: Henry Brahlinsky, Sam Silver, Sarah Hanser, Ben Steinberg.

(Ottawa Jewish Archives)

galvanizing moment for Canadian Jews. Over the course of one night, Jewish homes, shops, and buildings throughout Germany were ransacked and destroyed, Jews were beaten to death, thousands of synagogues were ransacked with hundreds set on fire, and 30,000 Jewish men were taken to concentration camps. The pogrom was well-publicized throughout the world and was clearly understood by observers to be a new and sinister stage in Nazi policies against Jews.

Jews in Canada were shocked by the events of *Kristallnacht* and quickly came together in protest and solidarity. Nationwide demonstrations, many organized spontaneously and including both Jews and Gentiles, took place across the country in the wake of the pogrom. The Canadian Jewish Congress proclaimed November 20, 1938, a day of mourning, and at memorials and meetings held across Canada on that day Gentiles and Jews voiced their revulsion and indignation at the events in Germany. Telegrams, resolutions, petitions, and letters

A Young Judaea Group in front of the Queen Street Synagogue in Kingston, Ontario, in 1943.

(Ontario Jewish Archives # 3056)

engulfed the offices of Prime Minister King and members of Parliament, calling on them to help European Jews and do something to stop Hitler. As Abella and Troper note, the largest meeting in Toronto passed a resolution demanding that Canadians "show their moral courage by taking action together with other liberal and democratic countries to provide havens of refuge for the victims of Nazi brutality."

At a meeting on November 23, 1938, an impressive group of Canadian Jews—members of Parliament and the leaders of all the Jewish community organizations in the country—implored Prime Minister Mackenzie King to admit even a small number of Jews into Canada, offering to guarantee that they would not become a financial burden. The prime minister was understanding and polite, but the response of the government remained negative. Indeed, Prime Minister King and his cabinet had already held a meeting the day before and had decided they would not modify their stand even in the face of the coast-to-coast demonstrations and worldwide condemnation of *Kristallnacht*. King and his cabinet continued to feel that their concern for the national cohesion of Canada must override the humanitarian or moral considerations of helping Jews in Europe. Focused on the resolute opposition of Quebec MPs and the political

The sixth annual convention of the Hadassah-WIZO Organization of Canada in Ottawa on September 7, 1930.

(Canadian Hadassah-WIZO Archives)

nual Hadassah Convention. Ottawa, Sept. 7–1930.

consequences of altering Canada's immigration policy, King would not allow Jews fleeing from oppression to find either temporary or permanent haven in Canada. Jewish members of Parliament such as Samuel Jacobs, who had played an important part in launching King's political career a few decades earlier, were unable to make a dent in King's immigration policy, even when it was clear that the situation was desperate. The attitude of Canadian authorities toward the welfare of the European Jews was one of indifference.

Frustrated by the inaction of the Canadian government on refugee and immigration policy, most Canadian Jewish leaders nevertheless

A meeting of members of Poale Zion Labour Party, held in 1936, in Montreal.

(Canadian Jewish Congress National Archives)

The United Palestine Appeal Planning Committee in 1943. (Left to right) Joseph B. Lubotta, David Dunkelman, Samuel J. Zacks, and Morris Till

(Ontario Jewish Archives)

believed that nothing would be accomplished by increased agitation and advised quiet protest. They continued to lobby as best they could, hatching many plans that went nowhere and launching petitions that fell on deaf ears. They actively supported the efforts of Senator Cairine Wilson who spearheaded the establishment of the Canadian National Committee on Refugees and Political Persecution in late 1938. In response to thousands of letters for help from European Jews, Jewish leaders found themselves in the uncomfortable position of expressing outrage and sympathy, and then having to explain Canada's immigration policy and their failure to change it. It was an agonizing time for Canadian Jews.

5

The Second World War
Death and Rebirth

O N SEPTEMBER 1, 1939, GERMANY's invasion of Poland
initiated the Second World War. Within a week, Britain,
France, Australia, New Zealand, and Canada had all
declared war on Germany. By this time, nearly all Jewish companies
in Germany had either collapsed under financial pressure and declin-
ing profits, or had been forced to sell out to the Nazi government as
part of the "Aryanization" policies. In 1940, the Nazis began to force
Poland's nearly three million Jews into overcrowded ghettos that
lacked sufficient food, water, and sanitary facilities; many of the Jews
in the ghettos died from starvation or disease. By the end of 1940, the

Members of the Jewish
Brigade in the Second World
War. The brigade, which was
a part of the British army,
included a number of
Canadian volunteers but was
made up primarily of Jews
from Palestine. It served in
Egypt, the northern Italian
front, and in northwest
Europe.

Abe Bonder of Montreal cuts
a straight furrow on a kibbutz
in British Mandate Palestine,
1943.

Nazis had invaded Denmark, Norway, France, Belgium, Luxembourg, the Netherlands, and signed the Tripartite (Axis) Pact with Italy and Japan; they would later be joined by Hungary and Romania. In June of the following year, the Nazis invaded the Soviet Union and in December 1941 began to implement their "Final Solution to the Jewish Question," systematically deporting Jews from the ghettos and all occupied territories to extermination camps and sending out roaming killing squads to round up Jews town by town and murder them. In addition to their own lethal machinery, the Nazis also encouraged others to carry out pogroms against the Jews.

By the end of the war, the Jewish population of Europe had been all but wiped out. The Holocaust had nearly destroyed European Jewry physically and almost—but not quite—destroyed it psychologically and spiritually. In Poland, home of the largest Jewish community in the world before the war, more than 90 per cent of the Jewish population—about 3,000,000 Jews—had been killed. At least 70 per cent of the Jewish populations of Greece, Yugoslavia, Hungary, Lithuania, Bohemia, the Netherlands, Slovakia, and Latvia had been destroyed, as well as half of the Jewish populations of Belgium, Romania, Luxembourg, Norway, and Estonia, one third of the Jews in the Soviet Union, and a quarter of the Jewish populations of France and Italy. The number of Jews murdered by the Nazis and their allies was six million. As Gideon Hausner, chief prosecutor at the war crimes trial of Adolf Eichmann in Jerusalem in 1961 said, "Only in our generation has a nation attacked an entire defenceless and peaceful population, men and women, greybeards, children and infants, incarcerated them behind electrified fences, imprisoned them in concentration camps, and resolved to destroy them utterly." This, he asserted, was "a new kind of murder" that involved "calculated decision and painstaking planning; not through the evil designs of an individual, but through a mighty criminal conspiracy involving thousands; not against one victim…but against an entire nation."

The Yishuv's Response to the Holocaust

In the first years of the war, the *yishuv* responded in various ways. In the summer of 1940, it set up a Jewish Palestinian infantry battalion to co-operate with the British army. In addition, skilled Jewish labourers went to work at British military bases, while some Jews enlisted

Sydney Shulemson in front of the Beaufighter he used to attack and destroy a number of German warships and freighters off the coasts of France and Norway. Canada's most decorated Jewish warrior, the Montreal pilot also played a major role in collecting weapons and personnel for the armed forces of Israel, besieged at its rebirth in 1948.

(Canadian Jewish Congress National Archives, Montreal)

directly in the British army. But the *yishuv*'s response to the Holocaust changed dramatically as the war continued. Information about the Holocaust began to reach Palestine as early as 1942, but it was only during 1943 that the overwhelming evidence began to convince people of the magnitude of what was occurring. However, neither the Zionist movement nor the *yishuv*'s institutions made any attempt to establish direct, independent contact with those European Jews held in camps or ghettos, much less try to organize revolts or acts of sabotage. Instead, futile attempts were made to pressure the Allies to take in more Jews.

Jews of the *yishuv* finally took action at the end of 1943 and in 1944. Thirty-two volunteers parachuted into seven Nazi-occupied countries to conduct intelligence operations and organize and encourage the Jews of those countries. Only a few were able to carry out their tasks successfully. These individuals—Enzo Sereni, Hannah Szenes, Havivah Reik, and their comrades—symbolized the valour

Canadian Palestine Committee, 1944

At the 1944 convention of the Zionist Organization of Canada, Harry Batshaw, Canada's first Jewish judge, announced plans to seek the support of non-Jews in the bid to drum up support for the restoration of Jewish statehood.

The key personality emerging from this effort was Herbert Mowat, a former Anglican minister from Toronto, who energetically, enthusiastically, and effectively provided professional leadership to what became known as the Canadian Palestine Committee.

Mowat approached a number of non-Jews, and among those who joined the committee were Lady Flora McCrae Eaton, Senators Salton Hayden and Adrian Hugessen, poet F. R. Scott, and Quebec lawyer, Aimé Geoffrion.

The executive secretary of the B'nai Brith lodge in Welland, Ontario, wrote in 1945, after a visit by Mowat, "Mr. Mowat certainly sold the non-Jew the idea of Palestine as the rightful homeland of the Jews. I don't know of anyone who is more qualified to speak at non-Jewish audiences on the Palestine question with such sincerity as Mr. Mowat."

In his poetry, Scott described devastatingly the waffling and inaction of Prime Minister William Lyon Mackenzie King, including the prime minister's cold and calculating refusal, for political reasons, to help rescue threatened European Jews (even though he expressed sympathy in his diaries) in the critical years leading up to the Second World War. In "W.L.M.K.," Scott wrote,

He [King] blunted us. We had no shape, because he never took sides, and no sides, because he never allowed them to take shape.

and sacrifice of the *yishuv* and the Jewish people as a whole, and strengthened the ties between the *yishuv* and the Jews of Europe.

In July 1944, the British at last allowed the formation of a Jewish Brigade. The brigade enabled the *yishuv* to establish contact with the remaining Jews in Europe, engaged in rescue attempts like the ones mentioned above, encouraged the survivors, and helped to organize "illegal" immigration to Palestine after the war.

The *yishuv*'s efforts to assist the Holocaust victims were dangerous undertakings requiring sacrifice and courage. They extended a much-needed lifeline to the victims of the Nazi regime.

The Changing Zionist Agenda

At the beginning of the war, the main objective of the Zionist movement was to see a quick and successful conclusion to the conflict. But as the facts about the atrocities committed against European Jews filtered out, the defeat of Hitler and his war machine fuelled the desire for a broader Zionist agenda.

The Biltmore Program, named after the New York hotel that hosted a meeting of leading Zionists in May 1942, constituted the basis for the Zionist movement's political activity. The program was based primarily on three resolutions: a demand that Palestine be opened to mass Jewish immigration; a demand that all matters connected with immigration and development of the country for absorption purposes be entrusted to the Jewish Agency; and a call for the establishment of an independent Jewish commonwealth in Palestine.

Following the war, the *yishuv* became active in constructing an independent Jewish policy, the unequivocal objective of which was the establishment of a Jewish state in Palestine. Recruitment efforts were intensified in Canada and in April 1946 alone, seventy-six members of Parliament, members of provincial legislatures, and senators joined the Canadian Palestine Committee, which now included two federal cabinet ministers—Ian Mackenzie and J. G. Gardiner. This effort was vital as the San Francisco United Nations Conference on International Organization loomed, its purpose to draft a charter for the United Nations. For the Jewish world, a major concern was how the new international body would deal with the mandate over Palestine granted to Britain by the League of Nations.

The Canadian Jewish Community's Response

As a result of Canadian government policy, fewer than five thousand Jews entered Canada from 1933 to 1945. While the Canadian government was doing little to provide a safe haven for European Jews, the Canadian Jewish community was left on its own to help Europe's Jews as best it could.

Many Canadian Jews put on a uniform; many paid with their lives. Others, such as Samuel Bronfman, began to gather Jewish community support for European Jewry. Bronfman, who became president of the Canadian Jewish Congress in January 1939, had no previous leadership experience in the Canadian Jewish community outside of fundraising for Jewish causes in Montreal, and no base among Labour Zionist and Jewish immigrant communities. But he saw immediately that his most important task was to unite Canadian Jews, to encourage them to set aside their differences, and to address the Canadian government with a unified voice. Within months, he was able to mobilize such divergent groups as the established wealthy Jewish elite, the Zionist movements, and working-class members of Poale Zion.

At the top of Bronfman's agenda throughout the Second World War was securing entry for Jewish refugees into Canada. He already

Louis Bloomfield

Charles Orde Wingate was a legendary figure in the formation of a Jewish self-defence force in British Mandate Palestine who trained members of the Haganah to protect the Jewish community from Arab raiders. The British officer's groups were known as Wingate's Night Squads, and his trainees included future Israeli military commanders Moshe Dayan and Yigal Allon. His intelligence officer was Louis Mortimer Bloomfield, who worked with Wingate on the development of an intelligence network to prevent Arab attacks on Jewish settlers, and especially on the oil pipeline at Haifa.

Born in Montreal in 1910, Bloomfield joined the British forces and was assigned to work with General Wingate. He also spent the period from 1936 to 1939 in the training program for the Haganah. In 1942, when Franklin D. Roosevelt established the Office of Strategic Services, Bloomfield was recruited and given the rank of major. In 1947, the OSS evolved into the Central Intelligence Agency, and Bloomfield continued to work with them. He retained his interest in Israel and met with Prime Minister Ben-Gurion on May 4, 1949.

After his adventurous years, he settled down in Montreal and worked with the prestigious law firm Phillips and Vineberg.

had some experience of how futile lobbying politicians and bureaucrats in Ottawa could be. Through the 1930s, as joint chairman of the Jewish Immigrant Aid Society with member of Parliament Samuel Jacobs, Bronfman, and A. J. Freiman of the Zionist Organization of Canada took part in increasingly frustrating meetings with various levels of government. Nonetheless, as information about the dire situation of European Jews reached Canada, Bronfman and other Canadian Jewish leaders continued to look for ways to help.

Simon Belkin, L. Zuker, J. A. Cherniak, and Hannaniah Meir Caiserman joined with other Jewish individuals and organizations to form the United Jewish Relief Agencies and create a partnership with the worldwide Joint Distribution Committee—Sam Bronfman's brother Harry had been a member for several years—that was soon to become one of the most creative nation-building philanthropic institutions in the world. Under the executive direction of Saul Hayes, the new organization built a relief network that assisted thousands of threatened families.

Throughout the war, press reports detailed the death and misery in Europe and lobbying the government continued unabated. Frustration mounted, anger swelled, and Canadian Jews became demoralized by the lack of response on the part of their government. The Jewish Immigrant Aid Society met hundreds of refugees who arrived in Canada on their way to the United States or Australia. Since these immigrants were not allowed to stay in Canada, the JIAS, much to their displeasure, could only provide them with food and temporary shelter before they left the country.

The Canadian Jewish community's response to the war effort was diverse—triumphant in some ways, but undercut by the community's lack of power in the place that counted most, Ottawa. Could there have been an alternative response to the situation? It is unlikely, as Canadian historians Irving Abella and Harold Troper point out in *None Is Too Many*, "Without doubt, mass demonstrations, civil disobedience, hunger strikes and protest marches to Parliament Hill, although perhaps cathartic to a Jewish community seething with the anguish of rejection, would only have confirmed what many Canadians believed—Jews were a disruptive, selfish and dangerous group."

A sad but accurate reflection of an opinion that was widespread in Canada of the 1930s and 1940s.

Picking up the Pieces

After the war, the *yishuv* in Palestine made contact with the remnants of European Jewry in an attempt to bring the survivors of the camps back to life and hope. The Jewish Brigade, for example, began bringing together the Jews who had hidden in the mountains and monasteries of Italy and offered them help with problems of health, education, and organized Jewish life, and assisted them in "illegal" immigration to Palestine.

With the surrender of the Nazis in May 1945, tens of thousands of Jews were assembled in displaced persons camps in Europe. The survivors of the concentration and death camps made pilgrimages back to their old homes in Poland, the Soviet Union, and Germany, hoping to find family members who might have lived through the Holocaust and the war.

The dimensions of this return movement were enormous. For example, approximately 150,000 Jews returned to Poland from the Soviet Union in 1946, only to encounter more pogroms. Faced again with anti-Semitic hostility, many Jews left Poland and tried to settle in Czechoslovakia or find refuge in the displaced persons camps in Germany. More than 200,000 refugees were in Czechoslovakia by the end of 1946, awaiting emigration to Palestine or another country.

With few countries willing to accept European Jews, the *yishuv* tried once more to force open the gates in Palestine. As early as August and September 1945, the first boats carrying survivors began to arrive from Italian ports; others arrived by land, having come through Syria. Clashes between the *yishuv* and the British military authorities over these illegal immigrants increased. The British tried to halt the immigrant boats, sent illegal immigrants to camps in Cyprus, set up detention camps in Palestine, and imposed curfews in some cities. Despite all the measures the British took, at least 70,000 Jews sailed to Palestine in the period between 1945 and the establishment of Israel in May 1948.

6

The Struggle for Independence

IN 1938–1939, AS THE SITUATION for German Jews had become increasingly dire and the Second World War loomed, new leadership had emerged in the Canadian Jewish community. Three remarkable men—powerful businessman Samuel Bronfman, consummate organizer and diplomat Saul Hayes, and eminent lawyer Harry Batshaw—formed a powerful base from which Canadian Jews were able to respond to the challenges they faced in the wake of the war. Over the next three decades their legacy would mark every aspect of Canadian Jewish life.

Sam Bronfman and his brothers Allan and Abe had been donating large sums of money to Jewish causes since they arrived in Montreal from the Canadian West in 1924, but Sam had preferred to remain very much in the background. It was not until he assumed the chairmanship of the Jewish Immigrant Aid Society (JIAS) in 1931 and the presidency of the Federation of Jewish Philanthropies of Montreal in 1934 that he began to take on a public role as a leader in the Canadian Jewish community. Although he became the honorary Dominion Chairman of the United Palestine Appeal in 1936, Sam Bronfman did not consider himself to be an ardent Zionist. As Michael Marrus points out in his biography *Mr. Sam: The Life and Times of Samuel Bronfman*, Bronfman's charitable support for Palestine—as a refuge for persecuted Jews rather than as a focus for Jewish national aspirations—was completely consistent with his Canadian patriotism: "Those of us who live in a free country like Canada should express gratitude by making it possible for other Jews to find freedom and security in Palestine."

It came as something of a surprise then—not least of all to Sam Bronfman himself—that prominent Labour Zionist leader Moshe

Dickstein suggested Bronfman be named the new president of the struggling Canadian Jewish Congress in 1939. Bronfman had been somewhat involved in Congress through his leadership of JIAS—he had joined the Congress refugee committee that lobbied Prime Minister Mackenzie King to allow more Jews victimized by the Nazis to immigrate to Canada. In January 1939, he had also become chairman of the newly formed United Jewish Refugee and War Relief Agencies of Canada. Nonetheless, as a member of the wealthy and established Westmount Jewish elite, he had no standing among the Yiddishist immigrant Jewish community and the Labour Zionists of Paole Zion. He was not even a particularly strong supporter of the Canadian Jewish Congress—until that point his leadership in the Jewish community had primarily been limited to fundraising for Jewish causes. Still, Dickstein believed that Sam Bronfman was the kind of dynamic leader that Canadian Jews needed and convinced members of Congress to support the nomination—and convinced Sam Bronfman to accept. He held the position from 1939 to 1962, during which his two most consistent messages were that Canadian Jews should always remain patriotic Canadians and that they should speak with one united voice.

One of the people whom Sam Bronfman relied on the most throughout his leadership of the Canadian Jewish Congress was the brilliant Jewish advocate Saul Hayes. A graduate of McGill University Law School, Hayes had begun his career in Jewish public service as the driving force behind the Jewish Vocational Service and Guidance Bureau for Montreal in the mid-1930s. In the late 1930s, like many Jews, his focus shifted to concern for Jewish refugees who had managed to escape the Nazis. He started working for the United Jewish Refugee and War Relief Agencies of Canada, founded by Sam Bronfman, and in 1940 became the executive director. In 1942, Bronfman hired him as executive director of the Canadian Jewish Congress, a position he held until he was named executive vice-president of Congress. Throughout his long and illustrious career as Canada's foremost Jewish "civil servant," Saul Hayes put forward the cause of Canadian Jews with dignity, diplomacy, and consummate skill.

The third member of this new leadership group, distinguished Montreal lawyer Harry Batshaw, had already been active in a variety of Jewish and Zionist organizations for a decade when he was made chairman of the United Zionist Council's public relations committee in May 1941. One of his first projects was to establish a committee of

Christians and Jews sympathetic to the Zionist cause to spread their message and lobby the Canadian government. Son of an immigrant carpenter, Batshaw became the first Jewish member of a Superior Court in Canada when Prime Minister Louis St. Laurent appointed him to the Quebec Superior Court. He also played an important role in changing anti-Semitic policies in Canada as founding director of the Canadian Human Rights Foundation, and founding chairman of the International Law Association's Committee on Human Rights. Over the course of his public career, he served as honorary vice-president of the Zionist Organization of Canada, president of Young Judaea Canada, and co-chairman of the Canadian Council of Christians and Jews, and helped found Amitiés culturelles Canada-Français-Israël. In 1983, a foundation was established in his name to subsidize the Karem Institute, which trained secondary-school humanities teachers in Israel.

Fight for a State

Canadian policy in international affairs became much more activist after the war. Canada supported the United Nations and cast itself as an international conciliator; the label "peacekeeper" would be applied later. From 1945 to 1948 Canadians took part in the talks on the future of Jews and Arabs in Palestine at the United Nations and played a decisive role in the international negotiations that led to the establishment of the State of Israel.

It was customary for Canadian prime ministers to simultaneously hold the position of Secretary of State for External Affairs, and Prime Minister Mackenzie King had firmly held onto the reins of foreign policy throughout the war. In September 1946, however, he relinquished the External Affairs portfolio to Louis St. Laurent and, at the same time, Lester B. Pearson took over the number two post of departmental under-secretary. The two men differed markedly from King in two important respects: neither shared the prime minister's devout emotional attachment to Britain and both saw a future role for Canada in the diplomacy of conciliation among the great powers.

Lester Pearson had been Canada's chief delegate to the 1945 San Francisco conference that drew up the UN charter and after 1946 served as head of the Canadian UN delegation and chairman of the UN Political and Security Committee. He was highly involved in international discussions about possible resolutions to the situation

The Pioneer Presidents

The first president of the Federation of Zionist Societies of Canada was Clarence de Sola of Montreal, who held the position for a remarkable twenty years, from 1899 to 1919. He was succeeded by A. J. (Archie) Freiman of Ottawa, whose presidency ran an extraordinary twenty-seven years, from 1919 to 1944. In 1925 the organization was renamed the Zionist Organization of Canada.

From 1944 to 1946, a presidium of three members—Michael Garber and Samuel E. Schwisberg of Montreal and S. J. (Sam) Zacks of Toronto—shared leadership responsibilities. Zacks later assumed the presidency alone and continued in office until 1949. Samuel Schwisberg served again as co-president with Edward E. Gelber of Toronto from 1950 to 1952. Gelber continued as president from 1952 to 1956, and Michael Garber of Montreal succeeded him for the period 1956 to 1958.

in Palestine and the Zionist movement benefited from his central role in the negotiations. Rooted in the Protestant millenarianism and mysticism that was widespread at the time, Pearson's childhood education had fostered a strong emotional attachment to the Holy Land. After the war this was compounded by his sympathy for the plight of Jewish survivors of Nazi atrocities. From the very beginning, he devoted his energy to making the United Nations work as an agency for the peaceful resolution of international conflicts.

In the spring of 1947, the UN General Assembly decided to set up a committee of investigation on the Palestinian question and charged Pearson's Political and Security Committee with overseeing the initiative. Through the discussions and negotiations on the terms and scope of the investigation, Pearson soon proved his impartiality by resisting Arab and Soviet attempts to have the inquiry's frame of reference limited in a manner that would serve their own goals. In May, the United Nations Special Committee on Palestine (UNSCOP), composed of delegates from Australia, Canada, Czechoslovakia, Guatemala, India, Iran, the Netherlands, Peru, Sweden, Uruguay, and Yugoslavia, was established to investigate all questions and issues relevant to the problem of Palestine. Canada's representative to the UNSCOP was Supreme Court Justice Ivan C. Rand.

A United Nations Special Committee

At the first formal session of the UN Special Committee on Palestine on May 26, 1947, UN Secretary General Trygve Lie informed the delegates that there would be no formal hearings in New York. Instead, the committee members would be leaving for Palestine to commence their investigation in June. Before leaving New York, the UNSCOP members decided to invite the "interested parties"—the

Jewish Agency, the Arab Higher Committee, and the British—to appoint liaison offers to work with them through the process. The Jewish Agency, which had been established under the terms of the British Mandate to administer the affairs of the *yishuv*, appointed as their representatives future Israeli diplomat and politician Abba Eban and economist David Horowitz, who later became governor of the Bank of Israel. The British appointed Donald C. MacGillivray, former deputy district commissioner at Acre, as their liaison officer. The Arab Higher Committee refused to appoint any liaison officer to work with the UN committee, declaring a complete boycott of the whole initiative.

The members of the UNSCOP arrived in Jerusalem on June 15, 1947, and awoke the following day to find that the Arab Higher Committee had called a general strike to protest their arrival. Although the committee was able to meet with Arab representatives later in Beirut, the Arab Higher Committee maintained a boycott of the hearings in Palestine itself. Nonetheless, the UN committee persevered and began their open hearings. The investigation lasted ten weeks and involved a 3,500-kilometre fifteen-day tour of Palestine, a five-day trip to Lebanon and Syria, a one-day visit to King Abdullah of Transjordan —now the Hashemite Kingdom of Jordan—in Amman, and a 4,350-kilometre seven-day tour of displaced persons' camps in Germany and Austria. The committee heard from thirty-seven representatives of six Arab states and fifteen Jewish organizations in thirteen public hearings, in addition to holding four private hearings and a total of thirty-nine private meetings.

Rand and other members of the UN committee were clearly impressed by the level of achievement evident in Jewish settlements. At the same time, two specific events that occurred while the UNSCOP was in Palestine convinced them that it was time for the British Mandate to come to an end. On the committee's first day in Jerusalem, the British military court had sentenced three members of Irgun, a militant Zionist group, to be hanged for taking part in a raid on the prison at Acre. Despite an appeal by three of the UN committee members, including Ivan Rand, that the sentence not be carried out, the three men were hanged, sparking retaliation and further violence. The second event was the arrival of the ship *Exodus 1947* in Haifa harbour on July 18, 1947. The *Exodus 1947*, carrying about 4,500 European Jewish refugees who wished to settle in Palestine, set sail from France and was intercepted at sea by the British. The passengers resisted British attempts to remove them from the ship and in the violence that ensued, three refugees were killed and many were injured. After being transferred to three British ships, the passengers were forcibly returned to displaced persons camps in Germany. These two events, in addition to the pages of testimony gleaned through the hours of hearings and private conversations, underscored to the UNSCOP members that the British Mandate government had lost control of the region and was incapable of administering any kind of peaceful settlement between the Jews and Arabs in Palestine. The committee members' experiences in the displaced persons camps in Europe furthered emphasized that any solution to the situation in Palestine had to take into account the plight of Jewish refugees. As the UNSCOP deliberated in Geneva, Switzerland, it became clear that the only solution was to establish separate Jewish and Arab states in Palestine.

Aliyah Bet and the Shadow Fleet

As more and more Jews sought to escape persecution in Europe and settle in Palestine between 1920 and 1948, and the British administration restricted the number of Jews allowed to enter the region, Jewish refugees—with the help of Zionist activists—found ways to evade British immigration quotas. The most effective method of transportation used for this clandestine immigration was travel by ship. This came to be known by the Jews as Aliyah Bet—secret or unofficial immigration to the Land of Israel. In 1938, when the situation for European Jews worsened dramatically, the Jewish leadership in Palestine established the Mossad l'Aliyah Bet (Organization for "Illegal" Immigration) to co-ordinate the movement of refugees. Aliyah Bet continued throughout the Second World War, but the conditions were much more dangerous—hundreds of Jewish refugees died at sea. Nonetheless, sixty-two voyages were organized between 1937 and 1944.

After the Second World War, the number of Jewish refugees rose substantially as tens of thousands of Holocaust survivors living in displaced persons camps sought to make their home in Palestine. The Mossad l'Aliyah Bet organized an underground network known as the Brihah—Hebrew for flight—to move the refugees from the displaced persons camps or places in eastern Europe to port cities in Italy, France, Yugoslavia, or Greece. Their perils hardly ended when they finally left Europe and set sail for Palestine, however. Many of the boats that the Mossad l'Aliyah Bet could obtain were old, substandard cargo ships, and they were often overcrowded with passengers when they set sail. More than 90 per cent of the ships were intercepted by the British navy and the refugees forcibly moved to detention camps in Cyprus. By 1948, over 100,000 people had travelled through the Brihah, including more than 70,000 Holocaust survivors; by the same year, the British held over 50,000 Jewish refugees in internment camps on Cyprus.

With so many Jewish refugees anxious to leave Europe in the immediate aftermath of the Second World War and not enough vessels to transport them to Palestine, a Quebec branch of Mossad l'Aliyah Bet purchased two Canadian corvettes as "freighters"—the *Beauharnois*, renamed the *Josiah Wedgwood*, and the *Norsyd*, dubbed *Aliya Bet Haganah*. Volunteer Jewish crews manned the ships when they sailed out of Montreal and picked up passengers bound for Palestine from a port in southern France. Both ships were intercepted by a Royal Navy destroyer in the Mediterranean off the coast of Palestine, however, and the Jewish refugee passengers were interned first in Palestine and then moved to British detention camps in Cyprus.

Interestingly, the vessels purchased by Canadian Jews to assist in Aliyah Bet later became an important part of Israel's defence. In 1948 the corvettes, then moored in Haifa harbour, were re-activated and renamed the *Hashomer* (guard) and the *Haganah* (defence). They became the core fleet—along with a converted passenger boat bought by Sam Zacks of Toronto and a former U.S. Navy icebreaker—of the fledgling Israeli navy. Although the British wouldn't let the Jews have access to the ships before the State of Israel achieved independence, plans were launched for the "shadow fleet" of the Israeli forces even as the vessels were rusting away alongside the breakwater inside Haifa harbour.

Once Israel declared its independence, Jewish volunteers who had served with the Royal Canadian and other navies manned the ships and trained Israelis to operate them. The vessels boldly engaged Egyptian warships, bombarded enemy positions, and patrolled the shoreline. Their biggest coup came on August 24, 1948, when the former Canadian corvettes seized a huge cargo of arms intended for the Arab armies. In what was called "Operation Pirate's Booty," the *Hashomer* and the *Haganah* intercepted the *Argiro*, a ship sailing under the Italian flag and with an Italian crew. When they boarded the vessel, the Israeli crew members found eight thousand rifles and ten million rounds of ammunition. The war matériel had originally been aboard another Italian vessel, the *Lino*, that had been sunk several months earlier in the port of Bari, Italy, by operatives from Israeli intelligence, the Mossad. The cargo had been recovered and placed in the holds of the *Argiro*, which then set sail for Egypt. En route, two Mossad agents boarded the vessel, convinced the Italian crew they would never make it to Alexandria, and arranged for the Israeli sailors to board the vessel and confiscate the cargo.

In another naval encounter on October 19, 1948, the *Haganah*, the *Hashomer*, and two other Israeli craft engaged an Egyptian corvette and three Spitfire fighters. They shot down one of the Spitfires and damaged the corvette; the Arab warship scuttled back to its base in Port Said. On October 22, 1948, the four Israeli craft met a much more formidable opponent in the *King Farouq*, flagship of the Egyptian navy. They sank the *Farouq* and damaged an Egyptian minesweeper. In the same month, the Israeli warships bombarded retreating Egyptian forces in the Ashkelon area and prevented Egyptian naval vessels from evacuating fleeing Arab soldiers.

In their yeoman service immediately before and after May 14, 1948, these two former Canadian vessels represented yet another way in which Canada contributed to the founding of the State of Israel.

Seeking Compromise

The United Nations Special Committee on Palestine finally put forward a Partition Plan with a number of recommendations that the members approved unanimously: the earliest possible end to the British Mandate; the granting of independence to Palestine after a brief transition; the recognition of the sacred character of holy places and a guarantee of free access to them; the neutrality of Jerusalem, which would be administered by a joint international trusteeship; the need for the United Nations to address the issue of resettling European Jewish refugees; the establishment of democratic principles and minority rights throughout Palestine; peaceful relations between the Jewish and Arab communities; and economic union. It was a painful compromise, which the Jewish leadership grudgingly accepted, preferring the proverbial half loaf to none at all, and which the Arab leadership denounced completely.

The areas on which the committee members could not agree were put forward separately in a majority report—endorsed by Canada, Czechoslovakia, Guatemala, the Netherlands, Peru, Sweden, and Uruguay—that called for the partition of Palestine into separate Arab and Jewish political entities within one economic union, and a minority report—put forward by India, Iran, and Yugoslavia—that advocated the creation of a single, federal state. John D. L. Hood, the Australian representative on the committee, abstained because of the lack of unanimity.

The Arabs both inside and outside Palestine had boycotted the UNSCOP sessions, but their allies had put forward their case at meetings in Beirut and Amman. In essence, the Arab leaders rejected unequivocally any justification for an independent Jewish state in Palestine—as far as they were concerned, all Jewish immigration to the region since the Balfour Declaration was illegal and Zionism was the source of all conflicts between Arabs and Jews in Palestine.

The UN General Assembly, constituting itself as a full committee to discuss all proposals regarding Palestine, set up separate subcommittees to examine each of the reports. Lester Pearson chaired the subcommittee examining the partition proposal. On November 29, 1947, the General Assembly passed Resolution 181, the Partition Plan for Palestine. The Canadian Cabinet had not given any direction in advance of the vote—beyond showing respect for Justice Ivan Rand's carefully considered endorsement of the majority

Arming

Aware of the Arab states' oft-proclaimed declaration that they would destroy the Jewish state at birth, prime minister-to-be David Ben-Gurion formed a team to collect the arms that would be desperately needed if Israel were to survive an assault by troops from eight Arab countries.

One of the more colourful underground arms merchants was a Winnipegger, David Harris. Harris, who lived in Israel for a time, used Ben's Delicatessen in Montreal as his "purchasing office." Bent over a table, Harris quietly negotiated deals with a variety of suppliers, working with a code based on the restaurant's menu. Harris's teenage son, Eiran, would occasionally be brought along as his father made deals in the noisy deli.

Canadian Arab reaction, 1947

Commenting on Canada's role in the passage of the Partition Resolution by the United Nations General Assembly, M. S. Massoud, president of the Arab League of Canada, said that the Arab World "would remember" Lester B. Pearson and Mr. Justice Ivan C. Rand, "who did their utmost to impose upon Arabs the infamous partition scheme."

recommendations as a distinguished member of the Supreme Court of Canada—and directed Pearson to seek advice from Ottawa as the deliberations progressed. In the end, the government accepted that UNSCOP's majority report presented the only possibility of a resolution to the situation in Palestine and was the only proposal that had

"Two-Gun" Cohen Helps Out

At the 1945 United Nations Conference on International Organization in San Francisco, the Canadian Jewish delegation was, like other non-governmental delegations, having difficulty getting information about what was going on in the closed-door sessions until Morris "Two-Gun" Cohen, one of Jewish history's most colourful personalities, introduced himself to Saul Hayes. Unlikely as it seems, Cohen was at the conference as part of the Chinese delegation and was happy to help. He not only kept the Canadian Jewish delegates informed, he introduced Sam Bronfman, then president of the Canadian Jewish Congress, to Dr. Wellington Ku, Chinese ambassador to Washington, and to the young Soviet ambassador to the U.S.—Andrei Gromyko.

Two years later, as the United Nations prepared to consider a plan to partition Palestine, "Two-Gun"—his nickname came from the time he was nicked by a bullet while serving as bodyguard to Sun Yat-Sen (founding president of modern China) and started carrying a second gun—came to the Jewish community's aid once again. A one-time general in the Chinese army, he had survived the Second World War (even though the Japanese had captured him in Hong Kong and threatened to behead him) and had found his way to Montreal, eager to start a new life. RCAF Squadron Leader Sydney Shulemson—Jewish Canada's most decorated warrior—contacted Cohen and sought his help on two matters: obtaining for Israel some of the two hundred Mosquito bombers earmarked for shipment to China, and influencing the Chinese vote at the UN. The UN then was a much smaller body—fifty-seven states—so every vote was crucial.

At the meeting, Two-Gun pulled out a letter addressed to him from Sun Yat-Sen stating that "the Chinese people should never do anything to harm the Jewish people." Armed with the letter, Shulemson's associate, Harry Venis, and Cohen arranged to meet with China's ambassador to Canada, who was also their representative at the UN. The letter impressed the ambassador, who had planned to oppose the partition resolution and campaign to have it defeated. With the new information, the diplomat decided that China would abstain, and he would not seek to influence others to oppose it. The abstention helped push the resolution through. The final vote was thirty-three for, thirteen against, ten abstentions, and one absent.

Israel was, however, unable to acquire any of the Chinese bombers.

any chance of achieving a two-thirds majority at the General Assembly. The head of Canada's delegation, Minister of Justice James L. Isley, put Canada on the record as supporting partition.

The Canadian government thus reluctantly accepted that they had no choice but to support the partition of Palestine, but Lester Pearson saw something more momentous in the passage of Resolution 181. Several years later he wrote, "It seemed imperative, moreover, after the annihilation of six million Jews in various centres in Europe,

The United Nations Vote on Partition, 1947

Jews throughout much of the world were transfixed as they listened to the live radio broadcast of the United Nations General Assembly vote on Resolution 181 calling for the partition of Palestine into Jewish and Arab states.

The secretary began a roll call of the nations. Two of the big powers—the United States and the Soviet Union—voted yes. The Zionist representatives attending the historic event were astonished to hear the Soviet delegate, Andrei Gromyko, tell the Assembly, "The Jewish people had been closely linked with Palestine for a considerable period in history. As a result of the [Second World] War, the Jews as a people have suffered more than any other people. The total number of the Jewish population who perished at the hands of the Nazi executioners is estimated at approximately six million. The Jewish people were therefore striving to create a state of their own, and it would be unjust to deny them that right."

Canada, with South Africa, New Zealand, and Australia among the Commonwealth nations, voted in favour, along with thirteen Latin American countries. Following the final tally thirty-three votes in favour of partition, thirteen opposed, ten abstained, and one absent—the Arab delegates stalked out angrily and prepared to go to war. Around the world, Jews celebrated the coming re-emergence of a Jewish state into the family of nations.

that arrangements should be made in at least one country in the world for the Jewish people to be definitely freed from the limitations and the fears imposed by minority status." This moral perspective, more than any other factor, set Pearson apart from most of his UN colleagues in dealing with Israel.

Support for Israel

Within only a few days of the new State of Israel's declaration of independence on May 14, 1948, armies from eight Arab countries poured over the borders. The small, ill-equipped Israeli forces faced approximately 1,000 Lebanese, 5,000 Syrian, 5,000 Iraqi, 10,000 Egyptian, and 4,000 Transjordanian troops, aided by volunteers from Saudi Arabia, Libya, and Yemen. The Arab countries had flatly rejected the UN partition plan and declared UN Resolution 181 and the State of Israel to be illegal. They unilaterally declared in its place the United State of Palestine. In response to these events, thousands of volunteers—both Jews and non-Jews—rushed to help defend the fledgling Jewish state that had scarcely had time to draw its first breath. Approximately 3,500 overseas volunteers came from forty-three

Lester B. Pearson with Leon Crestohl, who, in 1948, was head of the United Zionist Purchasing Committee that acquired vital supplies for Israel. He was a Liberal member of Parliament from 1950 to 1963.

(Canadian Jewish Congress National Archives, Montreal)

countries to join the Machal—an abbreviation for Mitnadvei Hutz La'aretz (volunteers from abroad)—to fight for Israel. Most were Second World War veterans who brought with them crucially important military experience and skills to shape the newly emerging Israel Defense Forces.

In addition to troops and technical experts, the *yishuv* also desperately needed armaments. A number of Canadian Jews had formed a Haganah committee to support Israel's War of Independence. The procurement team was made up of many people from across the country and included, among others, Sydney Shulemson and Joe Baumholz in Montreal, Max Brown in Toronto, and Alex Glanz in Windsor. The team also worked with Jewish

Pearson and Rand

Two Canadians were major figures in the creation of Israel—Under-Secretary of State for External Affairs Lester B. "Mike" Pearson and Supreme Court Justice Ivan C. Rand. Pearson, head of the Canadian delegation to the United Nations from 1946 to 1956, was elected as chairman of the UN General Assembly's Special Committee on Palestine in 1947. The Nobel Prize Committee, in its citation for Pearson's 1957 Peace Prize, states simply that "he laid the groundwork for the creation of the state of Israel." Israelis called the Canadian "the great facilitator" and "Balfour #2," referring to British foreign minister Lord Balfour who authored the Balfour Declaration in 1917. Mike Pearson was committed to the partition of Palestine in order to create a Jewish state and, in the small United Nations of 1947, pressed for passage of Resolution 181

that divided Palestine into Jewish and Arab states.

Mr. Justice Rand, as Canada's representative on UNSCOP, was critically important in drawing up the partition resolution. Commenting on Rand's role in the process, Israeli foreign minister Abba Eban said, "A key figure would be Justice Ivan Rand of Canada, an old-fashioned man of refinement, probity and independent temperament. He was the kind of man who would not be easily moved from any positions he would take and on whom there would be no prospect of influence by intimidation."

Lester Pearson, who served as prime minister of Canada from 1963 to 1968, received the Nobel Prize for his concept of UN peacekeeping forces, for his role in averting the Suez Crisis in 1956, and for his tireless work in seeking peaceful resolutions to international crises and avoiding war.

David Ben-Gurion proclaiming the rebirth of Israel, 1948.

(World Zionist Organization Archives, Jerusalem)

branches of the Canadian Legion—the Brigadier Frederick Kisch branch in Montreal, and the Orde Wingate branch in Toronto. They were occasionally able to procure items of considerable military value and, with a certain degree of ingenuity and subterfuge, get the matériel to Israel. Sales of surplus army vehicles and equipment were fortunately not subject to restrictions at the time, but the Canadian government would likely have taken a dim view of Canadians openly supplying the Israel Defense Forces with military hardware. The Canadians managed to get their hands on items as small as the consignment of nineteen signalling sets that provided Israel with its only communication network throughout the 1948 siege and as large as aircraft and a schooner.

Canadians Who Fought for Israel

"A great deal has been written about the gallant volunteers who went to Spain in the 1930s to fight in the International Brigade against Franco's Fascists. By contrast, almost nothing is known about the men—especially the Canadians—who volunteered to fight for Israel when it seemed that their quixotic mission was bound to end in death. A whole book could—and should—be written about the Canadians ... who fought to establish Israel in 1948. To give just an example of their contribution, Canadian pilots accounted for one-third of all Arab planes shot down in that war."

—Major Ben Dunkelman, DSO, *Dual Allegiance* (1976)

Arms for Israel

One mechanism that Canadian Zionists used to funnel much-needed arms for the War of Independence was the Victor Equipment and Supply Company at 422 McGill Street in Montreal. The "company," which had been established by a number of prominent Canadian Zionists including Samuel Schwisberg and Joe Frank, had only one employee—Walter Loewenson (succeeded later by Joe Baumholz, an engineering student from McGill University), who received information about Israel's specific requirements from operatives in New York and passed it on to the purchasing committee.

One of the Victor Equipment Company's most important acquisitions was a number of Harvard training aircraft—two-place monoplanes easily convertible into light bombers—that they purchased as scrap from an Ontario dealer. The problem they faced was how to ship military aircraft to Israel without alerting the Canadian government to what they were doing. At a meeting involving *Ottawa Citizen* newspaperman Moe Appel, who was also public relations director for the ZOC, an unidentified Ottawa lawyer, and Alex (Sandy) Skelton of the Canadian Trade and Commerce Department, the three men worked out a strategy for moving the huge crates that contained the parts of the disassembled aircraft. As historian David Bercuson describes in his book *The Secret Army*,

> The three met at night at Appel's office at 46 Elgin Street. Appel had just moved in and there were, as he put it, "just enough chairs and a desk for whiskey." They began to drink and had soon consumed the best part of a large bottle. Skelton said little; Appel and the lawyer did most of the talking.… In the midst of his doodling, Skelton suddenly exclaimed: "I've got it, goddamnit." He looked up: "Do you guys have a spring fair in Tel Aviv?" "No," Appel said, "but we can create one." Skelton seemed satisfied. "You draw a plan. We'll dismantle the goddamned things, put them in crates, and send them to the Tel Aviv Spring Fair." Not long after, several large crates painted red, white, and blue and addressed to the Tel Aviv Spring Fair left Canada. In Israel the contents of the crates were put back together, equipped with bomb racks, and pressed into service as dive bombers.

In addition to the Harvards, the Canadians also managed to acquire and deliver flamethrowers, shipped as "insecticide sprayers," and machine guns.

Sandy Skelton

Canadian Jews had few friends in Prime Minister William Lyon MacKenzie King's government, but one of them was Alexander (Sandy) Skelton, a friend of Zionist leader Sam Zacks, whom he had met while attending Queen's University. Skelton was the son of Dr. Oscar Douglas

Skelton, deputy minister of the Department of External Affairs, a senior policy adviser to King and unfriendly to the Jewish cause.

His son, Sandy, was a brilliant economist and had a different viewpoint—due in great part to his friendship with Zacks. After serving on a number of government agencies during the Second World War, the younger Skelton was appointed assistant deputy minister of the Department of Trade and Commerce, which put him in a position to arrange for export permits. The younger Skelton was a member—along with Moe Appel, public relations director for the ZOC, an unnamed Ottawa Jewish lawyer, and, by telephone, Joe Baumholtz of the Victory Equipment Company in Montreal—of an ad hoc committee formed to work out ways and means to export "questionable items" to Israel. Whenever a shipment was ready, Skeleton made sure that Baumholtz received the appropriate documentation, as well as advice on how equipment should be described on customs forms and how it should be shipped. Mountains of equipment were acquired through this operation and sent to assist the Israelis in the fight for their new nation.

All of the intrigues aside, the Canadian Jewish community did more than supply funds and matériel to Israel at this critical juncture—

A celebration of Israel's Declaration of Independence at Labour Zionist Headquarters, Montreal, May 14, 1948.

(J. Sommer Collection, Jewish Public Library Archives, Montreal)

Nova Scotia Fish Cakes for Israel

As the date for the British withdrawal from Palestine neared and Arab violence in opposition to the founding of a Jewish state increased, one of the biggest problems facing Israelis was hunger. One fervent Canadian Zionist who was determined to do something about it was Sam Jacobson of Halifax.

After considering the problem for some time, Maritimer Jacobson determined that the best way to provide Israelis with nourishment was through shipments of fish cakes. Since he lived in Halifax, surrounded by thousands of fishermen and dozens of canneries in the region, he also decided that Israelis would get the best-tasting fish cakes possible. With a

phone list on his lap, neglecting his own department store business and his family, he began telephoning every cannery and ordering from each a sample case of fish cakes. He assembled a committee—comprised of every member of his family, along with his friends and business associates—to cook fish cakes and eat them for breakfast, lunch, and dinner so that they could sample all the different cakes and help choose which was superior.

Working at a frenzied pace, Jacobson finally identified the brand he wanted to send by shipload to Israel, and he picked up the telephone to place his order—only to be told that his telephone had been disconnected because he had forgotten to pay his large phone bill!

Canadian Jews raised funds to equip the international volunteers who fought for the emerging Jewish state in Palestine immediately before and after independence and, in some cases, found ways to ship matériel to them directly.

(*The Globe and Mail*)

the Canadians who joined the Machal made the ultimate sacrifice for the new Jewish nation: they risked their lives.

Recruiting for Israel, 1948

When the new State of Israel came under attack from the Arab nations that surrounded it, over 250 Canadians heard the call and came to Israel's defence. The importance of their role in helping to establish

The Yacht and the Bren Gun, 1946

The Jews of Palestine had been desperately short of weapons for defence in the years immediately prior to independence and dreamed of setting up their own weapons-manufacturing facilities. In 1946, when the machinery needed to manufacture light machine guns became available in Toronto, members of the community set their minds to solving the problem of how to move the machinery to Palestine.

A group of Toronto Jews acquired Industrial Research Laboratories and looked for a way to move the plant—lock, stock, and barrel—to the emerging Jewish state. There was no problem shipping the basic equipment—it was the kind that would normally be used in a machine shop—but the metal dies were something else; they would be easily recognizable and their export blocked. So the group decided to send the dies to New York, where they could be slipped into transformers

and boilers being sent to the Holy Land. There was still the problem, however, of getting the dies out of Canada and into the United States without detection by customs officials.

They soon came up with a brilliant plan to send the crucial components from Toronto to New York aboard a thirty-foot pleasure yacht bought for the purpose by Sam Zacks. On the day of the shipment, a party of people boarded a boat loaded with fishing gear, a bar, and a generous number of picnic baskets and slipped out of Toronto harbour, obviously bound for a pleasant cruise on the placid waters of Lake Ontario. When the vessel had crossed the lake and arrived at the breakwater of the harbour at Rochester, New York, the happy group—cocktail glasses in hand—waved gaily at a customs inspector, who waved back. Once the boat was moored, Haganah agent Elie Schalit and his sister calmly stepped ashore, piled their heavy luggage into a waiting car, and drove off to New York.

the Jewish nation depended less on their actual numbers, however, than on their experience in combat and the contribution they could make to Israel's military organization and technical know-how.

Representatives from the Montreal and Toronto Jewish communities set up a Haganah steering committee to carry out two principal tasks: to create and operate an effective recruiting network and, since all Canadian recruiting would be financed locally, to raise the funds required to cover the expense of sending Canadian volunteers to Palestine. The head of the Canadian recruiting organization was D. Lou Harris of Toronto, and his many supporters included Sam Zacks, president of the Zionist Organization of Canada, and his wife, Ayala, who, as an underground agent in France during the Second World War, had helped downed Allied fliers escape the Nazis. Other key area recruiters included Hy Crystal in Calgary; Michel Finegold, Ben Adelman, Morley Kare, and Ben Pastinsky in Vancouver; Ralph

Hamovich in Winnipeg; and Bernard J. Finestone, Joe Venis, and Joe Frank in Montreal. Syd Shulemson was the head recruiter for eastern Canada, working with Moshe Myerson.

The recruitment of Canadian volunteers to fight for Israel began in January 1948 and every effort was made to keep it as secret as possible. When an anxious parent reported the activity to the Royal Canadian Mounted Police, however, the Mounties investigated and passed on what they learned to the Canadian justice minister: "The whole Jewish population of Canada appears to be wholeheartedly in support of the establishment of a Jewish state in Palestine." The RCMP admitted that even if they were to continue their investigation, few members of the Jewish community would co-operate with it and added, "Most of the prominent members of the Jewish community would not hesitate to do anything in their power to assist in the founding of a Jewish state."

The committee's initial recruitment target was 1,000 men, although the Jewish Agency later reduced it to 300. The Haganah committee felt that finding enough recruits would not be difficult as more than 18,000 Canadian Jews had served in the Canadian and Allied Forces during the Second World War. At the time, most Canadian Jews lived in Toronto and Montreal, and both cities had Jewish branches of the Royal Canadian Legion. Prominent among the Canadian Jews who helped with the recruiting efforts were, to name but a few, Lionel Druker, Louis Harris, Sam Zacks, Sydney Shulemson, Moshe Myerson, Ben Adelman, Leon Crestohl, Hy Cristall, Harry Freeman, Arthur Goldberg, and John Sector.

Thanks largely to the efforts of Sam and Ayala Zacks, Moe Myerson, Sydney Shulemson, Judge Harry Batshaw, and many other dedicated sympathizers, the fundraising campaign was an overwhelming success. By June 1948 the committee had collected $575,000 overall—$300,000 in Montreal, $100,000 in Toronto, and an additional $175,000 in other Canadian communities together. The Canadian Jewish community didn't just need manpower—it also need the funds to equip, clothe, and transport the recruits. The Haganah committee estimated that it would take $1,000 to get each battle-ready volunteer to Palestine, which meant that they would have to raise $300,000 in a fairly short time. Still, enthusiasm was high and meetings were quietly held across the country.

To lead the recruitment on the ground, the Haganah committee enlisted the help of Second World War veterans Major Ben

Benjamin Dunkelman (1913–1997)

Toronto-born Ben Dunkelman served with the Queen's Own Rifles of Canada during the Second World War, rising to the rank of major. He was in the second wave to hit the Normandy beachhead on June 6, 1944, and was awarded the Distinguished Service Order for bravery in the fierce battle along the Hochwald Ridge in Germany in February 1945. The campaign at Hochwald, during which Canadian forces suffered very heavy casualties, was part of the Allies' final push across the Rhine and an important step toward Germany's unconditional surrender on May 7, 1945.

In 1930, Ben Dunkelman's parents had given him a ticket to Palestine as a present for his seventeenth birthday. "As our train from Alexandria approached Jerusalem, I was gripped by excitement and anticipation," he wrote in his autobiography, *Dual Allegiance*. He stayed a year, working in the orange groves of Tel Asher, a small settlement north of Tel Aviv, and served with the settlement's defence forces.

Dunkelman's father, David Dunkelman, was the founder of the highly successful Tip Top Tailors and a lifelong Zionist. His mother, Rose Dunkelman, was a leader in Hadassah-WIZO Organization of Canada and also founded the *Jewish Standard* to counter the anti-Zionism of Toronto rabbi Maurice N. Eisendrath. Among the many significant visitors to the Dunkelman home was Chaim Weizmann, who later became Israel's first president. The Dunkelman residence became known as "the Canadian Zionist Embassy."

Ben Dunkelman had reluctantly remained in Canada in 1948 to help recruit dozens of Canadian veterans with valuable military experience, but when senior Israeli officers Shlomo Shamir and the legendary "Mickey" Marcus came to Canada to lend support to the recruitment efforts, they easily convinced Dunkelman to join them as a senior officer in the new Israel Defense Forces. To evade the British blockade on his way to Israel, Dunkelman sailed from Marseilles to Haifa with a forged passport using the alias of Mr. Fox from Twickenham. When he arrived and joined the Israel Defense Forces, his first commander was twenty-six-year-old Yitzhak Rabin, future prime minister of the Jewish state.

In Israel, he fought in the siege of Jerusalem, and then commanded the Hativa Sheva (Seventh Brigade), which included a significant number of Canadians and American volunteers in the 72nd (infantry) Battalion and the 79th (armoured) Battalion, throughout the War of Independence.

Dunkelman and Major Ben Adelman. War hero Ben Dunkelman had been anxious to enlist himself, but agreed to a request from the Haganah that he stay in Canada long enough to help recruit the hundreds of experienced Canadian war veterans who were willing to offer their services in defence of Israel. Dunkelman and Adelman were assisted in the recruitment drive by two extremely distinguished members of the Israeli military forces who had come to Canada for precisely that purpose—former U.S. Army colonel David "Mickey" Marcus, who would soon become Israel's first general, and former British Army officer Shlomo (Rabinovich) Shamir—also a future general.

When Dunkelman began his recruitment drive for Canadians to join the Machal, the first person he signed up was Lionel Druker of Sydney, Nova Scotia, a law student at Dalhousie University in Halifax. Druker in turn contacted Arthur Goldberg of Vancouver, British Columbia, who had already visited Palestine and was planning to volunteer. Goldberg brought with him a group of veterans from British Columbia to join the Machal.

The War of Independence

When the first Canadian Machal recruits arrived in Palestine in 1948, they were met by Ben Dunkelman. The Second World War veteran had arrived in early April and joined the Harel Brigade of Palmach—the acronym for Plugot Mahatz, or strike companies—as a supernumerary planning officer. He had originally wanted to keep the Canadians he had recruited together in one unit, but to his great disappointment, his attempts to form a Canadian unit in the new Israeli forces had failed because too many of the recruits had already scattered to various units throughout Israel.

1948—Major Ben Dunkelman of Toronto, a decorated Second World War hero, was one of the most outstanding Canadian volunteers who fought for Israel as commander of the Seventh Brigade, the highest ranking Canadian in the Machal.

(World Zionist Organization Archives, Jerusalem)

108

Lionel Druker

Lionel Druker was among the many Canadians who volunteered to fight for Israel during the War of Independence. A law student at Dalhousie University in Halifax who had been an intelligence officer with a Canadian armoured unit during the Second World War, he was galvanized by the idea of helping to build the new Jewish state. He abandoned his law studies and joined the Israel Defense Forces, rising to become a major and the first tank commander in the Israeli army. Using his previous war experience, Druker provided the army with its first instruction in tank maintenance and armoured battle tactics.

Following the war, Druker remained in Israel, married, and founded, together with fellow Canadian Arthur Goldberg, Tiyulim, which later on became Sightseeing/Greentours and United Tours. On a visit to Toronto many years later Druker had lunch with editors of the Canadian Press news agency, to whom he proudly showed two carbon-backed receipts written in Hebrew, from the IDF—the first for the receipt of "one Sherman tank"; the second, a receipt for a portable latrine.

Lionel Druker, first from left, perched on an Israeli tank in 1948.

(Machal Canada Archives)

The all-Canadian 52nd Battalion of the Givati Brigade—participants in Israel's 1948 War of Independence. Pictured are (front row) Allan Brown, Moe Dankevy, Gerry Gross, Art Lashinsky, Irving Kaplansky, Murray Cappel, Morris Lobe; (mid-row seated) Sam Cohen; (back row) Albert Spiegel, Joe Abramson, Murray Ginsberg, Abe Danovich, Sid Halperin, Ben Ocopnick, Jack Berger, bus driver (name not known), Joe Gerstl, and the Israeli commander, Yosef Horowitz; (reclining), and Avrom Siegal.

(Machal Canada Archives)

52nd Battalion, B Platoon,
Kfar Bilu, summer 1948.
(Rear) Irving Kaplansky, bus
driver M. Spiegel, Sid
Halperin, Max Freedman, Jack
Berger, Art Lashinsky, Abe
Danovitch, Sam Cohen, and
Joe Gerstl; (front row) Morris
Lobe, Av Siegel, Moe
Dankevy, Murray Cappel,
Gerry Gross, Joe Abramson.

(Machal Canada Archives)

One of Dunkelman's most valuable contributions to the war was his expertise in the effective use of heavy mortars to support advancing infantry. As the result of his efforts, the Israeli army created its first mortar battalion, which played a decisive role in many battles, particularly in the capture of Safed. As commander of the Seventh Brigade, he liberated Nazareth and the entire lower Galilee in Operation Dekel (Palm Tree). Former Israeli president Chaim Herzog said of the Canadian officer, "Ben Dunkelman singled himself out in command of the Seventh Brigade's campaign in Galilee."

One incident during that campaign stands out in particular. During Operation Dekel, the town of Nazareth surrendered to him with little resistance after both sides had signed a formal agreement that no harm would come to the civilians of the town. Not long after, in defiance of that agreement, Dunkelman received orders from General Chaim Laskov to expel the civilian population in the town, which he refused to do. "I told him I would do nothing of the sort—in view of our promises to safeguard the city's people, such a move would be both superfluous and harmful," Dunkelman wrote in his autobiography. "I reminded him that scarcely a day earlier, he and I, as representatives of the Israeli army, had signed the surrender document in which we solemnly pledged to do nothing to harm the city or its population. When Haim saw that I refused to obey the order, he left."

Barely twelve hours after Dunkelman's refusal, Laskov appointed

Buzz Beurling (1921–1948)

Another celebrated Canadian volunteer in the Israeli War of Independence was George "Buzz" Beurling, Canada's greatest fighter ace of the Second World War. Beurling turned down a princely offer of $2,000 a month from the Egyptians in favour of "meals and a chocolate bar" from the Israelis. As Ben Dunkelman recounted about his meeting with the pilot in his autobiography, "I told him we had no money to pay him, no uniform, and no airframes except for a few Piper Cubs. He said he didn't care about the money. He already had offers from three armies who wanted him. He told me, 'The Jews deserve a state of their own after wandering around homeless for thousands of years. I just want to offer my help.'"

Beurling unfortunately never made it to Israel. The Montreal pilot Sidney Shulemson had arranged for the ace to fly a Montreal-built Noorduyn Norseman first to an airfield near Rome (Urbe) in Italy and then on to Israel. But when Beurling took off from the Rome airport, his plane crashed and exploded, killing Beurling and his British co-pilot, Leonard Cohen. Cohen was known as the "King of Lampedusa," because he had crash-landed off the coast of the tiny Sicilian island in 1943 and convinced the entire garrison of 132 Germans to surrender to him because he was the "advance man" for a major landing of Allied Forces. There are many people who believe that Beurling's plane was sabotaged to prevent him from reaching Israel.

Why did Buzz Beuring turn down such lucrative offers to fly for Israel? Shulemson found out the answer a few months after Beurling's death, when he visited his family in the Montreal suburb of Verdun to discuss bringing his body back to Montreal for burial. He learned that Buzz had turned down all the offers because he belonged to the Plymouth Brethren, a small sect that believes that the Jews are the Chosen People and have an indisputable right to the land of Israel. Beurling's family was delighted when Shulemson assured them that their son could be buried in Jerusalem, according to their wishes. George Beurling was buried in Rome for two years and then interred in Mount Carmel Cemetery as a hero of the State of Israel.

another officer to replace him as military governor. "I complied with the order," Dunkelman recalls, "but only after Avraham [Yaffe] had given me his word of honour that he would do nothing to harm or displace the Arab population... I felt sure that [the order] had been given because of my defiance of the evacuation order." When Laskov appealed to David Ben-Gurion in his capacity as Minister of Defense, asking him to sanction Dunkelman for his insubordination, Ben-Gurion vetoed Laskov's order. The Arab inhabitants of Nazareth were never forced to evacuate. A bridge near the Lebanese border is still known as Gesher Ben, Ben's Bridge.

John McElroy

Israel's top ace in the War of Independence was Canadian John Frederick McElroy, a Second World War ace with the Royal Canadian Air Force. McElroy, a non-Jew, had been recruited to fly for Israel by Canadian fighter pilot George "Buzz" Beurling in the pivotal early days of the Arabs' attack on the new state. McElroy in turn persuaded sixteen other pilots to join him in the struggle. Credited with 10.5 kills in the Second World War, he is listed as having destroyed 13.5 enemy planes in the War of Independence.* The RAF supplied the Egyptian Air Force with Spitfires and armed and led the Jordanian Legion. Of thirty-three Israel Air Force fliers killed and missing during the War of Independence, nineteen were Machal (overseas volunteers) and six of them were Canadians. The official Israeli figure for Canadians in Machal is 250, and eleven of them lost their lives.

A 1942 photograph of John Frederick McElroy, Canada's top ace for Israel.

*Where two fighter pilots work together to destroy an enemy aircraft, the kill is halved and credited to each airman, hence they each get half a kill.

Canadian Machal

Approximately 250 Canadians (not all Jews) volunteered to fight for Israel in the War of Independence. Among them were 147 veterans of the Second World War who provided vital guidance to the newly established Israel Defense Forces. The Canadians were especially helpful in organizing the Israeli air force. Of the ninety-seven Canadians who helped build Israel's first air force, nine were killed in action, two were listed as missing and presumed killed, and seven were wounded in action. These were not mercenaries. Israel was unable to pay the high prices demanded by pilots for hire. Egypt was known to have made offers to such veteran pilots as "Buzz" Beurling, but there were apparently few or no takers. The Egyptian Air Force was far stronger and better equipped than the Israeli air element, but it performed poorly during the war. Obviously, many of the Canadians who flew for Israel did so because they believed the cause of the Jewish state to be just.

The Canadian Machal landed in Israel during the *yishuv*'s most crucial hours, when it was struggling for its very survival. The arrival of contingents of brave volunteers from overseas fortified the spirit of the people and boosted their morale. In those desperately bleak days, Israelis realized that they were not alone. World Jewry stood behind

The Canadian ace George "Buzz" Beurling, who shot down thirty-two enemy planes during the Second World War, volunteered to fly, without pay, for Israel—turning down handsome offers from Arab states to join their air forces.

(19750372–015#3, George Metcalf Archival Collection © Canadian War Museum)

them, and with them.

Canadians fought and died in many important battles and operations during the War of Independence. They distinguished themselves in the drive on Shafa Amr and Nazareth in the Galilee. They participated in Operation Hiram to dislodge the Syrians from their superior positions in Meron, lift the siege of Kibbutz Manara, and clear the Northern Galilee up to the Lebanese border. In Operation Lightning they assisted in the capture of strategic Arab bases in the south, such as Ashkelon, Ashdod, Bet Daras, and Bashit. They helped capture Lod Airport, win the decisive battle at Auja-el-Hafir, and launch the assault on El-Arish.

The volunteers who made the ultimate sacrifice paved the way for the hundreds of thousands who made aliyah to the new state. They too dedicated their lives on a daily basis to the building of, in Theodor Herzl's words, "an old new land."

101 Squadron, 1948: This unit was the first formation in the Israel Air Force (IAF) in 1948, and 70 per cent of its pilots were volunteers, Jewish and non-Jewish, from Canada, the United States, South Africa, Australia, Britain, and twelve other countries. This group of pilots includes four Canadians—John McElroy of Kamloops, BC (top row left); Denny Wilson of Hamilton, Ontario (second row, fourth from left); Jack Doyle of London, Ontario (fifth from left); and Lee Sinclair of Winnipeg (bottom row, second from left). Ezer Weizman, future president of Israel, is second from the right in the second row. Many Canadians also served as technical personnel for an air force that was truly "born in battle."

(Canadian Machal Archives)

A Tribute to the Canadians Who Defended Israel

What appears on pages 118 to 125 is the most comprehensive and authoritative list of Canadians who served in Machal, fighting to defend the fledgling State of Israel in the 1948 War of Independence.

Israel's Egyptian Spitfire

Throughout the War of Independence Britain provided the Rolls-Royce–powered fighter planes known as Spitfires to the Egyptians, but refused to sell any to Israel. In May 1948, Israeli rifle fire brought down one of the Egyptian Spitfires on the beach near Tel Aviv. A Canadian aircraft engineer, Dave Panar, of Edmonton, Alberta, was driven to the seaside to examine the wreckage and determine whether the aircraft could be salvaged. Panar found that the Spit had torn off a wing in the crash and damaged its propeller. Undaunted, the Canadian asked to be taken to abandoned Royal Air Force bases in former Palestine, where he found a variety of aircraft parts that had been left behind when the RAF had pulled out. Panar went to work and, in the end, was not only able to make the Egyptian Spitfire flyable—the plane he rebuilt was Israel's first Spitfire to fly in both combat and reconnaissance missions—but also found enough spares to assemble a second fighter plane.

THE STRUGGLE FOR INDEPENDENCE

It was compiled by one of the veterans, Eddy Kaplansky, and was provided by Ralph L. Lowenstein of the College of Journalism and Communications at the University of Florida.

The Vancouver Squadron Commander

One of the unsung Canadian heroes of the Israeli War of Independence was Ralph Moster of Vancouver, who commanded the Negev Squadron of the newly formed Israeli Air Force. Moster was killed on December 7, 1948, along with his American pilot and mechanic, when his plane crashed into the Sea of Galilee. The squadron was equipped with single-engine light planes that carried out such dangerous tasks as medical evacuations, delivering supplies to isolated Israeli settlements, and even dropping small bombs on Egyptian attackers.

Swifty's Flying Fortress

In 1948, as Israel found itself under attack by its well-armed Arab neighbours, a Flying Fortress bomber with engine trouble was forced to make an emergency landing at the Shearwater Naval Air Base near Halifax. In theory, the aircraft's pilot, "Swifty" Schindler, president of the New England Air Navigation Training Company, was instructing eight student pilots. In fact, he was second-in-command of the airlift of arms from Czechoslovakia to the new State of Israel, and the American-built B–17 bomber was on its way to the Middle East to strengthen the tiny Israeli air force. The Czechs, with the approval of the Soviet Union, were the main arms suppliers to the Israelis during the War of Independence. The Israelis found themselves with few modern aircraft to combat the largely British-equipped Arab air forces.

As Swifty stood, discouraged, on the Shearwater tarmac, he was approached by a portly, balding middle-aged man who offered him a cigarette. "Keep the package," the stranger said. Inside the flap were the words "Follow me."

The mysterious stranger was Halifax businessman Samuel Jacobson, who had been directed by his contacts in Jerusalem to do what he could to free the pilot, even if it meant abandoning the bomber in Halifax. In the end, however, Schindler felt he couldn't abandon the aircraft and the eight experienced flyers who were volunteering to join the fledgling Israeli air force. So he took off at night—without lights—and flew to the Azores, where, under normal circumstances, he could have bribed the authorities to allow him to refuel. When he landed, however, he found that too much publicity about what he was doing had preceded him. Schindler was arrested and returned to the United States, where he served a two-year prison sentence.

Shimon Peres and Mr. Sam

Even after the 1948 War of Independence, the new State of Israel continued to face raids and threats from the well-equipped Arab armies and the Israel Defense Forces were still experiencing great difficulty in acquiring arms due to international embargoes. In 1950, when Israeli prime minister David Ben-Gurion discovered that Canada had thirty surplus weapons it was willing to sell—for $2 million—he sent a young Shimon Peres to acquire the weapons. As he prepared to make the trip, Peres learned from various people that Israel had a very wealthy and influential friend in the man who was president of both the Seagram Company and the Canadian Jewish Congress, Sam Bronfman.

In his autobiography, *Leo: A Life*, businessman and former Canadian Senator Leo Kolber tells the story of what happened when Peres arrived in Montreal. The Israeli envoy turned up at the gates of the Seagram plant in Ville Lasalle, a suburb of Montreal, without an appointment, only to find that the security guards would not let him in. Peres pleaded with them to check with Mr. Sam (as Bronfman was popularly known), and finally met with success. He was escorted to Sam Bronfman's office, where he explained the mission that had brought him to Canada. Bronfman listened attentively and when Peres had finished, he snapped, "That's too much money." He picked up the telephone on his desk and called C. D. Howe, the powerful Minister of Industry and Commerce to arrange a meeting in Ottawa for the next day.

En route to Ottawa in a Bronfman limousine, accompanied by businessman and lawyer Sol Kanee, the three men were huddled against the winter cold under blankets, fortified—at Bronfman's insistence—with some Seagram's V.O., when Bronfman noticed with dismay that Peres was wearing white socks. Always an elegant dresser, he was horrified, and had the driver stop at a menswear shop to buy dark hose for the man who would one day be prime minister of Israel.

At the Ottawa meeting with the minister, Bronfman wasted no time in negotiating a 50 per cent reduction in the price of the armaments. On the way back to Montreal, Mr. Sam asked Peres, "Where will you get the $1 million?"

"From you," responded the Israeli representative hopefully.

The next night, Saidye and Sam Bronfman had "a few people" over to their Westmount mansion and raised the required sum. Not long after, the Israel Defense Forces had thirty new weapons—and it didn't cost the young state a penny.

Pierre Elliott Trudeau—Arrested in Embattled Jerusalem, 1948

In the summer of 1948, future Canadian prime minister Pierre Elliott Trudeau was arrested in Jordanian-occupied Jerusalem and charged with being a "Jewish spy." The twenty-nine-year-old Trudeau—sporting a beard and a fez—arrived in Amman, Jordan, only weeks after Israel had declared its independence and the war began.

Despite the dangers, Trudeau was determined to see Jerusalem. He boldly jumped aboard a truck carrying Arab soldiers to the front, and after rumbling across the Allenby Bridge, arrived in Jerusalem. In *Memoirs*, his autobiography, Trudeau describes what he encountered on his way to visit a monastery in the ancient city: "It was with immense pleasure that I walked through [Jerusalem], a pleasure mixed with other strong emotions, since I had to cross a street on the outskirts of the Old City under Israeli-Arab fire." Returning to his hotel in the company of a Canadian priest, Trudeau wrote, "Two Arab soldiers grabbed me by the collar and without any further formalities threw me in jail." He was told he would be charged with spying for Israel, but the priest intervened and explained that he was a student, not a spy. Nevertheless, Trudeau was repeatedly threatened with death until the British embassy in Amman had him cleared of all charges.

At the celebration of Israel's thirtieth anniversary in 1978, Trudeau delivered the keynote address to 20,000 people at the Montreal Forum, in which he said, "The Jews who gathered in the Holy Land to form the State of Israel brought to it all the wealth of spirit and intelligence, all the qualities, virtues and gifts that I have mentioned. In a few decades, their presence, the legitimacy of which cannot rightfully be questioned, has literally brought back to life a land that was being eaten away by the desert…a new democracy has been set up." At the same time, the Canadian leader was concerned about the fate of the Arab nations: "It is a situation made up of very complex and shifting forces, including neighbours strong in their own legitimacy."

Name	Hometown	Province	Unit
Abrams, Joe	Toronto	ON	Army
Abramson, Joe	Winnipeg	MB	Army
£ Alterson, Morris	Yorkton	SK	Army, Navy
Anger, Stanley	Toronto	ON	Air Force
Bagelman, Harry	Toronto	ON	Army
Baltman, William (Bill)	Toronto	ON	Air Force
Baron, Jack	Toronto	ON	Navy
Beckwith [Beck], Morris	Ottawa	ON	Air Force
Belkin, Jack	Calgary	AB	Army
Benn, Jacob (Jack)	Toronto	ON	Air Force
Berger, Jack	Toronto	ON	Army
Beube, Sidney	Toronto	ON	Army
† # Beurling, George F. "Buzz"	Verdun	QC	Air Force
Binder, Sam	Toronto	ON	Air Force
¥ Blank, Jack	Toronto	ON	Army, Navy
† Bradshaw, William "Blacky"	Dundas	ON	Air Force
Braverman, Immanuel	Montreal	QC	Army
† Brodigan, Charles	Vancouver	BC	Air Force
£ Brown, Allan	Toronto	ON	Army, Navy
Brown, Max	Toronto	ON	Army
Cadloff, Syd	Montreal	QC	Army
Calman, Mike	Vancouver	BC	Army
Camerman, Sam	Vancouver	BC	Air Force
Cameron, Rod "Tiny"	Toronto	ON	Air Force
# Canter, Wilfred	Toronto	ON	Air Force
Caplan, Alexander	Montreal	QC	Air Force
Cappell, Murray	Toronto	ON	Army
Chapnick, Allan	Winnipeg	MB	Army
Chen, Meyer	Montreal	QC	Air Force
Chetner, Sydney	Calgary	AB	Army
Chinsky, Eddie	Windsor	ON	Air Force
Cohen, Aaron	Kamsack	SK	Air Force
Cohen, Bob	Montreal	QC	Army
¥ Cohen, Eli	Montreal	QC	Navy
# Cohen, Harvey	Toronto	ON	Army
Meyer, Cohen	Montreal	QC	Air Force
Cohen, Sam	Toronto	ON	Army
Cooper, Morry	Toronto	ON	Army

Legend:
† Christian
# Killed in Action
£ Served in other Branches
¥ Served in both Aliyah Bet & Machal

118

Name	Hometown	Province	Unit
Cossman, Howard	Montreal	QC	Army
Covent, Perry	Toronto	ON	Air Force
Dankevy, Morris	Toronto	ON	Army
Danovich, Moe	Montreal	QC	Army
Danovitch, Abe	Montreal	QC	Air Force
Dari, Y.	Montreal	QC	Army
Dinkin, Harry	Toronto	ON	Air Force
Dlin, Norman	Edmonton	AB	Army
† Doyle, John (Jack)	London	ON	Air Force
Druker, Lionel	Sydney	NS	Army
Drutz, David	Toronto	ON	Air Force
Dunkelman, Ben	Toronto	ON	Army
Dworkin, Alec "Pee-Wee"	Montreal	QC	Army
Edelstein, Stephen	Pembroke	ON	Air Force
Eisen, Robert (Bob)	Toronto	ON	Army
Epstein, Alex	Toronto	ON	Army
Epstein, Morris	Toronto	ON	Army
† Etchells, David	Hamilton	ON	Air Force
Fagen, Sam	Montreal	QC	Army
Fine, Len	Toronto	ON	Army
# Fisher, William (Willy)	Winnipeg	MB	Air Force
† # Fitchett, Leonard	Vancouver	BC	Air Force
Floom, Harold	Winnipeg	MB	Air Force
Forster, Sam	Montreal	QC	Army
Fox, Jack	Winnipeg	MB	Navy
Fox, Leonard	Toronto	ON	Army
Freedman, Jack	Montreal	QC	Army
Freedman, Max	Winnipeg	MB	Army
£ Freedman, Nathan	Winnipeg	MB	Air Force
Freeman, Harold	Vancouver	BC	unknown
Freeman, Lionel	Toronto	ON	Toronto
Freeman, Solomon (Sol)	Toronto	ON	Army
Garbovitsky, Morley	Winnipeg	MB	Air Force
Garfin, Ansel	Edmonton	AB	Air Force
Gelmon, Alvin D.	Vancouver	BC	Army
Gerstl, Joe	Toronto	ON	Army
Gertzbein, David	Toronto	ON	Army
£ Ginsberg, Murray	Toronto	ON	Army, Navy

Name	Hometown	Province	Unit
Gold, Irving Mark	Vancouver	BC	Army
Gold, Jack	Montreal	QC	Army
Goldberg, Arthur	Vancouver	BC	Army
Goldberg, Samuel	Winnipeg	MB	Air Force
¥ Goldberg, Sol	Montreal	QC	Navy
Goldstein, Jack	Montreal	QC	Air Force
Goldstep, Myer	Winnipeg	MB	Army
Good, Philip M.	Toronto	ON	Army
Goodman, Harvey	Montreal	QC	Army
Goodman, Henry (Hank)	Calgary	AB	Army
Gordon, Machen	Preston	ON	Air Force
Gordon, Sam	Vancouver	BC	Air Force
Gorin, Reuben	Winnipeg	MB	Army
₤ Gross, Gerry Joseph	Montreal	QC	Army, Navy
Halamish, Joseph	Winnipeg	MB	Army
Halperin, Sidney	St. Catherine	ON	Army
Hambourg, Irving	Toronto	ON	Army
Heaps, Leo	Montreal	QC	Army
Horne, Salk	unknown	unknown	Army
Hurtig, Jack	Winnipeg	MB	Air Force
Hyman, Len	Regina	SK	Navy
Jacobs, Sol	Toronto	ON	Air Force
Jacobson, Sydney M.	Winnipeg	MB	Army
Joffe, Yale	Vancouver	BC	Air Force
Jolson, George	Winnipeg	MB	Army
Kahane, Bernard	Winnipeg	MB	Army
Kahansky [Kahan], Laz	Montreal	QC	Navy
† Kane, James	Windsor	ON	Air Force
Kaplansky, Dave	Montreal	QC	Air Force
₤ Kaplansky, Irving	Montreal	QC	Army, Navy
¥ Kaplansky, Yedidia (Eddy)	Montreal	QC	Air Force
Kare, Moshe (Morley)	Winnipeg	MB	Army
Kastner, Meyer	Montreal	QC	Air Force
Kates [Katz], Harold	Toronto	ON	Air Force
Katz, Jack	Winnipeg	MB	Army
¥ Katz, Moshe	Montreal	QC	Navy
Katz, Percy	Toronto	ON	Army
Kessiloff, Edward (Eddie)	Winnipeg	MB	Army

Legend:
† Christian
# Killed in Action
₤ Served in other
   Branches
¥ Served in both Aliyah
   Bet & Machal

Name	Hometown	Province	Unit
Kettner, Frank	Calgary	AB	Air Force
Kipness, Arnold	Calgary	AB	Army
Klein, Hyman (Hymie)	Vegreville	AB	Army
¥ Kogan, Bernard	Montreal	QC	Navy
Kopstein, Jack	Winnipeg	MB	Army
Kushner, David ("Art")	Vancouver	BC	Air Force
Langer, Albert	Toronto	ON	Air Force
Lashinsky, Arthur "Lash"	Toronto	ON	Army
Laurie, Louis	Quebec	QC	Army
Leff, Norman Arthur "Alter"	Toronto	ON	Army
# Leisure, Sidney	Toronto	ON	Army
¥ Leith, Nathan	Edmonton	AB	Air Force
Lenett, Harold N.	Vancouver	BC	Army
Leventhal, Philip	Toronto	ON	Army
Levi, Norman	Victoria	BC	Army
Levin, Ernest Max	Windsor	ON	Army
Levine, Abraham (Abe)	Whitby	ON	Army
Levitan, Elkan	Montreal	QC	Air Force
Lewis, Julius	Toronto	ON	Army
Lewis, Morrie	Downsview	ON	unknown
Liberson, Albert	Winnipeg	MB	Air Force
¥ Liberson, Joe	Winnipeg	MB	Navy
Lipschitz [Lipton], Edward	Toronto	ON	Air Force
Lobe, Morris	Trail	BC	Army
# Lugech, Ed	Toronto	ON	Army
Macillin, Joe	Winnipeg	MB	Navy
Mahan, Irving	Dorval	QC	unknown
£ ¥ Maltin, Manny	Vancouver	BC	Army, Navy
Manolson, Will	Calgary	AB	Air Force
Margolis, Robert (Bob)	Winnipeg	MB	Army
Matlow, Irving L.	Toronto	ON	Army
† McElroy, John F.	Vancouver	BC	Air Force
† McGunigal, Jim	Vancouver	BC	Air Force
Merovihtz [Mervin], Harry	Winnipeg	MB	Air Force
Merson, Leonard	Montreal	QC	Air Force
Meyers, Joseph	Winnipeg	MB	Navy
Meyerowitz (Meyers), Hank	Winnipeg	MB	Army
Miller, Stanley	Calgary	AB	Army

Name	Hometown	Province	Unit
£ Morris, Samuel	Vancouver	BC	Air Force, Navy
# Moster, Ralph	Vancouver	BC	Air Force
£ Naturman, Meyer	Montreal	QC	Air Force
† Nelson, Edward	Windsor	ON	Air Force
Newfield, Frank	Toronto	ON	Air Force
¥ Nezinsky [Lewis], Morris	Toronto	ON	Navy
Novick, William (Bill)	Montreal	QC	Air Force
¥ £ Ocopnick, Ben	Toronto	ON	Army, Navy
Olfman, Jacob (Jack)	Winnipeg	MB	Air Force
Olfman, Mitchell Moses	Kamsack	SK	Army
Orloff, Harold	Vancouver	BC	Air Force
Ostrovsky [Osten], Syd	Edmonton	AB	Air Force
Panar, David	Edmonton	AB	Air Force
Parness, Victor	Montreal	QC	Navy
† Pears, James	Hamilton	ON	Air Force
Perry, Norman	Toronto	ON	Navy
Pierce, Morris	Kingston	ON	Army
¥ Pleet, Yakov	Ottawa	ON	Navy
¥ Pomerantz, Haim	Montreal	QC	Navy
Poskanzer, Aliza	Winnipeg	MB	Air Force
Potter, Manly	Winnipeg	MB	Army
Pressman, Julius	Ottawa	ON	Army
Prussick, Sam	Montreal	QC	Army
Quitt, Gordon	Toronto	ON	Army
£ Reiter, Walter	Toronto	ON	Army, Air Force
Robinson, Max	Winnipeg	MB	Army
Rosen, Al	Montreal	QC	Army
Rosen, David	Vancouver	BC	Army
£ Rosenberg, Gerald S.	Toronto	ON	Army, Navy
Ross, Benjamin "Barry"	Calgary	AB	Air Force
¥ Rostoker, Ben	Montreal	QC	Army
¥ Rostoker, Willie	Montreal	QC	Navy
Roth, Eddie M.	Toronto	OC	Army
# Rubinoff, Sidney	Toronto	ON	Army
Rudin, Raymon	Edmonton	AB	Army
Ruvinsky, Aaron "Art"	Winnipeg	MB	Air Force
Sack, Louis	Toronto	ON	unknown
Sacksner, Lionel	Montreal	QC	Army

Legend:
† Christian
# Killed in Action
£ Served in other Branches
¥ Served in both Aliyah Bet & Machal

Name	Hometown	Province	Unit
# ¥ Schiff, Reuben "Red"	Toronto	ON	Army, Navy
Schwartz, Morris (Mo)	Toronto	ON	Army
Segal, Hy	Montreal	QC	Army
Shanas, Leibel "Ed"	Winnipeg	MB	Army
Shnitka [Shaw], Sam	Calgary	AB	Air Force
Sidorsky, David	Calgary	AB	Army
Siegel, Avrom V.	Toronto	ON	Army
Siegel, Joseph	Glace Bay	NS	Air Force
£ Silver, Melvin (Mel)	Calgary	AB	Army, Air Force
† Sinclair, George Leslie "Lee"	Winnipeg	MB	Air Force
Singer, Samuel	Winnipeg	MB	Army
Sirulnikoff [Sirlin], Harvey	Winnipeg	MB	Army
Slutsky, Jack	Montreal	QC	Army
Smith, Harry	Toronto	ON	Air Force
Smith, Jack	St. Georges	QC	Army
Smith, Jack	Winnipeg	MB	Air Force
Smith, Morry	Toronto	ON	Air Force
Sober, Stanley	Toronto	ON	unknown
Sokolow, Moshe	Toronto	ON	Army
Solsberg, Albert	Toronto	ON	Air Force
Spector, Israel	Winnipeg	MB	Army
£ Spiegel, Albert	Toronto	ON	Army, Air Force
† Spink, Thomas	Vancouver	BC	Air Force
Steinberg [Halamish], Joe	Winnipeg	MB	Army
Steinberg, Otto	Montreal	QC	Air Force
† # Stevenson, Fred	Vancouver	BC	Air Force
Stitz, Oscar "Al"	Montreal	QC	Air Force
Stitz, Frank	Portage La Prairie, MB		Navy
Sturrey, Ben ("Red")	Winnipeg	MB	Air Force
Sures, Lawrence	Winnipeg	MB	Army
Sussman, Joe	Toronto	ON	Air Force
† Sutton, Bernard "Terry"	Vancouver	BC	Air Force
Swartz, Morris	Toronto	ON	Army
Talksy, Joe	Toronto	ON	Army
¥ Taller, Abraham "Archie"	Ottawa	ON	Navy
Tate, Daniel	Toronto	ON	Army
Troube, Avraham "Al"	Toronto	ON	Air Force
Tunis, Joe	Vegreville	AB	Army

Name	Hometown	Province	Unit
† Wadman, Charles "Bill"	Calgary	AB	Air Force
Waldman, Leonard (Len)	Montreal	QC	Army
Waldman, Maurice H.	Assiniboia	SK	Army
Warner, Joseph	Toronto	ON	Army
Wasser, Samuel (Sam)	Toronto	ON	Army
Waters, Philip	Downsview	ON	unknown
¥ Weiver, Herky	Toronto	ON	Navy
Weiner, Joseph	Montreal	QC	Army
¥ Weinstein, Manny "Wingy"	Montreal	QC	Army, Navy
Weinzweig, Avrum Israel	Toronto	ON	Army
Werner, Herky	unknown	unknown	Army
† Wilson, Clifford "Denny"	Hamilton	ON	Air Force
£ ¥ Wittenoff, Julius	Montreal	QC	Army, Navy
£ Wohl, David	Edmonton	AB	Army, Air Force
Wolfson [Lam], Bessie [Batya]	Toronto	ON	Air Force
Workin, Alec D.	Montreal	QC	Army
£ Wosk, Saul	Vancouver	BC	Army, Air Force
Wright, David Isadore	Hamilton	ON	Air Force
† Wygle, Brien	Vancouver	BC	Air Force
Yurman, Shlomo	Winnipeg	MB	Air Force
Ziev [Sivkin], Nachum	Montreal	QC	Air Force

Legend:
† Christian
# Killed in Action
£ Served in other
  Branches
¥ Served in both Aliyah
  Bet & Machal

Montreal Jews celebrate the first Yom Ha'atzmaut, the anniversary of Israel's independence, May 15, 1949.

(Allan Raymond Collection, Jewish Public Library Archives)

7

Building Israel and Jewish Identity

U NITED STATES PRESIDENT HARRY TRUMAN granted de
    facto recognition of the new State of Israel immediately
    following the proclamation by the Jewish Provisional
Government on May 14, 1948. The Soviet Union granted de jure
recognition three days later. Canada, however, continued to hold back.

The United Kingdom put pressure on the Commonwealth
nations to prevent their recognition of Israel and Prime Minister
Mackenzie King insisted that Canada continue to back British policy
as a matter of course.

As he wrote in his diary on May 20, 1948, the day after Britain
declared that it would fulfill its treaty obligations and provide military

Golda Myerson (later Golda
Meir, prime minister of Israel)
is the guest speaker at the
launching of the 1948
Combined Jewish Appeal in
Montreal. She is seated below
the portrait of Israel's first
president, Chaim Weizmann.

(Canadian Jewish Congress National
Archives, Montreal)

Halifax Jews celebrate the rebirth of Israel in 1948 at a Jewish National Fund dinner.

help to several Arab states: "I, myself, was much amazed at this statement to be made at this time, but I am sure it is not without reason on the part of Britain.... I feel that the British have the best of reasons, having the most to lose from the course they have pursued."

In June 1948, Israeli diplomat Michael Comay travelled to Ottawa to discuss the matter personally with secretary of state for external affairs Louis St. Laurent and a number of other senior ministry officials. Although he strongly made the case that, as one of the states that had both drafted and supported the UN Partition Plan, Canada should immediately recognize the State of Israel, Prime Minister Mackenzie King's government, loathe to break openly with Britain, continued to demur.

Canada's subservience to British foreign policy ended when Louis St. Laurent succeeded Mackenzie King as prime minister of Canada on November 15, 1948. Earlier that fall, on September 10, Lester Pearson had taken over St. Laurent's portfolio at external affairs. An internationalist, Pearson saw Canada's new role as one of broker between the great powers rather than being strictly allied with any of them. In the UN General Assembly's First Committee meeting on November 22, 1948, Pearson put forward Canada's new position on Palestine, one that would form the basis of Canada's policy on the Middle East for many years. He contended that the existence of the Jewish state should be internationally recognized, that the Arab

Future Montreal member of Parliament Leon Crestohl, an outspoken friend of Israel, stands between two unidentified Arab leaders in Beersheba in 1948, shortly after the vote to partition Palestine.

(Canadian Jewish Congress National Archives, Montreal)

nations should accept both the fact of the existence of Israel and the fact that a separate Arab state in Palestine had not emerged, that the final determination of the details of the partition should be made by the Israelis and the Arabs themselves—either directly or through mediation—and that further settlement of the region should be carried out peacefully.

Over the course of the next month, the UN grappled with the questions of Israeli membership in the UN, the boundaries of the new Jewish state, the conflicting positions of the U.S., Britain, and the Soviet Union, and the terms of the proposed Palestine Conciliation Commission. While these various issues were being debated, the UN Security Council continued—with Canada's support—to delay the matter of Israel's membership in the international body. Finally, Pearson made the case to Cabinet that Canada could give de facto recognition to the Jewish state touching on the other aspects under discussion and, on December 24, 1948, the secretary of state for external affairs announced that, "The State of Israel was proclaimed on 15 May 1948. During the seven months that have elapsed, the State of Israel has, in the opinion of the Canadian government, given satisfactory proof that it complies with the essential conditions of statehood. These essential conditions are generally recognized to be external independence and effective internal government within a reasonably well-defined territory."

Pearson then sent a message to Israel's foreign minister, Moshe Sharett that read,

> I have the honour to inform you, on behalf of the Government of Canada, that Canada recognizes *de facto* the State of Israel in Palestine, and that it also recognizes *de facto* the authority of the Provisional Government of Israel, of which you are a member.
>
> This recognition is accorded in the knowledge that the boundaries of the new State have not as yet been precisely defined, and in the hope that it may be possible to settle these and all other outstanding questions in the spirit of the Resolution adopted by the General Assembly on 11 December 1948.

Canada's Reluctant Recognition of Israel

Canada remained caught between Britain and the U.S. on the question of recognizing Israel throughout the summer and fall of 1948. On November 29, just as the UN General Assembly was about to begin meeting in Paris, Israel upped the ante by applying to the UN Security Council for admission to the UN. Moshe Sharett, Israel's first foreign minister and future prime minister, had been counting on Canada, as a member of the Security Council, to back Israel's application. He met with Lester Pearson—now an elected member of Parliament and secretary of state for external affairs—to ask for Canada's support. Despite his own position in favour of recognizing the new Jewish state, Pearson only committed himself to referring the matter to Ottawa and suggested that Israel defer its application until the UN had completed its deliberations in regards to setting up the Palestine Conciliation Commission. Nonetheless, Israel's application

went forward and Canada, realizing that support for UN membership would be tantamount to recognition, abstained.

Concerned Zionists turned to their most influential Liberal Party ally, Montreal lawyer Lazarus Phillips. Phillips immediately contacted Brooke Claxton, who was acting secretary of state for external affairs while Pearson was in Paris.

Phillips met Claxton for dinner and stated his position in favour of Canada recognizing Israel. He was apparently convincing—the acting minister, despite the late hour, telephoned Prime Minister Louis St. Laurent to explain the need to change Canada's position. As Phillips later recounted, "After listening to my case, the prime minister instructed Claxton to phone Pearson in Paris, even though it was 5 a.m., Paris time, and ask him to change the vote to an affirmative."

Mr. Justice Ivan C. Rand, who wrote the United Nations Resolution calling for the partition of Palestine into Jewish and Arab states, is honoured at the 1949 Zionist Convention. Others at the head table for the presentation are (left to right) Israeli foreign minister Abba Eban, future Canadian member of Parliament Leon Crestohl, Sam Zacks, Michael Garber, Saidye (Mrs. Samuel) Bronfman, and Sam Bronfman.

(Canadian Jewish Congress National Archives, Montreal)

Not long after, in January 1949, Britain followed suit and recognized the State of Israel.

Israel was admitted into the United Nations as a full member on May 11, 1949, at which time Canada accorded it de jure recognition. On May 19, 1949, provisional recognition was granted to Israel's first consul general to Canada, Abraham Harman, who arrived on July 18. Later, the two governments would exchange ambassadors, initiating full diplomatic relations.

Israel's Ambassadorial Residence in Ottawa 1948

One of Israel's first diplomatic appointments was Michael Comay, who was named ambassador to Canada in 1948.

Comay called on a number of Jewish leaders to let them know that he had arrived in Ottawa and was able to help build Canadian support for the new Jewish state.

One of his earliest visitors was the wealthy and influential Sam Bronfman, certainly the most generous supporter of Israel in Canada at the time.

"Mr. Sam" was shocked to find that Israel's "ambassadorial residence" was a room in Ottawa's Château Laurier Hotel. "This won't do!" he snapped and immediately made arrangements for the purchase of a splendid residence on Clemow Avenue to serve as home to Israel's ambassadors.

As Bronfman said to Saul Hayes, "This is the first time in 2,000 years that a Jewish nation is being recognized in world capitals and Ottawa is one of them."

Dov Yosef (1899–1980)

A native of Montreal, Bernard Joseph played an important role in supporting the Zionist cause in both Canada and Israel. He became involved with Zionism in his teens, helping to organize Canadian Young Judaea and serve as its first president. In 1918, he joined the Jewish Legion and served in the battle to free Palestine from the Ottoman Turks. He stayed in Israel after the First World War and became known as one of Palestine's leading lawyers. Joseph, who changed his first name from Bernard to Dov and the spelling of his surname from Joseph to Yosef, became legal adviser to the Jewish Agency in Jerusalem. When the Second World War began, he helped recruit volunteers for Jewish units in the British Army. His role in Jewish Agency activities was important enough for the British to detain him, along with other Jewish leaders, at Latrun, in 1946.

When the War of Independence broke out, Israeli forces were able to hold only a portion of Jerusalem, which—under the United Nations Partition Plan—was to be internationalized. With the city divided between the Israel Defense Force and the Jordanian Legion, the Israeli government proclaimed, on August 2, that areas controlled by Jewish fighters would be considered "Israeli-occupied" territory, and Dov Yosef was appointed military governor of Jerusalem. Three days later, the Israeli government, with important input from Governor Yosef, rejected any proposal to internationalize the city. Later, Yosef would write, "My hardest task as Military Governor was also the longest and slowest: helping to secure recognition by the world that Jerusalem had become irrevocably part of Israel."

Yosef was governor of the embattled city for five crucial months—from August 1948 through January 1949. According to the *Encyclopedia Judaica*, "his energy and determination played a vital part in the city's successful defense during the critical siege."

In December 1949, David Ben-Gurion put the final nail into the coffin of internationalization of the city, telling the Knesset, "We regard it as our duty to declare that Jerusalem is an organic and inseparable part of the State of Israel, as it is an inseparable part of the history of Israel, of the faith of Israel."

After the war, Dov Yosef represented Mapai, precursor of the modern-day Israeli Labour Party, in the Knesset from 1949 to 1965, holding a variety of portfolios.

The Links Grow Stronger

Israelis such as Abraham Harman, Moshe Rivlin, Michael Comay, and Eppie Evron fostered close ties between Canada and Israel and Israel and the Canadian Jewish community. They saw themselves not only as official envoys to Canada but also as links between the Jews of Israel and the Jews of Canada.

The Canadian Jewish community's strong bonds of solidarity between the two nations was enhanced by its material contributions in

Saul Hayes, executive vice-president of the Canadian Jewish Congress (far left) with Lord Jenner, a leader of the British Jewish Community (center left). Dov Yosef, military governor of Jerusalem (centre right).

(Monteal Jewish Publication Society)

the early years of Israel's statehood—they were among the highest in the world. On a per capita basis, the community's contribution was twice that of its American counterpart.

Canadians in Israel made their mark as well. As minister of rationing and supply from 1949 to 1950, the veteran Bernard Joseph, who became known as Dov Yosef, took on the unenviable task of guiding Israel through the *tsena*, the years of austerity. From 1951 to 1952 and from 1961 to 1966, the Canadian lawyer served as Israel's minister of justice.

Virtually every area of endeavour—culture, education, tourism, trade, commerce—was marked by collaboration and mutual support. But above all, Canadian Jewry continued to give its children to the new state, as Israel influenced Canadian Jews in redefining their identity and giving the community new meaning.

New Activities for Canadian Zionists

Canadian Zionists were overjoyed by the establishment of the State of Israel. However, the fulfillment in 1948 of the dreams harboured by a few Jews who had come out on a wintry night in 1898 to establish the first Zionist society did not mean that the end was in sight. There was still much work to do if the Jewish homeland was to flourish and serve the needs of Jews throughout the world, and it was to this end that the Canadian Zionist movement turned its attention after 1948. As the pre-state focus on efforts to establish the state shifted in the post-establishment era to the need to strengthen the new Jewish state, the organizational structure of Canadian Jewry changed. The "Parliament" of Canadian Jewry, the Canadian Jewish Congress, played a major role in the coordination of Jewish communal activities on a national basis and represented the needs and interests of the Canadian Jewish community to the various levels of government. It was a powerful voice that articulated the ties between

Samuel Zacks

Sam Zacks, a native of Kingston, Ontario, and a graduate of Queen's University, played an immensely important role in the history of Canadian Zionism. In 1938 he was one of the founders of the United Jewish Welfare Fund in Toronto. He served two terms as president of the Zionist Organization of Canada in the critical years from 1943 to 1949. He was a vigorous campaigner in the frustrating effort to change Canada's unsympathetic attitude toward Jews seeking to escape Nazi Germany. He served on the executive of the National Committee on Refugees, which helped re-establish 3,000 German Jewish refugees before and after the Second World War. He was involved in almost every Canadian effort to help Jews in Palestine and elsewhere. He was the only Canadian member of the Sonneborn Institute, the fictitous New York-based organization founded by

Rudolf Sonneborn to secretly supply arms to the Jews of Palestine before and during the War of Independence.

Sam Zacks also helped establish the Canada-Palestine Committee under the chairmanship of Sir Elsworth Flavelle and was a co-founder of Canadian Friends of Hebrew University and the Weizmann Institute of Science. In the 1960s, he was the first Jewish chair of the board of the Art Gallery of Ontario, and was a key figure in the first expansion of the gallery by the architect John C. Parkin in 1974 and the creation of the Henry Moore Pavilion. Through their generous donation to the AGO, Sam and Ayala Zacks gave their world-famous collection of modern art to the people of Ontario. The Zacks were also responsible for construction of a building in Hazor, Israel, to display artifacts from King Solomon's summer palace.

the Jewish community and Israel and communicated those ties to the non-Jewish world.

Material support such as fundraising was coordinated in Jewish community federations across the country—led by, among many others, Sidney Zack in Vancouver, Joseph Shoctor in Edmonton, Tevic Miller in Calgary, and Max Forman in Halifax. These community federations became the fundraisers and fund distributors, and eventually formed the National Budgeting Committee of Canadian Jewry (NBC) that effectively controlled various communal and overseas allocations, including those to the United Israel Appeal.

In addition, a number of Israel-based organizations—such as the Jewish National Fund (JNF), Israel Bonds, and committees for various Israeli hospitals, universities, and other institutions—either came into being or expanded their activities. Following the establishment of the State of Israel, virtually every aspect of Jewish life, from synagogues to fraternal organizations such as B'nai Brith, reflected the mainstreaming of Zionism among most Jews and almost all Jewish organizations.

Early on, the JNF raised funds to purchase forest lands throughout the State of Israel. In 1954, there was a fundraising drive to support the planting of a forest of one million trees outside Ein Kerem. The drive was completed over several years, and the area has taken on the name of the Canada Forest. Two more Canadian-sponsored forest projects were subsequently completed: the Canadian Centennial Forest near Amatzya in the Lachish Region in 1964, and the Canadian Friendship Forest near Nashua in 1968.

Israel Bonds

Israel Bond activities in Canada began in the early 1950s and since then have represented a real investment by Canadian Jewry in both their future and that of the State of Israel. Canada's Israel Bonds program began in 1951 when Israel's first prime minister, David Ben-Gurion, asked Samuel Bronfman to form an effective bond organization to raise funds for the Jewish state. Bronfman, with the assistance of Professor Maxwell Cohen of McGill University in Montreal, obtained a Canadian Charter in 1952, incorporating the bond organization under the name Canada-Israel Securities Limited (CISL).

Bond sales have fluctuated over the last 60 years, depending on the perceived needs of Israel. In the first year, sales totalled $4,524,050. And, until 1967, the yearly sale of bonds averaged between $4 and $5 million.

In 1967, as a result of threats to the state of Israel by Egypt during the Six Day War, bond sales doubled to $10 million and increased modestly each year until 1973. In 1973, the year of the Yom Kippur War, sales rose to $46 million. In 1982, during the Peace for Galilee Campaign, sales were $54 million, and, in 1989, sales of $69,487,310 were recorded. Two decades later, sales had more than doubled, with Israel Bonds purchased in Canada averaging between $150 million and $175 million a year in the first years of the twenty-first century, an impressive percentage of Israel Bonds' annual worldwide sales of $1.25 billion.

Many people have contributed immeasurably to the organization and sale of bonds in Canada. Among them were Kurt Rothschild, Ray Wolfe, Alex Grossman, Eph Diamond, Charles Bronfman, Rubin Zimmerman, Thomas Hecht, Melvyn Dobrin, Benjamin Guss, R. A. Kanigsberg, J. M. Goldberg, S. Hartgreen, and Isadore Namerow. Israel Bonds, usually sold following banquets, at synagogues, during High Holy Day appeals, and through a vigorous marketing and public relations program, have become a prominent aspect of Jewish community fundraising.

Alberta Young Judaeans at their camp in 1949. Among them is Mel Hurtig, (centre back row) who later published *The Canadian Encyclopedia*.

(Jewish Archives and Historical Society of Edmonton and Northern Alberta)

Israel as Inspiration

After Canada's recognition of the State of Israel in 1948, Canadian Jews, regardless of ideology, began to flock to Israel not just as pioneers, but as students and tourists. What had once been a hope or dream now became almost a commonplace experience that subtly reshaped the character of Canadian Jewry and changed the perspective of countless thousands of Canadian Jews who happily took for granted the fact that Israel was part of their lives.

Working together as a unified community, Canadian Jews have contributed to the creation of a multi-faceted, worldwide, coherent, and integrated fundraising network of welfare funds such as Combined Jewish Appeals, United Jewish Appeals, and so on, supported by new research in community planning, education, Jewish sociology, and demography. In this atmosphere, the activities of the formal organizations of Canadian Zionism took on new importance. Public education, school programs, assistance to those wishing to make aliyah, and public advocacy of Israel's continuing struggle for recognition all became part of the new direction for the Zionist undertaking.

Aliyah as a Goal

The word *olim*, which in Hebrew means "those who ascend," is also used to refer to immigrants. Their move to the Promised Land is called aliyah, which for Zionists is intended to denote something more meaningful than simply migrating from one country to another. From the Zionist viewpoint, aliyah is truly a pilgrimage. Indeed, "making aliyah" remains Zionism's first credo. The movement's second credo, or article of faith, was originally that Jewish settlers coming back to Zion should give up their previous lives as city dwellers and "return to the land itself." In other words, the *olim* would become agriculturalists engaged in tilling Zion's soil.

In the 1920s and 1930s, as anti-Semitism was growing in Canada and elsewhere, individual Canadians as well as some Canadian families chose to settle in Palestine on kibbutzim, moshavim, or alone. But in general, Zionist organizations viewed aliyah with disfavour until 1950—Canadian Zionists saw themselves primarily as suppliers of necessary materials for the *yishuv*. In fact, Canadian Jews' love for Canada has made Canadian Zionists ambivalent

Israel's first major warship, the
Strathadam, 1949.

(George Metcalf Archival Collection
© Canadian War Museum)

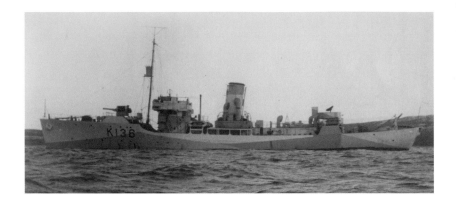

Israel's first major warship, the frigate *Strathadam*, was acquired in 1949 from Canada. The vessel had been constructed in 1944 and had seen only a few months service escorting convoys across the Atlantic before it was moth-balled.

A Royal Navy officer, Allan Burke, was asked to sail it to Israel, but that was not a simple task because, as the Israelis knew only too well, Arab countries would do all they could to block their acquisition of the warship. Burke had the *Strathadam* re-registered under the Panamanian flag and then sailed to Marseilles, France, where a crew of Jewish volunteers came aboard.

Burke was aware of threats to the vessel, noting later that "Intelligence reports said that Egyptian frogmen aboard an Egyptian mer-chantman berthed nearby might try to sabotage it." Refugees from a nearby camp, waiting for passage to Israel, helped mount round-the-clock security.

Burke learned that the night for the Egyptian attack had been set, and though repairs to the warship's engine and boilers had not been completed, the skipper took on only enough fuel to reach Haifa and sailed—in a thick fog—on "engine trials."

On arrival in Haifa, Burke was appointed officer-in-command of the Israeli Flotilla.

about the role of immigrating to Israel in building a Zionist iden-tity. When the State of Israel achieved independence and conditions began to improve, the attraction of settling there intensified. In 1950 the Zionist Organization of Canada finally endorsed aliyah as a suitable undertaking for its youth wing, Canadian Young Judaea. Overall, however, North American aliyah has been negligible, a tes-tament to how at home Jews feel in both Canada and the United States.

בתי ילדים אלה מוקמים צ׳ני לעזרה ושקום באמריקה ע״י ועד פועלים
LABOR ZIONIST COMMITTEE. FOR RELIEF AND REHABILITATION

וזרן אינגנובית דורכן ... גישטעט ... כירג ... איבכר...

The Canadian Aliyah

Many Canadians who settled in Israel rose to prominence and contributed to the building of the country. As mentioned, former Canadian Jewish Legionnaire and founding president of Canadian Young Judaea, Dov Yosef, served as military governor of Jerusalem during the 1947–1948 seige of the city, and as minister of justice, Jewish Agency treasurer, and a member of the Knesset from 1949 to 1959 and 1961 to 1966.

In 1922, Lillian Cornfeld of Montreal was one of the first women among Canadian *olim*. Upon her arrival at the port of Jaffa,

A Farband (Labour Zionist) convention held at an Israeli kibbutz in the 1950s. The Canadian delegates are easily identified; they are the only ones wearing ties!

(Canadian Jewish Congress National Archives, Montreal)

Ben-Gurion and Canada

David Ben-Gurion looked on Canada as a friendly country. He wrote in his diary on September 13, 1950, "Canada is acting friendly. Lester [Pearson] is helping out. Young McNaughton [the son of Canada's chief of staff during the Second World War] is our representative. The Canadians have sold us 5,000 armour-piercing shells, 200 used machine guns [$80 each instead of $1,300]; repairs will cost $20 apiece. A license has been obtained to buy Mosquitos."

Mosquitos were light fighter bombers built by de Havilland Aircraft of Canada. The planes were flown to Israel by volunteer pilots, but one disappeared during the flight and was never found. At that time, El Al, the Israeli national airline, had one aircraft and it was diverted in a vain search for the two missing flyers.

Delegates to the Maritime Young Judaea Conference in Saint John, New Brunswick, 1950.

(Saint John Jewish Historical Museum)

The State of Israel float in Vancouver's annual Victoria Day Parade, 1950. The entry won second prize. On the float (left to right) are Nessi Raels, Pearl Raels, Lila Israel, Stephen Bricker, Lorilee Mallek, Cyril Boas, and Alan Carr.

(British Columbia Jewish Historical Society)

she was greeted by none other than Bernard Joseph. Cornfeld went on to be known as the Mother of Israeli Cuisine because of her cookbooks and her recipes published in the *Jerusalem Post*. She also initiated the first program for women on Kol Yisrael, Israel's national radio station.

Molly Bar-David, another Canadian, expanded on Cornfield's work. In 1963, Bar-David wrote an authoritative book on the folk origins of cooking in Israel's various ethnic communities—an important tribute to Israel's melting pot that incorporated people from Europe, Asia, and Africa. She also published a book in 1954, titled *My Promised*

Land, about her experiences in Jerusalem during the War of Independence.

Betty Dubiner, wife of Sam Dubiner, made an enormous contribution to the State of Israel by setting up a voluntary welfare organization administered along American lines, the first such organization established outside the framework of the welfare services provided by the government of Israel. In 1952, she created the Ilanshil (Israel) Foundation, known since 1964 as ILAN, whose aim was to relieve the suffering of Israeli children who had become ill during a polio epidemic. Dubiner also organized the first summer camps for handicapped children, initiated a voluntary program for polio immunization, organized the first March of Dimes campaign in Israel, founded the ILAN Sport Centre for the Disabled, and worked for the Soldiers Welfare Organization. All in all, her contribution has been an impressive humanitarian effort for one person.

Montreal Zionist leader Ben Milner (circa 1950s) worked tirelessly for the cause.

(Zionists-Revisionists Archives)

The New *Olim*

The growing affluence of the Canadian Jewish community and the concurrently changing needs of the State of Israel combined to diminish the influence of *chalutz*-oriented youth movements. The Professional and Technical Workers Aliyah (PATWA) was formed to

Anna Raginsky, founder of the first Hadassah branch in Canada (in Toronto), meets Israel's first prime minister, David Ben-Gurion. Raginsky, then honourary president of Canadian Hadassah-WIZO, was attending the Fourteenth World Conference of the Women's International Zionist Organization in Israel in 1962.

(Canadian Hadassah-WIZO Archives)

induce people with advanced professional education to lend their skills to Israel. As a result of their efforts, Canadian Jews work in a variety of professions, including law, medicine, dentistry, social services, and government. Members of PATWA are highly respected throughout Israel.

In another form of aliyah, businessmen or members of their families frequently establish themselves in Israel in order to oversee a business endeavour. To facilitate this immigration, the United Israel Appeal set up a Israel Residents' Committee to provide a forum for Canadian Israelis and visiting Canadian delegations. The committee has also offered, directly or through the Association of Americans and Canadians in Israel (AACI), supplementary mortgages to help Canadian settlers acquire apartments or start businesses.

Aliyah from Canada increased in 1950, but it reached a higher level in the mid-1960s, fed in part by the large migration of Jews from Montreal between 1960 and 1980 as a result of growing French-Canadian nationalism. While there were few examples of violent French-Canadian anti-Semitism—and there were some positive instances of tight alliances

Ben Milner and the Zionist-Revisionists of Canada

To distinguish themselves from the heavily socialist Labour Zionist mainstream, the national political faction of Zionism dubbed themselves Revisionists. Ben Milner was one of the founders and greatest supporters of the Zionist-Revisionists of Canada, working with what he called "a handful of supporters" in 1955 to organize the group. In 1970, he was named president of the Montreal chapter and in 1976 national president.

The Polish-born Milner was waiting for his papers to go to Palestine—"We were Zionists," he said of his family)—when the Second World War broke out. After a few weeks of resistance, the Polish armed forces virtually collapsed, and Milner, then in the army, found himself "wandering around the countryside in defeat."

He spent the remainder of the war in Russia, where he found and married his childhood sweetheart, Rose. They returned to their native town in Poland only to find "nothing—nobody. They were all gone—killed in the Holocaust."

The Milners immigrated to Canada, where Ben established Avalon Hosiery, with two manufacturing facilities and three hundred employees. He then travelled to Israel and became a close friend of leader of the Likud Party, Menachem Begin. Every time Begin visited Montreal, he stayed with the couple. "I wouldn't let him stay anywhere else," Milner recalls.

The politician was obviously a great source of inspiration to Milner. "I was so impressed with his dedication. The only way to fight to free Israel was to stand up." Begin, he asserted, "wasn't a terrorist—he was a freedom fighter."

A joint meeting of the Sydney and Queen Esther Chapters of Hadassah in Sydney, Nova Scotia, 1950.

(Evelyn Davis photo collection)

and effective bridge-building—the overwhelmingly Anglo-Canadian Jewish community felt unwelcome and sometimes threatened, especially by some of the more militant separatist elements. Most of the migrants settled elsewhere in Canada, but many went to Israel.

According to the historian Michael Brown, many historical forces played a large role in aliyah: "The surge of 1950 occurred in the first year of stability in Israel after the War of Independence, which was also the first year of open immigration. Many prospective *olim* in North America and the U.K. had been waiting for years to make aliyah, but were held back by British regulations, because of the preference given to Europe's endangered Jews, and by wartime conditions. The high numbers of 1968 and 1969 are one of the results of the Six Day War. Israel's unexpectedly easy victory in June 1967, seemed finally to prove the country's military viability."

The 1970s were a period of low aliyah partly because of the anxiety following the Yom Kippur War of 1973. In addition, runaway inflation took hold of Israel in the late 1970s, which may have contributed to the lower number of Canadians immigrating to Israel.

Along with the historical factors that affect aliyah, the organized Zionist movement in Canada continues to play a large role in creating an attractive awareness of the society, culture, institutions, and lifestyle of Israelis. Even when people did not make the decision to move, they at least felt intimately tied to the country. Between 1950 and 1987, approximately eight thousand Canadian immigrants arrived in Israel. Since the Canadian Jewish community is relatively small, the scale of aliyah from Canada is not numerically large. However, those who do make aliyah have contributed significantly to the growth and prosperity of Israel.

The New Canadian Israelis

Young Canadians make aliyah to Israel for a whole host of reasons—many are dedicated to the future of Israel; some believe it is the only country where they want to raise their children; some have had such wonderful and memorable times during organized trips, vacations, or study periods that they cannot wait to return on a more permanent basis; and some fall in love with their future spouses while in Israel.

For family members whom *olim* leave behind, particularly parents, an organization in Canada and the United States called Parents of North American Israelis (PNAI) provides a support system. It helps parents, for example, to become comfortable with the distance between themselves and their children.

Beyond organizations and movements, there is a new spirit that forms a bridge between Israel and the Jewish community of Canada. The new Canadian Israelis are the modern-day *chalutzim* in the vanguard of the new Zionism. They are equally at home in Canada and Israel, equally comfortable in Hebrew and English, and equally attached to Canadian and Israeli culture. They do not belong to only one generation. They might be people of business, industry, and commerce like the Azrielis and the Zimmermans; professionals like the architect Moshe Safdie; innovators and inventors like Benny Landa; advocates for women's rights like Faigie Zimmerman; or university students and young couples making new lives for themselves as Jews in a Jewish homeland.

Secret Canadian Documents

Secret documents of Canada's Department of External Affairs prepared in 1953 showed an understanding of Israel's difficult situation in military terms.

A communication from L. W. Wilgress (undersecretary of state for external affairs), marked "secret," stated, "Arms should be denied to the Arab states until they undertake to co-operate in the defence of the Middle East as a whole and show a greater disposition to make peace with Israel, as suggested in the eight-power draft resolution approved by the Ad Hoc Political Committee of the [United Nations] General Assembly on December 11, 1952."

In another "secret" document, dated May 28, 1953, C. S. A. Ritchie (deputy undersecretary of state for external affairs) notes that "ever since early 1950 we have been freely exchanging with [United States authorities] on a bi-monthly basis, information on all exports of arms to the Middle East."

At this time, the young State of Israel was trying to strengthen its armed forces in the face of continued, repeatedly expressed hostility from such states as Egypt and Syria.

All these recent Canadian Israelis have redefined themselves, their Jewish identity, and Zionism.

1960s and 1970s

The 1960s and the 1970s reflected the growth of the relationship between Canada and Israel in times of peace and of war. And it was during this period that the Canadian Zionist Federation (CZF) was established.

Emerging out of the Zionist Organization of Canada, the CZF represents people of diverse political leanings, some closely related to parties in Israel. More important, it gives structure and cohesiveness to the efforts organized Zionism undertook on behalf of Israel and the Jewish community. Organizationally, the Canadian Zionist Federation serves as a link between Canadian Zionism and the Jewish Agency and its activities reinforce the mutually enriching ties between the Jews of Israel and the Jews in Canada. It is a vehicle for strengthening Jewish identity in Canada and, at the same time, for the expression of support by Canadian Jews for Israel.

Fundraising Works Both Ways

Fundraising and support for a Jewish home by individual Canadians and their agencies have been ongoing since the beginnings of the

Israel's seventh anniversary is celebrated in Toronto in 1955.

(Ontario Jewish Archives)

Dignitaries at the 1954 National Convention of Hadassah-WIZO in Halifax, including (left to right) Mrs. D. P. Gotlieb, Premier Henry Hicks, Mrs. S. Sherman, Mr. Justice L. D. Currie and Nina (Mrs. Harry) Cohen.

(Library and Archives Canada/PA 119032)

Zionist movement. Such activity was not seen so much as an act of charity as the expression of Jewish commitment to the restoration of their people in their renewed home. Fundraising and material contributions by Canadian Jews strengthened their own sense of identity and vouchsafed their national future.

United Israel Appeal of Canada

The United Israel Appeal is the major conduit for contributions to Israel. Funds raised by the UIA in small and large communities across

A 1954 Zionist meeting in Montreal.

(Canadian Jewish Congress National Archives, Montreal)

Canadian Mizrachi leader Rabbi Seymour Zambrowsky with Israeli prime minister David Ben Gurion during a visit to Israel (circa 1960s).

(Jewish Public Library Archives)

The 1955 Young Judaea Convention in Sydney, Nova Scotia.

(Evelyn Davis Photo Collection)

Israeli general Moshe Dayan strides into the 1958 celebration of Israel's tenth birthday in Montreal.

"I first visited Israel in 1958, on the occasion of the tenth anniversary of the founding of the state. I was absolutely knocked out. I was totally impressed with the dedication of the people and their sense of purpose. It was one of the most exciting experiences of my life."
—John Bassett, chairman, Baton
    Broadcasting, on visiting Israel

"It seems to me that an essential, indeed, a first requirement, is that the Arab states should recognize the legitimate and permanent existence of the State of Israel. That, as I see it, necessitates abandonment by them of the impractical stipulation that we must return to the United Nations resolutions of 1947 which provided for a divided Palestine. The Arab states took up arms to prevent these resolutions becoming effective and I do not see how they can claim the right to have them accepted now as the price of peace in the area. The people of Israel have the right to know that their national existence is not at stake."
—Lester B. Pearson, speaking in the
Canadian House of Commons, January
24, 1956

Abba Eban and Lester B. Pearson

Israel's eloquent foreign minister Abba Eban enjoyed a close relationship with Canada's Lester B. Pearson. Here is a telling passage from Eban's 1977 autobiography:

"From Paris I went on to fulfill a previously arranged visit to Ottawa. I was in friendly conversation with an old acquaintance, Prime Minister Lester Pearson, when I got a sudden call from Washington. Last-minute difficulties had arisen in our negotiations for the supply of the Skyhawk aircraft. It would have been a great disappointment at the beginning of my ministry for this vital prospect to subside. Lester Pearson offered me his private plane to make my way to Washington for talks with President Lyndon Johnson and Secretary Robert McNamara. Within a few days the crisis was disentangled and our delighted air force began to prepare for a new stage in its technological and operative progress." (*Abba Eban: An Autobiography*, Random House, 1977)

Canada are centrally transferred and disbursed in Israel. The impetus for the founding of the UIA came in the late 1960s, when federal legislation in Canada relating to charities and their operating procedures was amended. People such as Alan Rose, Saul Hayes, and Jacob M. Lowy were instrumental in organizing UIA as Canada's central fundraising mechanism for Israel. The UIA's legal status empowers it to manage funds destined for Israel and to ensure that these funds are disbursed and managed in Israel in accordance with terms set by

A meeting of the National Fundraising Council, in Toronto, involving (left to right) Lawrence Freiman, Israeli ambassador Arthur Lorie, and Sam Bronfman.

(Canadian Jewish Congress National Archives, Montreal)

Hadassah-WIZO President Lottie Riven in Jerusalem in 1959 with Belgian Queen Mother Elizabeth, at the Nahalal Agricultural school, part of a Youth Aliyah Village.

A Canadian Israel Bond Leadership Mission meets with David Ben-Gurion in the 1950s.

(Jewish Public Library Archives)

Canada Revenue Agency. It also promotes a heightened awareness of Israel's human needs.

In Israel, most of the funds have been granted to the Jewish Agency for Israel. The agency, in turn, allocates them to various social welfare, humanitarian, and educational programs and projects. Among the many UIA-supported undertakings is the Jewish Agency's Immigration and Absorption Department, whose work includes operating transit

centres, homes for elderly immigrants, immigrant welfare services, pre-immigration preparation, assistance for needy students, and absorption centres. The Youth Service Program provides facilities and assistance for the social and cultural integration of youth and children who would otherwise remain outside the mainstream of Israeli society.

In the area of post-secondary education, UIA allocates funds to Israeli universities to assist selected foreign Jewish students in pursuing studies in Israel. At the beginning of each academic year, approximately fifty-five scholarships are granted to Canadians to study in Israel and a further 650 scholarships are granted to Israeli students who remain in Israel for their studies.

UIA supports and develops key areas in the Galilee, Negev, and Arava through the work of the Mariculture Centre in Eilat, which

A 1960 meeting of the Habonim Lodge, Halifax (top row) Hymie Jacobson, Jack Mintz, Hi Borshy, Joseph Glube; (second row) Frank Zilberman, Paul Kantor, Noah Heinish, Wilfred Mosher, Morton Kitaff, Jacob Nathanson, Sam Solomon; (front row) Bob Konigsberg, Alex Shore, Arron Solomon, Irving Nathanson, Jack Stein, Sam Glube.

(Sarah Yablon Collection)

develop techniques for rearing valuable fish for export, and the Settlement Study Centre in Rehovot, which consults around the world on issues related to development and agriculture.

Money is channelled by individual contributors through the UIA of Canada to specific projects. This process has led to the creation of eighteen youth centres; fourteen cultural centres; forty-two facilities for education, health and welfare, sports, and recreation; six youth dormitories; seven libraries; eleven synagogues; five absorption centres; and seventy-one kindergarten daycare centres.

The UIA's internationally acclaimed Project Renewal helps to improve socially and economically depressed urban neighbourhoods by "twinning" them with communities throughout the Diaspora. Project Renewal's spirit of partnership between Israelis and donors abroad may well be Diaspora Jewry's most enduring achievement. The effectiveness of the program stems from celebrating the strong ties and feelings of interconnectedness linking the Jewish people together in hands-on, significant projects that build enduring friendships while rebuilding depressed areas. Project Renewal evolved into Partnership 2000, linking Montreal with the Beersheba region and Toronto with the Eilat region, building ties person to person, institution to institution.

Leadership Development Missions to Israel are also organized under the auspices of UIA in order to familiarize people with the

William Gittes flourishes the honorary fellowship bestowed on him by Canadian Friends of Bar-Ilan University in 1961. The moment is shared by (left to right) Saul Tarnofsky, Rabbi S. M. Zambrowsky, Philip Vineberg, Professor Charles Liebman, and Rabbi Karpol Bender.

(Canadian Friends of Bar-Ilan University)

Nina Cohen (left) and Neri Bloomfield unveil a plaque in 1962, identifying the Canadian Hadassah-WIZO Forest in Israel.

(Library and Archives Canada/e003525034)

problems of Israel and its society, as well as to showcase UIA's accomplishments. In addition, UIA has participated in the March of the Living and youth leadership development.

Finally, each year UIA organizes the Hineni meetings, in which major contributors to local Jewish federations are invited for a three-day examination of issues confronting the Jewish people throughout the world, but particularily in Israel. And while UIA is the primary vehicle for Jewish material assistance to Israel, it is at the same time responsible for Canadian Jewry's most extensive youth education and leadership development programs. Fundraising indeed works both ways!

With the outbreak of the Arab-Israeli wars in 1967 and 1973, it soon became apparent that such reciprocal support was critical to the well-being of Israel and the Canadian Jewish community. Fundraising was only one component here. Leaders of the Canadian Jewish community worked hard to bolster Israel's morale and ensure continuing support for Israel by Canada and other leading Western countries in the United Nations and other international forums.

The Conference inaugurating the Canada-Israel Investment Corporation in Toronto in 1963. Participants include Jacob M. Lowy (left), Saul Hayes (fourth from right), and Allan Bronfman (front right).

(Canadian Jewish Congress National Archives, Montreal)

With Israel's stunning victory in 1967, it became obvious that the Jewish state would not continue to be seen as little David fighting Middle Eastern Goliaths. The "honeymoon" period that had endured since 1948 came to an abrupt end. Increasingly, Israel came under attack from a growing alliance of pro-Arab Palestinian forces and leftists, many of whom demonstrated a harsh, even sinister hatred of the Jewish state and the Jewish people while at the same time claiming to be benign and constructive critics of Israeli policies.

Two Jewish Toronto mayors —Phil Givens (second from right) and Nathan Phillips (right)—at a Zionist meeting with Ekliezer Dembitz (left) and Allan Grossman (second from the left) in the 1960s.

(Ontario Jewish Archives)

PART II:

Canadian Zionism in Action

8

The Canada-Israel Connection

U
NTIL THE LATE 1960s, informal intercession and quiet diplomacy was the basic approach of Canadian Jewish advocacy. The Canadian Jewish Congress and the Zionist Organization of Canada entered into a loose, ad hoc partnership in the late 1950s, and together they created the Joint Public Relations Committee (JPRC), made up of members from both organizations and chaired by Maxwell Cohen. The JPRC met when an emergency arose or when a special situation required that the community act with one voice. The committee was involved in meeting with governmental officials, setting policy, and determining strategy on matters of concern to the Jewish community.

During the 1950s and 1960s, however, their contact with government was usually informal, personal, and carried out by leaders such as Sam Bronfman, Lawrence Freiman, Saul Hayes, and Saul Kanee, as

The executive of the Maritime Young Judaea, in Saint John, New Brunswick, 1966.

(Saint John Historical Museum)

Leon Kronitz

Dr. Leon Kronitz was a major figure in the development of the Zionist movement in Canada.

Born in the shtetl of Kletzk, Poland, he attended the Tarbut Teachers' College, graduating at nineteen with a teacher's diploma. Two years later, he arrived in Montreal—a multilingual teacher who spoke five languages, but no English! He went to work for the Talmud Torah and when his English improved, he first attended McGill University and then the Jewish Theological Seminary in New York.

Kronitz became the first principal of Herzliah High School and then spent seventeen years as principal of the Solomon Schechter Academy.

When he left the field of Jewish education in 1972 to become executive vice president of the Canadian Zionist Federation, it was on the following two conditions: "Let me establish an educational department and elect me unanimously for the job."

Both conditions were met.

Dr. Kronitz had been active with the Zionists from his first days in Montreal (he was national president of the Labor Zionist Movement for nine years), and plunged enthusiastically into professional leadership of the Canadian Zionist Federation.

"The Canadian Jewish community, as a whole, is dedicated to the Zionist ideal," declared the longtime educator who won the title "Mr. Zionist" because of his lengthy and distinguished service to the movement. Under his leadership, the organization, which had 42,000 members of the 300,000 Jews then in Canada, placed great emphasis on education. "My philosophy," said Kronitz, "is that Jewish education in the Diaspora must be based on Jewish tradition. If we can transfer values, we would not have to worry about the future of our children."

well as others who had personal access to members of the government. While it may have been effective at the time, this approach stressed personal rather than institutional contacts.

The Canada-Israel Committee

The Six Day War in 1967 altered Israel's reality and that of the world Jewish community. As events in the Middle East took a turn for the worse in the spring, anxious Jews around the world once again came together to give moral and material assistance to Israel.

Following the war, the Jewish community of Canada and elsewhere experienced feelings of pride, relief, and joy. In Canada, however, pride in the success of fundraising and community organization was mixed with concern over the Jewish community's relations with both the Canadian government and the public. Many of the leaders of Canada's Jewish community sensed the need for an

June 1967

The Jewish world was horrified by the rhetoric from Israel's Arab neighbours who threatened in May 1967 to destroy the State of Israel and massacre its citizens. The mood of Montreal community leaders Sam Bronfman and Gordon Brown was grim as they flew to Quebec City in a Seagram private jet for a meeting with provincial government officials. What could they do to help? Bronfman, quite likely the only person who could pull it off, decided to call a meeting of top Jewish leaders from coast to coast at Montreal's Montefiore Club. His brother Allan got on the telephone, and a hundred of the country's most influential Jews hurried to the Montreal meeting. Sam, whose family donated $2 million annually to Jewish charities, dramatically announced that the family's gift to Israel would be tripled. And

he asked those present to follow his lead. Most of them did, and some contributed even more! When Sam arbitrarily set a campaign goal of $20 million, it seemed to be a pipe dream, but it was quickly reached and exceeded.

That was not the end of it. Bronfman's physician, Dr. Abe Mayman, recalled, "that dramatic episode, when people in the Montreal Jewish community were coming to his house on Belvedere with bags of money, their pensions, savings and everything, pushing it at him, asking him to put it to good use for Israel." A few days later, the Six Day War broke out, and Israel faced attacks from Egypt, Syria, and Jordan, and soundly defeated them all—capturing (and reuniting) Jerusalem, and seizing the West Bank, the Sinai Desert, and the Golan Heights.

A Canadian fact-finding delegation in Israel in the immediate wake of the Six Day War of 1967. In the picture are (left to right) Henry Blatt (arms folded), Gordon Brown, Allan Bronfman, and Mr. Justice Samuel Freedman (with cap) of Winnipeg.

(Montreal Jewish Publication Society)

independent and professional body to present Israel's case to the Canadian government. The concept garnered support from leaders such as Ray Wolfe and Sam Bronfman, although there was opposition from existing national organizations that believed that this kind of activity fell within their mandate.

David J. Azrieli with Israeli prime minister Itzkhak Rabin in the mid-1970s.

Canadian Clergymen

In 1967, when Arab nations were once more threatening to attack and destroy Israel, a group of Canadian Protestant and Catholic clergymen wrote to the Soviet premier, Alexei Kosygin, whose country was the principal supplier of arms to the Arab countries: "Once before in this century the leader of a nation proclaimed the aim of destroying the Jews. The world did not believe him.

"The world stood by. Again the leader of a nation has proclaimed the aim of destroying Jews— this time the State of Israel. Let us not believe that the unbelievable cannot happen again. This time let us not stand by. The undersigned speak as Christians who remember with anguish the Nazi holocaust and are filled with deep apprehension about the survival of the State of Israel."

Historically, the Canadian Zionist Federation (as the Zionist Organization of Canada became known in 1967), B'nai Brith Canada, and the Canadian Jewish Congress had conducted public relations for Israel. None of these organizations felt comfortable relinquishing this responsibility to an unproven group. Nonetheless, negotiations among the various interested organizations began, assisted, each in his own way, by Monroe Abbey, Hy Bessin, Harvey Crestohl, Saul Granek, Sidney Harris, Saul Hayes, Saul Kanee, Leon Kronitz, Herb Levy, Bill Morris, Aaron Pollack, Abel Sellick, Ray Wolfe, and Sidney Zack.

In 1970, the negotiations came to a close and the new Canada-Israel Committee (CIC) set up its first office in Toronto. Ray Wolfe was appointed chairperson, Aaron Pollack became deputy chair, and Sol Littman was named executive director. Unfortunately, communications between the CIC and other Jewish organizations remained loose and were plagued by political infighting. In the middle of 1971, Wolfe, increasingly frustrated, resigned and the office temporarily closed.

"Israel was left alone"
—A *Gazette* Editorial, 1967

"While pleas will be made—and rightly made—to Israel to co-operate with the United Nations in fostering peace in the Middle East, there must also be understanding for Israel's position. Faced with vicious threats of extermination from the Arab world, and the hostile acts of closing the Straits of Tiran to Israeli shipping,

the United Nations did very little to give Israel guarantees of security. When Nasser told the United Nations Emergency Force to withdraw, it packed up and left with barely a word.

"Israel was left to take care of herself; obviously no one was prepared to come to her aid."
—Montreal *Gazette* editorial, June 8, 1967, in the wake of Israel's stunning victory over Arab armies in the Six Day War.

Jewish National Fund
advertisement, 1969.

(Jewish Standard)

"In recent days Israel's right to live has been hammered out anew in blood and arms. Today in old Jerusalem, for the first time in many years, that portion of city occupied by Jordan is under Jewish control once more. The Garden of Gethsemane, scene of warfare in the last few days, the Wailing Wall, embodiment of Jewish resistance through all generations, King Solomon's Temple, today a Moslem mosque—these areas are now in possession of the Israelis. They should never have been outside of Israel in my opinion."
—John Diefenbaker, House of Commons, Ottawa, June 8, 1967, commenting on Israel's success in reuniting Jerusalem.

Despite this awkward beginning, both the Canadian Jewish Congress and the Canadian Zionist Federation recognized the need for such an organization and soon agreed to re-establish the CIC as the principal advocate for the Canadian Jewish community in all matters relating to Canada-Israel public relations. The new start was helped by the requirment that the organization identify its two sponsors, CJC and CZF, in all its public manifestations; B'nai Brith Canada shortly after became the CIC's third sponsor. Aaron Pollack became the CIC's national chairperson, and Myer Bick was appointed national executive director. Anne Gross was the chairperson for the Montreal Regional Committee and Rabbi Erwin Schild the chairperson for the

A national Israel Bonds meeting in Montreal in 1966 with the organization's president, Norman Spector, standing behind the podium. Among the community leaders gathered here are Rubin Zimmerman (seventh from left), Abe Stern (seventh from right), Bernard Bloomfield (sixth from right), and William (Billy) Gittes (right).

(Jewish Public Library Archives, Montreal)

National Labour Zionist
Convention, Kingston,
Ontario, 1968.

(Canadian Jewish Congress National
Archives, Montreal)

Toronto Regional Committee. Some other prominent national CIC chairmen over the next two decades included Rabbi W. Gunther Plaut (1975–1977) and Norman May (1977–1979) of Toronto and Harold Buchwald (1979–1983) and Sidney Spivak (1987–1991) of Winnipeg.

The structure of the CIC was fairly straightforward: A national board, comprised of an equal number of senior leaders from the three sponsoring organizations, representatives from regions and cities, and others who were recruited, set broad policy for the committee's major initiatives. It usually met every two months, although it would meet more frequently if deemed necessary. An executive committee was also established to oversee daily activities. It consisted of the presidents and senior professionals of the sponsoring organizations, the CIC

A Canadian Hadassah Mission
to Israel in the 1970s.

(Saint John Historical Museum)

national chairperson, the regional chairperson, and the national director. In addition, regional committees were formed in Montreal and Toronto to deal with local developments and issues.

It was natural for the CIC to establish an office in Toronto, Canada's media and business centre, where staff could develop contacts with people in the electronic and print media and provide them with quality background material and a point of view on pertinent issues. The office also monitored published material and broadcasts about Canadian Jews and the State of Israel.

The Montreal office, which housed a research department, fulfilled a number of interrelated functions. It prepared materials with a Canadian perspective, geared for Canadian consumers; became the main

"Mr. Sam" and the Campaigns for Israel

Sam Bronfman set the pace in Canadian fundraising for Israel for some three and a half decades, until his death in 1971.

Whenever funds needed to be raised, an invitation would go out from the red-brick Westmount mansion on the slopes of Mount Royal to leaders of the community. As Billy Gittes* has described, after a cocktail reception (featuring, of course, only Seagram brands), "Sam would meet with friends in the basement of the Belvedere house and undertake to contribute 10 per cent of the total on behalf of his family.... He'd get the group of us together and speak to us like newborn babes."

The target for the campaign was devised by "The Boys"—Sam's younger brother, Allan, Arthur Pascal, Sam Steinberg, Louis Reitman, Jacob Lowy, Moe Levitt, Maxwell Cummings, Phil Garfinkle, Billy Gittes, and Gordon Brown—and following the initial Bronfman pledge, Mr. Sam would start the roll call. One by one, the spokesman for each family represented would rise and announce the family commitment,

generally in descending order of the size of the pledge. With the passing years, the sons of the original donors turned up to carry the family banner.

The Bronfmans' gifts to Jewish charities were for decades the largest in North America. After Mr. Sam died, son Charles and his wife, Andrea, picked up the torch. For another twenty years they followed the same procedure from the living room of their Forden Street home—after a cocktail reception on the veranda—although Charles was far less dictatorial about setting goals. Despite splitting his time between his homes in the United States and Israel, Charles Bronfman continues to make very significant contributions to Jewish causes both in Montreal and in the Jewish state.

*Billy Gittes chaired the Israel Bonds Guardian Dinners for more than a decade and was chairman of the Awards Committee of Montreal's Combined Jewish Appeal for so long that no one could remember when he started playing that role.

Samuel Bronfman gathered the leaders of Canada's Jewish communities for an emergency fundraising effort in May 1967, when Arab nations were threatening to "drive the Jews into the sea."

The first Montreal Women's Mission to Israel, in 1971, co-led by Dodo Heppner (second from left) and Kappy Flanders (fourth from right, standing).

(Montreal Jewish Publication Society)

centre of information and resources on Canada–Middle East affairs and Israel and provided services for all the other CIC functions.

Since the foremost priority of the CIC was to maintain effective communication with members of the government of Canada, a regional office was also established in Ottawa, with Howard Stanislawski as its first professional director. The CIC now had closer access to members of the cabinet, members of Parliament, senators, and public servants.

The special cultural and linguistic realities of Quebec prompted a major CIC effort in that province. Jacques LaSalle and Michael Solomon undertook a diverse range of activities there, including the establishment of the Amitiés Québec-Israel, a separate organization of Quebec "friends"; programs with the labour movement and other interest groups; academic and media missions to Israel; and the founding of two publications, *Regards sur Israel* and *Canada-Proche Orient*.

1973 and Beyond

The Yom Kippur War of October 1973 shocked Israel and Jewry around the world and Canadian Jews quickly reacted to the events in a variety of ways. Leaders of the Jewish community held discussions with the federal cabinet, members of Parliament and senior public

servants. The CIC issued advertisements, position papers, and statements. Individuals and organizations wrote letters, initiated telegram campaigns, and held community rallies. Contacts were initiated with church, academic, and labour groups.

George Cohon and Israel Bonds

George Cohon, who was CEO of McDonald's in Canada for many years, was national chairman for Canada of Israel Bonds in the 1970s. Cohon targeted and achieved impressive sales of $30 million a year, but, when Israel was attacked on Yom Kippur in 1973, the businessman criss-crossed Canada and raised a hefty $45 million nationally.

The big breakthrough that year was the decision by Canadian banks to invest in Israel Bonds. Cohon persuaded the president of the Bank of Commerce, Don Fullerton, to buy a $1 million note. Charles Bronfman made a similar deal with the Bank of Montreal, and the Toronto-Dominion Bank later joined the ranks of investors in Israel. Another of George Cohon's accomplishments on behalf of Israel Bonds was his successful lobby to have a law amended so that Canadian insurance companies could invest in Israel.

Following the 1973 war, the CIC embarked on an outreach program to find support among individual Canadians who played an important role in their communities. In Winnipeg, representatives of the organization made arrangements to meet every member of Parliament and senator from Manitoba, held meetings with senior editors from Winnipeg's news media, delivered speeches at service clubs, and invited prominent Israeli officials to give talks to members of the public on issues relating to the Middle East. This program was extended to other cities throughout Canada. It produced a national network of outstanding people on whom the CIC could call to help Israel's cause. The network came to be essential to the CIC as it subsequently dealt with issues such as the Arab Boycott, the UN resolution equating Zionism with racism, terrorism and the PLO, and the 1982 war in Lebanon.

Sponsorship for the CIC broadened as major Jewish communities of Canada and the United Israel Appeal joined in the 1980s. The regional committees of Toronto and Montreal also gained strength and hired professionals to serve them.

During the evolution of CIC activities and programs, a number of other pro-Israel organizations developed to engage Jews and non-Jews in discussions about how to support and improve a thriving,

Bernard M. Bloomfield (left), president of the Jewish National Fund of Canada, with the Israeli president, Zalman Shazar, in 1972.

(Library and Archives Canada/e0035035)

Israeli Prime Minister Golda Meir at a meeting in Toronto in 1973 to raise funds for Israel. Allan Bronfman is at the microphone, and other prominent Zionist supporters in the picture include Thomas Otto Hecht (far left), Ray D. Wolfe (third from left), and Sam Chait (seated next to Mrs. Meir).

(Montreal Jewish Publication Society)

democratic Israel amid hostility from much of the world. These groups included the Canada Israel Foundation for Academic Exchanges, an independent body that organizes the exchange of scholars between Israeli and Canadian institutions of higher learning; the Canadian Professors for Peace in the Middle East, an organiza-

tion for academics who are interested in informed discussions on the Middle East; and Amitiés Quebec-Israel, which conducts programs throughout Quebec to promote better understanding between Quebecois and Israelis.

In summarizing the CIC's influence, Myer Bick, national director of the CIC until 1978, noted that "Canadian Jews should understand that the Canada-Israel Committee, first and foremost, represents the interests and concerns of Canadian Jews. What it can actually do for Israel is secondary. A strong, professional and active CIC bespeaks a proud, mature and resilient Jewish community. Together, they are telling Canadians that Israel is intrinsic to Jewish life and that the bonds of Jewish peoplehood are inseparable."

Milestones Become Paving Stones

In the years following the momentous events of 1967, Israel came to be accepted in Canada as part of the international political, economic, and cultural landscape. In this country, exchanges and activities on all levels became so commonplace that, in a very healthy sense, they were

Canadian Academics Make Their Mark in Israel

Dozens of Canadians have distinguished themselves in various fields in Israel. They include Professor Rachel Alterman, town planning, Technion; Professor Rebecca Bergman, nursing, Tel Aviv University; Professor Richard Breecher, political scientist and author, Hebrew University; Dr. Arza Churchman, town planning, Technion; Dr. Yehezkel Cohen, environmental sciences, Hebrew University; Dr. Richard Deckelbaum, pediatrics, Hadassah Hospital; Professor Sol Dreman, psychology, Ben-Gurion University; Professor Emil Fackenheim, philosophy, Hebrew University; Professor Theodore Friedgut, Russian studies, Hebrew University; Professor Jack Gross, cardiology, Hadassah Hospital; Rabbi David Hartman, religious stud-

ies, Hartman Institute; Professor Isaac Horowitz, physics, Weizmann Institute of Science; Professor Eliahu Kanovsky, economics, Bar Ilan and Tel Aviv universities; Professor Bryan (Baruch) Knei-Paz, political science, Hebrew University; Professor Ben Lappin, social work, Bar Ilan University; Dr. Mae Bere Mereminski, director, Histadrut Social Services; Dr. Michael Rosenbluth, director, Sha'arei Tzedek Hospital; Dr. Don Silverberg, chief medical officer, Tel Aviv Municipality; Dr. Ted Tulchinsky, director, public health services, Administered Areas; Professor Gdalyah Wiseman, engineering, Technion; Professor Abba Zuriel, drama, Haifa University.

(These accomplished people were all identified by Melvin Fenson in the second edition of *The Encyclopedia Judaica* 2006)

ON THIS SITE WILL BE CONSTRUCTED
THE TERRY AND LAWRENCE BESSNER BUILDING FOR ZOOLOGICAL RESEARCH

Members of the Montreal
Mission to Israel, organized
by the Canadian Friends of
Tel Aviv University, attend the
dedication of the Terry and
Lawrence Bessner Building
for Zoological Research in
1998.

almost taken for granted. What had previously been milestones on the
long road toward a substantial relationship between Canada and Israel
became the paving stones for the now frequently travelled two-way
street between the two countries. And, significantly, the Canadian
Jewish community's continuing commitment to Zionism that made

Brothers Maxwell (left) and
Nathan Cummings at the dedication of the community
building bearing their name in
Montreal. Both brothers were
vigorous supporters of Israeli
causes.

(Montreal Jewish Publication Society)

this street possible was now keeping it in good repair.

Ventures in co-operative development became more and more frequent. Pratt & Whitney Aircraft of Canada, for example, sold engines to Israel Aircraft Industries for use in the Aravah aircraft; Babcock & Wilcocks of Canada received a $70 million contract from the Israel Electric Corporation, and the Canada-Israel Joint Committee for the Development of Trade and Economic Expansion was established.

Such initiatives were followed by many others: the creation of a Canada-Israel air link, first with Montreal and then with Toronto; Canadian investment in opening the Super-Pharm chain based on the Shoppers Drug Mart model; and development of the hospitality industry capped by the opening of the Four Seasons Hotel in Netanya and a CP hotel in Jerusalem.

During this period, Israel became Canada's third largest trading partner in the Middle East and North Africa. This connection eventually led to a series of agreements, including a critical one on the exchange of technology in the 1990s.

Cultural and educational links between Canada and Israel also became more widespread and intensive. The Lady Davis Vocational School opened in the early 1960s and became the first of the now over one hundred technical schools within the AMAL network. Meanwhile, Canadian Friends organizations for Hebrew University, Tel Aviv University, Bar Ilan University, Haifa University, and Ben-Gurion University, as well as the Technion and Bezalel Academy of

Israeli general Moshe Dayan (centre) jokes with Montreal community leaders in 1971 including Thomas Hecht (far left) and Joe King (left) and Gordon Brown (right).

(Drummond Photo by Ruby Shulman)

Longtime community leader Gordon Brown (left) is named an honourary fellow of Hebrew University at a Montreal dinner in 1974. Sharing the moment are (left to right) Michael Greenblatt, Joe Schaffer, Dr. Ralph Halpert, and Consul-General Zvi Caspi.

(Montreal Jewish Publication Society)

Art and Design, initiated activities in all of Canada's major cities.

In the arts, the National Gallery of Canada sponsored exhibits in Israel by Canadian artists; Zubin Mehta, musical director of the Israel Philharmonic Orchestra, led the IPO on a Canadian tour; the Royal Winnipeg Ballet participated in the Israel Festival; the Canada-Israel Cultural Foundation was established, and the Ayala Zacks-Abramov Pavilion of Israeli Art opened at the Israel Museum in Jerusalem.

Diplomatic relations between Canada and Israel also warmed as the two countries grew closer. Building on support for the Zionist

Revolutionizing Retailing

"In 1982, I decided to bring one of the most modern innovations—the shopping mall—to one of the most ancient nations on earth—Israel. No one gave me the slightest chance of success. At the time, stores in Israel were half the size they are today, full of dust, without displays, without any regard for the customer or aesthetics. I realized that with all I had learned in Canada, I could change this. I was certain that Israel was ready for a modern shopping experience, where fashion

and services would be available ... I was certain that a well-designed space for people to get together and for commerce to take place would work in Israel, just as it works anywhere else.

"I opened the first mall—Canion Ayalon—in Ramat Gan in 1985, and then others in Tel Aviv, Jerusalem, and Beersheva.
—David J. Azrieli, C.M., C.Q., M.Arch, speaking at his eighty-fifth birthday celebration in May 2008

The remarkable Ayala Zacks-Abramov (left) was a major figure on the Israeli art scene after moving to the Holy Land from Toronto. (Following Sam's death, she married Dr. S. Zalman Abramov, an Israeli lawyer.)

(Canadian Jewish News)

Alan Rose, national executive director of the Canadian Jewish Congress, fought vigorously for Jewish causes in Canada and internationally, particularly on behalf of Israel. In the cause of his activities, Rose undertook a number of secret missions, details of which have never been revealed.

ideal shown by Mr. Justice Ivan Rand and Prime Minister Lester Pearson, leaders of Canada and Israel embarked on a series of visits to each other's country that deepened the friendship. Most Israeli prime ministers—David Ben-Gurion, Levy Eshkol, Golda Meir, Yitzhak Rabin, Shimon Peres, Menahem Begin, Yitzhak Shamir, Benjamin Netanyahu, and Ehud Barak, among them—came to Canada on state visits. The trips were reciprocated by Canadian leaders such as Lester Pearson, Pierre Trudeau, Joe Clark, Brian Mulroney, and Jean Chrétien. Contacts between foreign ministers and other cabinet ministers increased as they travelled back and forth and collaboration spread to new areas such as transport, science and technology, and communications.

Continuing to Make the Land Bloom

The Jewish National Fund (JNF), which had proved so successful in the pre-state period, continued to build Israel while fostering strong ties between the Diaspora community and Israel. Following the creation of the State of Israel in 1948, the JNF initiated an annual event known as the Negev Dinner to simultaneously honour outstanding communal leaders and raise funds for the development of the arid Negev desert region. The first Negev Dinner was held in Montreal, but they were subsequently held in communities large and small across Canada. Until recently, the proceeds of the Negev Dinners were used to foster settlement in the Western Negev region—approximately 60 per cent of the land in the new Jewish state—however, the funds are now devoted to projects all over Israel.

Throughout the 1970s, JNF projects included the construction of the John Bassett Sports Centre at Yotvata in the Arava Valley in southern Israel, the establishment of the infrastructure for a Canadian-adopted village in the Arava known as Samar, the development of a 7,500-acre Canada Park between Tel Aviv and Jerusalem, the Garden of the Rebuilders of Jerusalem, and the Ontario recreational area in the Jerusalem forest.

In the second half of the 1970s, the Jewish National Fund encouraged settlement in the Galilee. By the mid-1980s, Galil Canada made possible the infrastructure for the settlements of Eshcar, Kachal, Kalanit, Kamon, Kedarim, Kfar Hananya, Korazim, Livnim, Lotem, Masaad, Michmanim, Moran, Ravid, Tefachot, and T'zviah. In the mid-1980s, the JNF intensified its close partnership with the City of Jerusalem through the second phase of the Rebuilders of Jerusalem project, which sought to preserve and enrich the beauty and environment of Israel's capital. Most notably, the park at the base of the Old City was beautifully landscaped thanks to generous Canadians and the JNF.

The role of the JNF in the development of Israel has been tremendous. By the time it celebrated its centennial in 2001, the JNF had planted more than 220 million trees; reclaimed over 250,000 acres of dormant and arid land for agriculture, pasture land, villages, industry, and homesteads; created more than 400 parks and 110 playgrounds and recreational areas; built thousands of kilometres of roads; and constructed more than 150 dams and water reservoirs to improve agricultural productivity and provide water to more than 1.2 million Israelis.

New Challenges and New Opportunities

Despite the amazing growth and forging of new links between Canada and Israel, the late 1970s and the 1980s presented new challenges to Israel, to the Canadian Jewish community, and to the Zionist movement. Ironically, this period began in the shadow of what was seen as the beginning of the peace process. Israel's Prime Minister Menachem Begin and Egypt's President Anwar Sadat signed the Camp David Accords under American auspices on September 17, 1978, and it seemed that all the dreams of the century-old Zionist movement had been fulfilled.

Israeli leader Shimon Peres (to right of podium) at a 1979 Combined Jewish Appeal dinner in Montreal. To his right is Morton Brownstein, general chairman of the appeal, Montreal's central annual fundraising campaign on behalf of Israel's local and national needs. On Peres's left is Saidye Bronfman and her son Charles.

(Montreal Jewish Publication Society)

Senator Thérèse Casgrain
(third from right) is hailed as
the honoree for Hadassah-
WIZO Month, 1961. With
the senator are the Montreal
event's key organizers: (left to
right) Miriam Liberman,
Israeli Ambassador Yeshayahu
Anug, Mirial Small, Miriam
Peletz, and Susan Balinsky.

(Canadian Hadassah-WIZO Archives)

Students from Montreal's
Jewish People's and Peretz
School celebrating Yom
Ha'atzmaut atop Mount
Royal, 1980, an event spon-
sored and organized by the
Canadian Zionist
Organization.

(Photo by Howard Kay)

But this was not to be the case. Terrorism emanating from bases
in Lebanon, culminating in Israel's siege of Beirut to secure its northern border in 1982, saw Israel under attack by both diplomatic sources
and the international media. At the same time, many Jews were torn
between their support for Israel and concerns about Israel's linger-
ing involvement in the Lebanese quagmire. This dilemma was further
complicated in the late 1980s by the outbreak of what the Palestinians

Israeli general Moshe Dayan (seated to the right of the speaker) at a Combined Jewish Appeal meeting in Montreal in 1983 to raise funds for Israel. The campaign's general chairman, Norman Spector, is at the microphone, and others at the head table (left to right) are Arthur Pascal, Allan Bronfman, and Edward Bronfman.

(Montreal Jewish Publication Society)

called the *intifada*, the uprising. Here, too, the Jewish community was called on by political and press critics to answer many questions about Israel and the territories and the nature of the Israeli response to the intifada. At home, Canadian Jews also saw the emergence of new problems that required new responses. A resurgence of anti-Semitism in Canada was fuelled by revisionist historians who denied the authenticity of the Holocaust and whose views were disseminated by neo-Nazis like Ernst Zundel.

In the meantime, Israel continued to suffer attacks in the media and from representatives of major, hitherto neutral, organizations. Israel's international support continued to be eroded under the pressure of world events, and the Jews of Canada were called on to shore up support for Israel in Canadian government quarters. Canadian Jewish youth faced a number of conflicting challenges as the mood on campuses changed. Although a Jewish presence on a campus was now widely accepted, Israel and Zionism were targeted broadly, and often sloppily, with Israel caricatured by "politically correct" professors and many student organizations as the new South Africa, and Zionism libelled as racism or a form of apartheid.

Despite the various political, diplomatic, ideological, and demographic clouds, cultural, economic, philanthropic, and personal ties

The committee planning a 1984 visit by the Israeli Philharmonic Orchestra includes key members of the Combined Jewish Appeal (left to right) Carol Koffler, Bernice Brownstein, Sara Reisman, Milly Lande, and Lillian Gold.

(Montreal Jewish Publication Society)

between Canada and Israel continued to flourish. Canadians have been particularly instrumental in bringing changes to Israeli society in the area of the economy. The Bronfman Investment Corporation (among other initiatives) bought the Supersol chain of supermarkets and, beginning in 1958, revolutionized supermarkets in Israel. The Bronfmans also brought their International Distilleries enterprise to the country— Sabra, a liqueur developed in Israel and packaged in bottles made to look like ancient glass found at the Jerusalem excavations, has become a bestseller worldwide. Another Bronfman enterprise initiated during this period was Task Force, a group of top Jewish financiers and industrialists who helped Israel attain economic independence. The organization was founded and operated by Charles Bronfman, who spearheaded efforts to improve the marketing of Israeli exports and expand their overseas outlets. Murray and Leon Koffler, well known in Canada for their Shoppers Drug Mart chain, introduced a radical shift in mass-market retailing to Israel with their nationwide chain Super-Phrarm.

Canadian contributions to Israeli industry have paralleled those in marketing. Sam "Yo-Yo" Dubiner made Israel his home and became the driving force behind a variety of enterprises such as Amgo containers, B'nei Brak precision tools, the Cargal factory, Injection plastic products, Jerusalem Pencils, Kalit wires, and Zinkal irrigation pipes. He was also one of the founders of the Foreign Investors' Association and one of the purchasers of Japhet Bank.

The New *Chalutziut*

"I left my childhood home in Poland in September 1939, and spent three years on the run, living in fear and dread, always one step ahead of the Nazis. Arriving in Palestine in December 1942, splashing my way across the Jordan River in a shallow part of the stream, and taking refuge in Kibbutz Maoz Chaim, I could finally unburden myself. I was moved by the most profound emotion, a sense of personal liberation and destiny. I had always dreamed of going to Eretz Yisrael, and this goal had eased the continual stress of my journey. I now felt that all my dreams had come true.

Life in Palestine was intense and liberating. I got a job as an assistant auto mechanic, and was accepted to Technion to study my passion, architecture. My studies were cut short when I joined in the fight for Israel's Independence in 1948. Serving in the Seventh Brigade, I took part and was wounded in the battle to free the Latrun Pass and the road to the encircled city of Jerusalem. After centuries of persecution, wandering and hardship, the modern State of Israel became a reality. It was my greatest honour to be there and play a small role.

Although I chose to leave Israel in the 1950s to find the remnants of my family, I always knew I would find a way to go back and make a contribution. Over the years, I built a successful career in design and development and established a family in Canada, and I have an abiding love of this great country. But I never lost sight of my commitment to Zion. Through philanthropy and community work—including a very stimulating term as president of the Canadian Zionist Federation in the 1980s—I found ways to contribute.

My greatest opportunity to make a contribution to the vitality and future of the Jewish state came when I decided to go back to Israel as a builder in the mid-1980s. Looking back now, at the start of the twenty-first century, I can say that I am truly proud of what I have achieved in Israel—the numerous commercial complexes and buildings all over the country, and especially the Azrieli Centre in Tel Aviv. For me the commitment to Zion takes a specific form, which I describe with a phrase I have often used: the new *chalutziut* (pioneering spirit). It is still possible to be a Zionist pioneer in Israel, a *chalutz*, but the new *chalutziut* is economic in nature. Israel's new *chalutz*, for example, is a pioneer in advanced technology and design, or the salesman of Israeli products who allows Israel to compete on world markets. If I can say that I have bettered the State of Israel and its people economically, and I believe I have, I have achieved my own personal Zionist dream."

—David J. Azrieli, C.M., C.Q., M.Arch, speaking at his eighty-fifth birthday celebration in May 2008. On this occasion, he donated $1 million to his alma mater, Technion–Israel Institute of Technology.

Canada-Israel Cooperation

Along with the contributions of individual Canadians, the friendship between Canada and Israel is manifested in numerous bilateral relationships in the fields of science and technology, culture and communications, trade and industry, and education. There are at least two dozen bilateral agreements between the two countries that encourage co-operation in the arts and business, reward the establishment of joint ventures, and help to direct bilateral relations in a number of legal spheres. Current treaties affect employment, taxation, extradition, immigration, and tourism.

There are also important memoranda of understanding that provide for exchanges of specialists and scientists in agriculture, geology, academe, and health services. Canadians and Israelis have combined their resources and knowledge in various fields to improve the conditions in less-developed countries, distinguishing themselves individually and collectively in bringing Western expertise to poverty-stricken countries in Africa, Asia, and Latin America. From 1980 to 1985, for example, Canadian development resources and Israeli technical skill combined to support a dairy-farm community in the Dominican Republic, providing pre-processing facilities and the necessary infrastructure for milk production.

As Canada's third largest Middle East trading partner, Israel imports Canadian grain, paper and wood products, vehicles, aviation equipment, textiles, sulphur, assorted electrical goods and machinery, and unrefined metals and plastics. Canada, on the other hand, imports Israeli food products, chemicals, high-technology telecommunications and computer equipment, diamonds, textiles, and medical and laboratory equipment.

There is enormous future potential for Canada-Israel trade in high technology. Israel has made leading advances in the fields of agrotechnology, fine chemicals, computers and electronic hardware, solar energy, telecommunications, and medical electronics; and Canadian industry should take advantage of this know-how and continue to co-operate in research and development with Israel.

In all areas, the bilateral and co-operative arrangements between Canadians and Israelis help to create spinoffs that strengthen both countries' economies.

The Canada-Israel Cultural Foundation

The Canada-Israel Cultural Foundation (CICF) began in 1972 to build a cultural bridge by encouraging artists and performers to visit each other's country. Champion of the arts and violin virtuoso Isaac Stern played an important role in helping to found the CICF. Another of its staunchest supporters was Joel Slater, who headed the the Toronto branch of the organization for more than a decade. CICF's success can be seen in the constant exchange of musicians, actors, dancers, and writers between Canada and Israel, which has had a particular impact on the Canadian Jewish community. Israeli songs, dances, and celebrities have helped to shape Canadian Jewish culture, while the common Western culture that dominates both democracies has created a shared language. The CICF also provides scholarships for the study of the arts; assists programs that draw youth closer to the arts; supports major cultural institutions; and encourages gifts of art, musical instruments, and grants to specific institutions and projects.

Over the years, the foundation has contributed to bringing the Bat Sheva Dance Company to Canada and sponsoring the 1978 Israel Art Festival in Toronto and Ottawa. It has also organized concerts and recitals featuring Yitzhak Perlman, Shlomo Mintz, and others, and given financial assistance to Canadian artists travelling to Israel.

The CICF has also established a special committee for the Israel Museum and has donated gifts of art and financial assistance to other Israeli museums. The Israel Museum, the largest and most prominent

A National Officers' meeting of the Canadian Association for Labour Israel in 1986. The association raises funds for rehabilitation programs and assistance to immigrants.

(Canadian Jewish Congress National Archives, Montreal)

David Ben-Gurion Place, at the corner of Portage and Main in Winnipeg, was the logical spot for Mayor William Norrie (left) to welcome visiting guests from Israel's Ben-Gurion University. From the Winnipeg Chapter of the Canadian Associates of Ben-Gurion University of the Negev are chapter president Harry Walsh (second from left) and executive officer Ed Vickar (far right) with university president Amos Ben-Gurion (second from right).

(Canadian Associates of the Ben-Gurion University of the Negev)

of its kind in the country, is the centre of various art and cultural activities. By 1987, the museum had attracted one million visitors annually—half of them tourists from overseas, including numerous groups of Israeli schoolchildren. The CICF also helped develop T'zlil-Am (Sound of the People), a project designed to bring Israeli youth into the mainstream of the country's cultural life. To that end, T'zlil Am sends mobile units staffed by accredited music teachers to settlements and towns all over Israel.

Music

Canada's formal connection with Israeli music dates back to 1953 when the Canadian Jewish Congress assisted in the formation of the Montreal Jewish Music Council to arrange programs of Israeli and

Jewish music for both Jewish and non-Jewish communities. The council subsequently sponsored performances of orchestral and chamber works by Israeli composers such as Amiram Pugachov, Chaim Alexander, Paul Ben-Chaim, and Odeon Partos. The CICF also established an exchange program for musicians that brought the Israel Philharmonic Orchestra and the National Choir of Israel to Canada and assisted many Canadian musicians in making trips to Israel.

Increasingly, Canadian musicians visit Israel without sponsorship. The world-famous opera star Maureen Forrester toured Israel in the 1960s and 1970s. And many prominent Israeli musicians—Yitzhak Perlman and Pinchas Zukerman, to name two—have performed in Canada. The pianist Iliakim Taussig now lives in Toronto and is a founding member of the Camerata Chamber Ensemble. George Zuckerman, a bassoonist, lives and performs in Vancouver.

Film and Television

The links between Canada and Israel have encompassed both high culture and popular culture. The impetus for ties in the film and television industry, like so much else, has been the outgrowth of activities designed to bolster Jewish identity in Canada and increase support for the building of the national home first in Palestine and then in Israel.

Films, newsreels, documentaries, and the like became, over the years, a means of portraying life in Palestine and Israel. In the early years, when travel was difficult and expensive, it meant that the reality of Jewish national rebirth could be witnessed from afar by members of Hadassah, Mizrachi, the Revisionists, or simply members of Jewish communities who were making their contribution to the national enterprise.

The birth and early years of Israel's feature film industry were experienced in Canada as well. Many Canadian Jews eagerly awaited new films, attending showings organized as fundraisers

Chaim Herzog, 1989

A red letter day for Canadian Jews came in 1989 when Israel's president Chaim Herzog visited Ottawa with his wife, Aura. Dr. Herzog described the experience in glowing terms: "On 26 June 1989, Aura and I arrived in Ottawa, Canada, for a state visit. At the entrance to the grounds of Government House, we transferred to an open, horse-drawn carriage. A cavalry escort of the Royal Canadian Mounted Police preceded us through the gardens to the dais at the entrance to Rideau Hall, where we were received by the governor general, Madame Jeanne Sauvé, and her husband, Maurice Sauvé.

"On Tuesday, 27 June 1989, I addressed both Houses of Parliament in the Commons, an unusual honor. My predecessors on such occasions included Winston Churchill, President Reagan, President Bush, Prime Minister Thatcher, President Mitterand, Chancellor Kohl, and the Queen of Holland. The chamber was packed, and the public gallery was filled to capacity with representatives of the Jewish community."

Izzy Asper

On a visit to Israel, Israel (Izzy) Harold Asper (1932–2003) met, among other people, Prime Minister Menachem Begin and, reflecting later, asked himself, "What did those guys do in their lifetimes? They created a Jewish state. What have I created?"

If Izzy Asper needed a precise answer to that question it came in 2003, when—on his death at age seventy-one—Winnipeg's Shaarey Zedek Synagogue was filled to its thousand-seat capacity, with hundreds more lining the streets listening to the service broadcast over a public address system. Among the mourners were Prime Minister Jean Chrétien and Manitoba's premier, Gary Doer.

Izzy Asper was one of the most important broadcasters and publishers in Canada. In his tribute to the media mogul, Senator Jack Austin declared, "I considered him one of the four or five most dedicated people in Canada to the security of Israel and to the growth of the Jewish community in Canada."

In the 1960s, Izzy Asper worked with lawyer Harold Buchwald to garner political support for Israel, an effort that later crystallized as the Canada-Israel Committee. Among other contributions, Asper established a national scholarship fund to send Canadian students to Hebrew University. He also established the Asper Holocaust and Human Rights Studies Program that teaches Jewish and non-Jewish high school students across Canada about the Holocaust, culminating each year in a fully funded trip to the U.S. Holocaust Museum and Memorial in Washington D.C. Each student makes a commitment to "fight discrimination and advance human rights throughout their lives."

Asper planned as his final major project a Canadian Museum of Human Rights to be located in Winnipeg. The museum received the full support of the Canadian government in 2007 when it was declared a federal institution. Gail Asper—president of the CanWest Global Foundation, managing director of the Asper Foundation and Izzy's daughter— spearheaded the efforts to get the project approved.

Izzy Asper was born in Minnedosa, Manitoba, the son of musicians who had immigrated to Canada from Ukraine. He became a lawyer, as did his two sons and one daughter.

and community functions across the country. One of the most successful films made in the early years of the Israel film industry was *Sallah Shabati*, a 1964 comedy written and directed by Ephraim Kishon. Jews the world over delighted in the film's simple humour and vigorous spirit. Israeli film festivals soon became a part of many Canadian communities' cultural calendars, and Israeli films have also appeared occasionally in the Montreal and Toronto International Film Festivals.

Canadian Jews also became even more directly involved in the continuing growth of Israel's film and television industry. Well-known Canadian film producer, distributor, and philanthropist Harold Greenberg invested in Israel's premier production facility, United

Studios of Herzliyah, and the Bassett family of Toronto and its Baton Broadcasting invested in Israel's fledgling television broadcast industry. In fact, when Itzik Kol, director general of United Studios, visited Baton's CFTO television station in Toronto in the 1970s, he happened on an unused mobile black-and-white broadcast unit in the CFTO back lot. When he expressed interest in the unit, John Bassett, CFTO's head, said, "Take it—it's yours. It's my contribution to the Israeli television industry." This became Israel's first black-and-white mobile unit! Some time later, Kol visited Bassett again and handed him an envelope. Much to Bassett's amazement, rather than a request for more equipment, it was a cheque for Baton Broadcasting's share of the profits from the mobile unit. Bassett gave the cheque back to Kol to use as the down payment for Israel's first colour mobile unit.

Collaboration in the film and television industry became more frequent in the 1980s and culminated in the signing of a Canada-Israel co-production agreement. Today, film and television co-productions between the two countries are commonplace.

Art

The first organized art exchange between Israel and Canada took place in 1953 when a Canada-Israel Art Club, a group affiliated with the Canada-Israel Association, assembled twenty-seven works of art and donated the exhibit to the Jerusalem Museum of Art. In 1966, the Montreal Museum of Fine Arts exhibited of the works of twenty-five contemporary Israeli artists, which were brought to Montreal by the Department of Cultural Programming of the Canadian Jewish Congress. Over the past decades, Canadian and Israeli artists have had their works shown in a variety of museums and art galleries through-out both countries.

Bringing Modern Art to the Ancient Homeland

Ayala Zacks and her husband, Sam (fourth president of the Zionist Organization of Canada), were art lovers who helped enrich Israel's art world. Ayala studied art in Paris in the 1930s and with Sam acquired a large and remarkable collection of European works that reflected all the major trends in the development of twentieth-century art. Their collection features masterpieces by painters such as Bonnard, Chagall, Rouault, and Soutine; Cubist works by Braque, Léger and Picasso; and drawings by Degas, Gauguin, Matisse, and Renoir. Half of all the works collected by Sam and Ayala Zacks are on display at the Israel Museum

"The creation of the State of Israel is one of the epochal events of this century. For Canadians, Israel is not simply a place on the map. Israel is a tribute to the deep spiritual beliefs and the unfailing personal courage of a remarkable people. Israel is a monument to the indomitable spirit of man."
—Prime Minister Brian Mulroney introducing President Chaim Herzog of the State of Israel in the Canadian Parliament, June 27, 1989

and the Tel Aviv Museum, on permanent loan from the Art Gallery of Ontario.

A few years after the death of her husband in 1971, Ayala settled in Tel Aviv, where she established the History of Art Fund for guest professors at the Hebrew University in Jerusalem. In 1976, she married Dr. S. Zalman Abramov, and, at the urging of Jerusalem mayor Teddy Kollek, the couple opened the Ayala Zacks-Abramov Pavilion at the Israel Museum in 1985. This pavilion is divided into two sections: the first is a historical section devoted to Israeli works of art produced in the early days of the Bezalel Art Academy; the second is a contemporary art wing, which houses the works of some of Israel's avant-garde painters and sculptors.

An Archaeological Treasure Trove

A Polish-born, naturalized Canadian citizen, distinguished scholar, writer, and lecturer, Elie Borowski became a world-renowned archaeologist and authority on the art and artifacts of the ancient Near East—which comprises the lands and peoples mentioned in the Bible, the birthplace of the Jewish people and their belief in one God, the

Kurt Rothschild (left), national president of the Canadian Zionist Federation (1985–2004), presents the 1988 Jerusalem Award to Alan Gotlieb (centre) and Phil Granovsky "as staunch friends of the State of Israel."

faith that inspired the two other great monotheistic religions, Christianity and Islam. With his wife, Batya, Borowski co-founded the Bible Lands Museum in Jerusalem in 1992 and donated almost three thousand of the works they had collected over more than four decades. The objects reflect the intricate pattern of material and spiritual life that prevailed in this region in antiquity.

In addition to his own activity as a collector of ancient Near Eastern artifacts, Borowski, while living in Switzerland from 1953 to 1979, acted as an adviser to important European art and antiquity collectors. During this time, he became one of Europe's leading dealers in ancient art. He made substantial contributions to building such great public collections as the Liebighaus in Frankfurt, the National Prehistoric Museum in Munich and West Berlin, the Glyptothek in Copenhagen, the Badisches Landesmuseum in Karlsruhe, and the J. Paul Getty Museum in Los Angeles, California. His work has been applauded around the world.

In 1976, while cataloguing 1,879 objects from the Borowski Collection in Basel, Dr. Wilfred G. Lambert, Assyriologist and member of the Royal Academy in London, reported that it had "more in quantity and of distinction than the national and other museums of certain Western countries which take an interest in Near Eastern antiquities." It was this expertise and commitment that Borowski brought to Israel, thereby enriching its cultural life. Elie Borowski died in 2003.

Israel in Canadian Literature

Not surprisingly, many Canadian Jews—incuding Naim Kattan, Mordecai Richler, Jean-Guy Pilon, Moshe Klein, Miriam Waddington, and Guy Nemer, to name but a few—have been inspired to write about Israel. In 1982, a book titled *Twenty-five Top Canadian Prose Writers: An Anthology*, edited by Marion Richmond and Robert Weaver, was translated into Hebrew. The book was published in cooperation with the Canadian Publishing Foundation and the Canada Council in order to acquaint Israelis with Canadian literature.

The Second Century

The 1990s marked the beginning of the second century of Canadian Zionism. The first hundred years saw the nurturing of the *yishuv*, the Holocaust, the establishment of the State of Israel, strong moral and material support for Israel in war and in peace, and the strengthening of a Canada-Israel connection in many domains.

During the Oslo interlude—the seven years between the 1993 announcement of secret negotiations that created an Israeli-Palestinian peace process and the Palestinian turn from negotiation to terror in 2000—the relationship between Canadian Zionists and Israel reached a certain maturity. Some tensions developed as both Israelis and Canadian Jews sought to establish the right tone for their partnership. But there was also a healthy mutuality that developed, most notably in the great success of the "Israel Experience" for young people. In fact, if the major challenge of the twentieth century was survival, a twenty-first-century challenge is the search for the greater meaning through Israel and Jewish nationalism. Canadian Jews are remarkably free, proud, and settled. But they, like so many other moderns, seek anchors, traditions, and deeper connections, which Israel helps provide, especially through programs such as birthright israel.

The Jewish community also now faces a "continuity problem"—assimilation and intermarriage—as a threat to the Jewish future in North America. After maintaining a strong sense of Jewish community and identity in the face of thousands of years of persecution, the intermarriage rate in the U.S is estimated to be at least 50 per cent of all new marriages. The intermarriage rate has been considerably lower in Canada; the demographic debate in Montreal in the 1990s centered on whether the intermarriage rate was 6 per cent or 13 per cent. Still, on both sides of the border, concern over Jewish assimilation has grown.

Israeli trips for youngsters—known as the Israel Experience—emerged as one of the most effective tools for re-energizing Jewish identity. Recent research shows that such "24/7 Judaism"—intense

In 1997, Israeli prime minister Benjamin Netanyahu (second from left) confers in Toronto with (left to right) Sidney Greenberg, national vice-president CZF, Lou Rosen, president Central Region, 1977–81, and Max Shechter, president Central Region, 1973–77 and 1985–89.

(*Canadian Jewish News*)

Canadians and Israel

Canadians have been among the strongest supporters of Israel throughout its brief modern history.

Since the State of Israel was declared in 1948, eight thousand Canadian Jews have moved to the Jewish state. Making the move from Canada to Israel is admittedly not easy, however, and the Association of Americans and Canadians in Israel was formed to assist new immigrants making Israel their home.

Tens of thousands flock to the Jewish state annually as tourists—many of them participating in various organizational study missions. In 2004, 34,000 Canadians visited Israel—an increase of 34 per cent over the previous year. The birthright israel program has taken more than 11,000 young Jews to the Jewish state since 2000—when it was launched—through 2004.

Canadian investors have "transformed the country's way of life," in the words of Yair Ofek, deputy director-general of the Israel Export and International Cooperation Institute.

Ofek drew particular attention to "Canadian architect and land developer David Azrieli, who introduced shopping malls to Israel" and to the "Koffler family that started the Superpharm chain that has proliferated all over country." Ofek added, "It's hard to imagine Israel without the shopping malls or pharmacy chains" brought in by Canadians.

The volume of trade between Canada and Israel has been steadily increasing. In 1981, it was $125 million, but in recent years, it has topped the $1 billion mark. And the direction of the flow of commerce has changed, too. Israel now exports more goods to Canada than it imports.

In 2005, speaking in Tel Aviv, Pierre Pettigrew, the Canadian Foreign Affairs minister, praised the activities of the Israel-Canada Chamber of Commerce and Industry. Pettigrew noted that "since the implementation of the Canada-Israel Free Trade Agreement in 1997, we have seen our bilateral trade more than double."

group experiences with Jewish peers in the Jewish people's homeland—has a tremendous impact and can often help jump-start young Jews' journey back toward tradition and forward to an exciting Jewish future. Such positive experiences were the impetus behind the launch of the birthright israel program, which Charles Bronfman and Michael Steinhardt hoped would create a new Jewish rite of passage, as natural as a bar or bat mitzvah, that would put young Jews in touch with themselves, each other, and their people in their homeland.

In addition to being an altruistic and effective gift from "one generation to another," as Bronfman has often said, birthright israel reflects a new, more mature, more equal partnership between Israel and the Diaspora. More proactive and positive, less reactive and crisis-driven than other Zionist initiatives, birthright israel portrays Israel and Israelis as a

birthright israel

In 1999, Canadian Charles Bronfman—in partnership at the time with American Michael Steinhardt—created "birthright israel," a program that sends thousands of students to the Jewish state for a ten-day visit at virtually no cost to them. The program is aimed at "Jewish adults 18-26 who have little previous knowledge of Judaism and have not been to Israel previously on an educational program." Mr. Bronfman originated the program, which soon developed into a $210 million partnership of philanthropists, federations, Keren Hayesod, and the Jewish Agency for Israel.

By 2005, the program had eight thousand young people from North America, including nine hundred from Canada, participating annually.

During a meeting in Israel with students, Mr. Bronfman was asked, "Why is it you choose to give so much to the birthright program?" And the philanthropist responded, "I personally felt that we cannot be Jewish without having a knowledge of and understanding of Israel."

source of answers to modern Jewish needs, and not as a needy recipient of assistance.

The fact that the tours began in late 1999 and early 2000—when Israel was intoxicated by the hopes of peace and the dot-com prosperity of the 1990s—fed participants' euphoria and optimism. Unfortunately, hopes soured when Yasser Arafat led his people away from negotiations and toward a terror campaign directed against Israeli schoolchildren, commuters, seder-attendees, and bar mitzvah celebrants. The scourge of suicide bombing, the randomness of the strikes, the lethality of the blows, and the ubiquity of the fear combined with a relentless international attack on Israel for reacting in self-defence, cast Israel again as the troubled, problematic partner in the relationship between Canadian and Israeli Jews. Israel Experience attendance dropped as Diaspora Jews feared becoming victims of terror.

Yet as hostilities increased, the balance in the relationship was restored. Israelis displayed remarkable dignity and fortitude in the wake of the onslaught. After Al Qaeda's terror attacks against the United States on September 11, 2001, Jews realized that all Westerners had become targets, and that Israel was a key fighter in eradicating the worldwide scourge of terrorism. Remarkably, birthright israel continued running trips throughout the entire time, bringing more than 70,000 students to Israel during its first five years, from 1999 to 2004. During this period, Canadian Zionists worked hard to defend Israel—and their fellow Jews at home and throughout the world. Anti-Semitic incidents surged, especially in Montreal and Toronto, while in its attempt to appear "evenhanded," Prime Minister Jean Chrétien's government often chastised Israel. After a slow start, members of the community published hundreds of articles, generated thousands of emails, and sent millions of dollars to Israel. Canadian Jews felt the sting personally, as Toronto-born Chezi Goldberg was murdered in a Jerusalem bombing, as synagogues were attacked, and as anti-Semitic immigrants hostile to Israel firebombed the library of the Montreal Jewish day school, United Talmud Torah, and a few years later, a yeshiva (a boys' Torah seminary).

In September 2002 out-of-hand demonstrations at Concordia University in Montreal brought out riot police and prevented former prime minister Benjamin Netanyahu's lecture at the school. Hostility toward Israel had been festering on many campuses for years, and tensions at Concordia had run high for years. The out-

Charles Bronfman, in 2001, meets with participants from Canada in the birthright program that sends eight thousand students a year to Israel from North America.

burst of actual violence mobilized students while galvanizing the community. Thanks to a combination of grassroots activism and behind-the-scenes negotiations, the pro-Arab Concordia Student Union became less hostile—although Jewish students never succeeded in securing permission to re-invite Netanyahu or even to host former prime minister Ehud Barak after the atmosphere had improved. Other campuses also experienced tension. At York University in Toronto, and elsewhere, Jewish students worked effectively to celebrate Israel's commitment to peace and democracy while countering the Palestinian activists who launched campaigns accusing Israel of practicing South African–style apartheid.

In an attempt to lobby the government more effectively, the Canada-Israel Committee reorganized. The Canadian Council for Israel and Jewish Advocacy Public Affairs Committee (CIJA-PAC) emerged as a national outreach organization to champion the Canadian Jewish community's interests to politicians and other opinion leaders and decision makers across Canada. B'nai Brith proved effective as an aggressive pro-Israel voice, and several grassroots coalitions developed. Most notably, Montreal's 2007 Israel Independence Rally, which attracted 7,500 people, including leading politicians from the Conservative and Liberal parties, resulted from an informal coalition of Jewish activists and community groups who insisted on holding the celebration downtown. Editorial pages and columnists, especially in the *National Post*, were articulate and eloquent in defending Israel, and the *Canadian Jewish News*, ably edited by Mordechai Ben-Dat, celebrated Israel's accomplishments and Zionism's continuing positive vision.

The inside-outside strategy worked. Paul Martin's Liberal government from 2003 to 2006 was appreciably more supportive of Israel than Jean Chrétien's—although Canada sometimes voted in favour of resolutions critical of Israel at the United Nations. In addition to Martin's sympathies, his justice minister, human rights activist Irwin Cotler, was a strong champion of Israel, often arguing against the current anti-Israel bias in the United Nations. Cotler was also active in combatting new forms of anti-Semitism that often arose out of the common cause made by progressive forces and dictatorial regimes in singling out Israel for discriminatory treatment.

In 2006, Martin was replaced by a Conservative government led by Stephen Harper, whose government has been strongly supportive of democratic Israel in the face of growing extremist threats. During the Second Lebanon War in the summer of 2006, Prime Minister Harper condemned Hezbollah as part of the broader scourge of terrorism internationally. The Canadian Jewish community mobilized, raising over $45 million as part of the $359 million collected throughout North America by the United Jewish Communities' Israel Emergency Fund. This money went directly to alleviating the misery of the communities in the north of Israel that were terrorized by Hezbollah's Katyusha rockets. After the war, Canadian students flocked to the area to help rebuild damaged houses. During the conflict, Prime Minister Harper stood his ground, even as ugly demonstrations demonized him—and once again uncovered a limited but virulent hostility toward Canadian Jews as well as Israel.

Shocked by the hatred at home and abroad, and forced to deploy armed guards in schools and synagogues, Canadian Zionists nevertheless continued to embrace a positive Zionist dream, investing in their sister communities in Israel, sending missions to Israel, maintaining a disproportionately high percentage of birthright participants from North America, and re-evaluating curricula and community strategies to emphasize all Israel's successes.

During these years, Canadians helped spearhead a Zionist revival. The bestselling book *Why I Am a Zionist: Israel, Jewish Identity and the Challenges of Today* by McGill University professor Gil Troy sold more than 20,000 copies throughout North America, after being hailed by many leading Zionists as a "must read" and touted by the *New Republic*'s Martin Peretz as the most "persuasive presentation of the case" in decades. Nefesh b'Nefesh, Soul to Soul, an organization encouraging aliyah from the West, helped over seven hundred Canadians settle in Israel between 2001 and 2007.

From the gleaming white of the magnificent hockey rink at the Canada Centre at Metullah in northern Israel—where Torontonian

Sidney Greenberg became chair of the Israel Ice Hockey Federation in 2008—to the dazzling yellow of the Negev sands being transformed into a rich green in the south, Canadians have built bridges of generosity, creativity, and friendship with Israelis. Business tycoon Gerry Schwartz and his bookstore-chain-owner wife, Heather Reisman, established the Heseg Foundation (Keren L'Chayalim Bodedim) to support lone soldiers serving in Israel's army whose families live outside of Israel. The foundation plans to build up to an annual donation of $3 million a year to fund three hundred full scholarships for immigrant soldiers. Schwartz and Reisman also donated a library for the Shimon Peres Peace Center, funded an exchange program linking the University of Manitoba with Tel Aviv University, and supported the Alyn Center for Disabled Children in Israel.

The "Canadian friends" organizations of the various Israeli universities were particularly successful. Dinners honoured leading Canadians, including former prime minister Brian Mulroney and the Toronto couple spearheading the fight by non-Jews against anti-Semitism, Tony and Elizabeth Comper. In September 2006, Toronto-based mining magnate Seymour Schulich donated US$20 million to the Technion, which named the school's chemistry faculty after him. Coincidentally, a few months later, another mining magnate, Peter Munk, donated US$16 million to establish the Peter Munk Research Institute at the Technion.

Funding students at all seven leading universities, the Quebec real-estate developer Marcel Adams allocated US$20 million in spring 2005 so the Israel Academy of Sciences and Humanities could offer generous fellowships to "the best and the brightest" science students pursuing doctoral studies. In 2007, the Azrieli Foundation allocated $30 million to establish another prestigious graduate funding program. The aim of the Azrieli Fellows Program—which offers generous grants to Israeli and international graduate students studying at Israeli universities in the fields of applied sciences, architecture and education—is to create a network of leading professionals and academics who will raise Israel's profile internationally and maintain strong links between Israel and the rest of the world.

In standing up to the terrorist onslaught but continuing to sing and dance with Israelis, not just fight and mourn, Canadian Zionists demonstrated that remarkable mix of realism and romanticism that characterized the first century of Zionism—and shaped the old-new Jewish state. This same combination of fortitude and farsightedness will keep Canadian Zionists working, building, planning, and dreaming for a State of Israel that is not only a source of greatness and pride, but also functions as the emotional, ideological, spiritual, political, and moral epicentre of the Canadian Jewish community—and the entire Jewish world.

9

Canadian Zionist Organizations

WHILE THE RELATIONSHIP BETWEEN Canadian Jews and the Jewish homeland—both before and after the declaration of the State of Israel—has been strong ever since the earliest days of nineteenth-century Hovevei Zion in Montreal, it has also evolved, adapting to new domestic, international, and regional realities as they have arisen. This combination of a strong foundation and dynamic adaptability can also be seen in the organizational expressions of Canadian Zionists over the years.

In general, the years between the establishment of Israel in 1948 and the outbreak of the Six Day War in 1967 were a time when Canadian Jews consolidated the Zionist component of their modern identity. Significant financial support to Israel-based organizations and causes increased in the years after 1948 and, as David Goldberg noted in "The Post Statehood Relationship: A Growing Friendship" (*From Immigration to Integration: The Canadian Jewish Experience*, 2001), a disproportionate number of Canadian Jews chose to make aliyah before or shortly after statehood.

At the same time, the existing Canadian Zionist organizations were not as vocal in their public advocacy for Israel in this period as they had been in the immediate pre-state period—their approach harkened back to the quiet "don't rock the boat" advocacy of the 1920s and 1930s. There were, as Goldberg argues, a number of reasons for this. The first is that the reality and consolidation of Israel as a functioning democratic modern state removed a sense of urgency and relieved Diaspora communities of the immediate need to provide the wherewithal for both development and defense in the new state. And, from a pragmatic point of view, Canadian Jewish organizations that focused on the needs of the

"In defining myself as a Zionist, I have never defined myself as a supporter of any political party or movement. This was also true when I served as president of the Canadian Zionist Federation in the 1980s, when I came out strongly for a message of unity among the various groups in Canada, and undivided support for Israel as our public message. I have always been honoured to speak to, or be consulted by, leaders of Israel regardless of political stripe, because at bottom there is something common to all of them that is more important than their political affiliation: their commitment to the State of Israel."
—David J. Azrieli, President, Canadian Zionist Federation (1987–1989)

Jewish communities at home rather than on the goals of Zionism had greater resources than their Zionist counterparts. But perhaps most importantly, the Canadian Jewish community of the 1950s and 1960s was only beginning to feel fully accepted in Canada and worried about being too vocal in its political advocacy for a foreign country. It was, Goldberg notes, better "to follow the time-honoured tradition of entrusting a handful of prominent *shtadlans* to make Israel's case privately in the corridors of power."

A turning point for the Canadian Jewish community came with the 1967 war, as it did for Jews all over the world. The ominous beginning of the war revived the sense of urgency for Jews around the world and they once again united in the common cause of defending the Jewish homeland. In the rush of exhilaration and pride that followed the successful outcome of the war, Canadian Jews, like Jews throughout the Diaspora, understood the need for continuing support for Israel and the importance of maintaining strong ties among all Jews, both inside and outside Israel. Instead of focusing on the political advocacy role that was now being led by the Canada-Israel Committee, Canadian Zionist organizations after 1967 were rejuvenated by what they saw as their renewed mandate to educate Jews and non-Jews about Israel, to promote aliyah and travel to Israel, and to create and build stronger social and cultural ties between Canada and Israel.

For more than thirty years following the Six Day War, the leading role in these activities was played by the Canadian Zionist Federation and its constituent organizations. Established in 1967 as the successor organization to the Zionist Organization of Canada, its mandate was to serve as the national federation for Zionist organizations across Canada and to provide programs to educate and nurture young people, to help them preserve their identity as Jews by instilling in them a deep commitment to Israel. At the start of the twenty-first century, new realities in Canada and the Middle East and on the international stage raised new and difficult challenges for Zionists, and the Canadian Jewish community once again embarked on a process of organizational renewal. Nonetheless, the various organizations continued to focus on strengthening the Zionist component in the identity of Canadian Jews, in keeping with the inspiring history of the contributions Canadians have made to the Jewish national dream from the turn of twentieth century to the inauguration of the twenty-first.

The Canadian Zionist Federation

The Canadian Zionist Federation was established in 1967 to represent all Canadian Zionists—transcending party differences—to foster and advance a common purpose among its constituent organizations, and to be the official representative of the World Zionist Organization in Canada. The CZF is expressly committed to Jewish education, Jewish culture, and the centrality of Israel in Jewish life. Over the course of more than forty years, the organization has realized its commitment to Jewish education through its Israel-oriented educational activities for youth, by providing assistance for aliyah through its Aliyah Centres, by promoting *hasbarah* (public information) with its Israel-focused program materials, by bringing *shlichim* (emissaries) from Israel to act as instructors and youth counsellors, and by working in remote and small Jewish communities in Canada.

To achieve these objectives and continue to carry out the mandate of the Zionist movement in Canada, the CZF organized itself to serve the widest possible range of Jewish needs. With main offices currently in Montreal and Toronto, the organization at one time had regional offices in six regions across the country: Atlantic (based in Halifax); Eastern (based in Montreal); Central (based in Toronto); Midwest (based in Winnipeg); Western (based in Edmonton); and Pacific (based in Vancouver).

The Canadian Zionist Federation has a large membership across Canada in distinct constituent Zionist organizations. As an umbrella organization, the CZF brings these respected, independent bodies together with the common aim of enhancing Zionist activities and promoting the crucial role of Israel in Jewish communities across the country. The constituent organizations include, among others: Achdut Ha'avoda Poale Zion, the Canadian

Presidents of the Canadian Zionist Federation

Over the past twenty-five years, the presidency of the Canadian Zionist Federation has swung back and forth between representatives from Toronto and Montreal.

Samuel Chait 1967–1970
Hy Bessin 1970–1972
Philip Givens 1972–1984
Neri J. Boomfield 1984–1986
David J. Azrieli 1987–1989
Kurt Rothschild 1990–2004
Norman Stern 2004–

The Canadian Zionist Federation

A FÉDÉRATION SIONISTE CANADIENNE מנורה בקרה

...STERN REGION

Sephardi Federation, the Confederation of United Zionists of Canada, Emunah Women of Canada, Friends of Pioneering Israel, Herut-Likud, Hadassah-WIZO of Canada, Herut Women, ARZA, the Labour Zionist Alliance of Canada, the Labour Zionist Movement of Canada, Mercaz Canada, the Mizrachi Organization of Canada, Na'amat Canada, and Tehiya Canada. With the support and collaboration of the CZF, as well as on their own, these organizations initiate and participate in a wide variety of Zionist projects, activities, and programs.

Constituent Organizations

The Canadian Zionist movement, like Zionist movements throughout the world and throughout Zionist history, encompasses a wide range of ideological, political, and religious tenets. The many organizations in Canada demonstrate the Zionist movement's diversity. The ideological focus and activities of the different organizations reflect their specific orientations. Overall, they can be categorized according to their main ideological focus as belonging to one of four groups: the National Camp, Labour Zionism, Religious Zionism, and General

Zionism. The categories express the political origins of Zionism in Europe and its evolution, first in Palestine, then in Israel. However, like all Jewish movements, they have been transformed by their North American and Canadian histories.

The National Camp

The organizations that form the core of the Zionist National Camp in Canada are Herut Canada, Herut-Likud, and Herut Women. The Herut movement in Canada has participated actively in Jewish community life since the early 1930s. There are two branches to this movement—Herut-Likud, which is based in Israel and acts as a counterpart to the other branch, Herut Canada. Both organizations were founded on the teachings and ideology of Zeev Jabotinsky (1880–1940). Born in Russia, Jabotinsky dedicated his life to the rescue of the Jewish people. Shortly after witnessing the Kishinev pogrom in 1903, he organized the Haganah in Palestine, a Jewish self-defence organization designed to enable Jews to fight back against individual and group expressions of anti-Semitism. He urged all

Thirty teachers from Montreal's Solomon Schechter Academy on a visit to Israel in 2000. The tour was planned to help the teachers explain the reality of Israel to their students and to strengthen ties with the Afik school in Beersheba.

threatened Jewish communities to organize themselves into self-defence units and helped raise the funds necessary to purchase ammunition. His activism and doctrine of Jewish self-reliance in the defence of Jewish lives and communities has marked the National Camp's ideology throughout its history.

In addition to Jabotinsky's self-defence activities and exploits, he was involved in the creation of Hebrew day schools and universities in the Diaspora and the establishment of the Hebrew University in Jerusalem. He was also the guiding light behind the formation of the Jewish Legion, known as the Zion Mule Corps, that fought in the First World War. Some of the *yishuv*'s most distinguished leaders fought with this unit in places such as Gallipoli.

A Canadian group inspired by Jabotinsky's nationalist principles and teachings established a presence in Canada in 1935. Known as the Zionist Revisionist Movement, its supporters included Issie Brat, Morris Feinstein, and Sam Sokoloff. As was the case with Revisionist Zionist groups in Europe and Palestine, the founding of a Canadian organization constituted a break with mainstream and Labour Zionism. In the mid-1950s, the movement was re-energized when Polish-born Montrealer Ben Milner and a group of friends became involved. Considered one of Canada's greatest supporters of Revisionist Zionist ideals, Milner became national president of the Canadian organization in 1976.

Today, Herut Canada, like other organizations within the National Camp, is part of the Canadian Zionist Federation. It acts as the Canadian arm of one of Israel's strongest conservative political parties—the Likud, successor to Herut and then Gahal. Herut Canada and its members have been involved in many different Jewish community and Zionist activities over the years. In Israel, for example, it has entered into various co-operative projects with the Jewish National Fund, including a forest outside Jerusalem in memory of Aliza Begin, the late wife of former prime minister Menahem Begin, and a youth camp near the outskirts of the ancient Shuni Fortress in memory of Teddy Schwartz. Herut Women supports daycare centres and group homes in depressed areas of Israel. They also care for and educate pre-school children and troubled teenagers. In Canada, Herut's activities include, among other undertakings, an ongoing media watch, lobbying on behalf of oppressed Jewry, children's programming, *hasbarah* seminars and newsletters, fundraising, regular conferences with prominent Israeli figures, and family events.

Labour Zionism

The Labour Zionist movement emerged in the late nineteenth century out of the Jewish workers' movements of Central and Eastern Europe. In contrast to Theodor Herzl's political Zionism, which concentrated on building support in the international community for the creation of a Jewish state, the focus of the Labour Zionists was to build a Jewish state through the efforts of a Jewish working class settling in Palestine. David Ben-Gurion, one of the architects of the modern State of Israel and its first prime minister, was an ardent Labour Zionist. Reflecting the ideals of A. D. Gordon—the Russian-Jewish Zionist leader whose writings inspired a generation of young pioneers to make aliyah to Palestine—Ben Gurion saw the aims of Zionism as a return to labour and the soil of the homeland.

National renaissance and social justice are the cardinal principles of Labour Zionism. Although its ideology is clearly many-faceted and eclectic, some general and shared principles of Labour Zionism are: a belief in the unity of the Jewish people, the goal of social justice as expressed by collective ideals, and the need to fortify the national consciousness and internal strength of Jewish communities. The Labour Zionist movement embraces the religious and the secular, self-realization and collectivism, the practical necessity of settlement of the homeland, and Jewish organizational and cultural autonomy in the Diaspora.

At the beginning of the twentieth century, groups of young Jews who called themselves Poale Zion (Labourers of Zion or Labour Zionists) appeared in Canada and other countries throughout the world. Poale Zion was committed to a platform that included establishing a Jewish state; building a society on the foundations of social justice; participating in the World Zionist movement; facilitating immigration to Palestine; fostering democratic Jewish community institutions around the world; uniting Jewish workers in the Diaspora; supporting an organization of Jewish workers in Palestine; and participating in democratic, socialist, and labour movements throughout the world.

The Labour Zionist movement has made many impressive contributions to Israel and Jewish life. For much of the twentieth century, Labour Zionism was the central mainstream vehicle for rebuilding the Jewish homeland. It counteracted anti-Zionist and assimilationist influences among Jewish workers in the Diaspora during the first three decades of the century and organized Jewish workers in support of Israel. It brought together labour organizations in support of the Histadrut, Israel's trade union movement. Labour Zionism dominated Israeli politics and government for the first thirty years of the state's existence.

In Canada, Labour Zionist groups worked vigorously for the establishment of the Canadian Jewish Congress as the voice of Canadian Jewry. They also established educational institutions and published works of Yiddish authors in Canada. They supported Jewish defence in Eastern Europe and Ha-Shomer (an organization of Jewish workers founded in 1909) in Palestine before the First World War. In general, the Canadian Labour Zionist movement worked to garner support from all the major Jewish and non-Jewish labour organizations in North America for Zionism and the State of Israel. The Labour Zionist movement also promoted the creation of Hechalutz, a pioneering youth organization.

A number of constituent organizations make up the Labour Zionist movement, among them the Histadrut Campaign, the Labour Zionist Alliance, Na'amat Canada, Achdut Ha-Avoda Poale Zion, and Friends of Pioneering Israel.

Through the Histadrut Campaign, created by Canadian Labour Zionists in 1924, the movement fundraises in support of labour and co-operative institutions in Israel. In the years after 1967, this organization—known also as the Canadian Association for Labour Israel—has focused mainly on raising funds to assist Histadrut (Israel's trade union movement) in its programs aimed at settling and integrating newly arrived immigrants in Israel. A vital component of Histadrut is the Canadian Friends of AMAL, whose goal is to encourage and develop vocational education in the numerous schools devoted to that purpose in Israel. The AMAL schools, dotted throughout Israel, provide an opportunity for needy children to obtain a comprehensive vocational and high school education; on graduation they are skilled in one of more than one hundred different trades.

Na'amat Pioneer Women was founded in 1925 as a North American group that included both Canadians and Americans. The group is committed to the ideology and philosophy of such notable figures as David Ben-Gurion and Golda Meir (who was a founding member of the organization). In 1966, Na'amat Pioneer Women became two autonomous organizations in the United States and Canada. Since then, the Canadian organization—known as Na'amat Canada—has expanded in Canada to become one of the premier

groups working in support of Israel. Na'amat Canada is affiliated with Na'amat Israel, and maintains close links with the World Labour Zionist Movement in Israel and its fraternal organizations in Canada. Na'amat Canada is dedicated to the social and economic enhancement of a free, democratic, progressive society in the State of Israel, based on social justice, economic equity, respect for human rights, and freedom of religious and cultural expression. It is also committed to providing support for the welfare and education of under-privileged women, teenagers, and children throughout Israel. Fundraising is conducted for daycare centres; for the maintenance and expansion of homes for orphans; for legal services and counselling for bereaved families and victims of domestic violence; for vocational training schools for young people; and for community centres that provide educational and recreational programs for women. Since 1966, Na'amat Canada has funded the construction of a children's home in Haifa, community centres in Migdal Ha'amek, Givatayim, Ramat Gan, Katamon Gimel, and Holon, a daycare centre in Jerusalem, and an agricultural boarding school and science centre in Israel. It has also been involved in promoting tourism to Israel; the construction of the Canada Na'amat Children's Centre and Women's Educational Centre in Givatayim, and the Canada Na'amat Centre in Petach Tikva; and

Na'amat Montreal celebrates seventy-five years of service to Israel with a candle-lighting ceremony in 2002. Fifteen presidents, past and present, participated.

(Na'amat Canada Montreal)

intensive cultural programs to help perpetuate Jewish traditions, language, culture, and heritage. Na'amat Canada also plays a political advocacy role in Canada, petitioning the Canadian government on matters that concern them as Canadians, as women, and as Jews.

Achdut Ha-Avoda Poale Zion, another mainstay of Canadian Labour Zionism, was established in Toronto in 1923 by a group of newly arrived immigrants from Poland. The majority of the *chaverim* (members) were workers, and they soon became active in the trade union movement, particularly in the needle trade. Many held leadership positions in unions such as the Hat, Cap and Millinery Workers, the Amalgamated Clothing Workers of America, and the International Ladies' Garment Workers. As a result of its participation in union activities, the Zionist organization gained the friendship and understanding of the mainstream Canadian labour movement (represented by the New Democratic Party and the Canadian Labour Congress).

Achdut Ha-Avoda was also active in the field of Jewish education in Canada—for example, it was one of the groups that helped start the Borochov School and Kindergarten in 1932. During the Second World War, it assisted in the fight against anti-Semitism, worked for the rescue of Jews from Nazi-occupied countries, assisted the underground movement, and helped in the resettlement of survivors in Canada. The organization issued *Unzer Veg* (Our Way)—a political and literary periodical, as well as bibliographies, works on social subjects, and a number of translated works by Ber Borochov, the founder and leader of Poale Zion.

Religious Zionism

For many Jews and most of the founders of Zionism, the ideals and goals of Judaism and the underpinnings of Jewish civilization are best expressed through actions that promote social justice. Labour Zionists, by far the strongest and most active group in the early years of the Zionist movement, frequently abandoned the rituals and practices of formal Judaism in favour of the more political expression of social and economic reform. In contrast, religious Zionists worked hard to synthesize modern nationalist concepts with traditional Jewish religious ones.

Religious Zionists are a large group within the Zionist movement who were and are inspired by the religious tenets of Judaism to build a flourishing Jewish state in the land of Israel. The roots of religious Zionism date back to 1862, when the Prussian Orthodox Rabbi Zvi

Hirsch Kalischer published an important tractate entitled *Derishat Zion* (Seeking Zion). Kalischer argued that the salvation of the Jews, promised by the Prophets, can come about only through self-help. In the twentieth century, influential religious leaders such as Rabbi Abraham Isaac Kook argued that young religious Jews should support efforts to settle the land and try to influence the secular Labour Zionists to give more consideration to the religious tenets of Judaism. For most religious Zionists the resettlement of the Jewish people in its homeland is part of a divine scheme that will bring salvation (*geula*) to Jews and to the entire world.

The ideas and goals of religious Zionism were not widely accepted in the early years. Indeed, as the Zionist movement began to flourish all over the world in the late nineteenth century, many religiously observant Jews were opposed to Zionism, seeing it as a secular heresy. In this view, only the Messiah could re-establish a Jewish homeland in Israel, and any attempt to do this by human agency was understood as an expression of disbelief in God's salvation and power. The exceptions to these views in the early years were the supporters of Orthodox Mizrachi and Ha-Poel Ha-Mizrachi organizations. Later, in the immediate pre-State days, almost all Orthodox Jews came to support the theological arguments made by Rabbi Kook, and nearly all Orthodox synagogues, in Canada as elsewhere in the Diaspora, rallied to the cause of a Jewish state and worked to raise money in support of the realization of the national dream.

For very different reasons, Reform Judaism also rejected the idea of Jewish peoplehood or nationalism in the late nineteenth and early twentieth centuries. Reform Judaism is based on both the central tenets of Judaism—God, Torah, and Israel—and recognition and acceptance of a wide diversity in Jewish beliefs and practices. Early Reform Judaism was anti-Zionist, arguing that the seeming acceptance and success of European, and especially German, Jews in all areas of society would allow them to be "a light unto the nations" with no need for a national home. This continued to be the guiding hope until the late 1930s—when the looming tragedy in Europe began to make the failure of assimilation fully apparent. The Columbus Platform of 1937 formally affirmed Reform Judaism's shift to a belief in "the obligation of all Jewry to aid in building a Jewish homeland."

Unlike the Orthodox and Reform branches of Judaism, Conservative Jews advocated for the Zionist cause from very early on. Arising out of the intellectual currents in Germany in the mid-nineteenth century, Conservative Judaism is a modern stream of Judaism that combines a positive attitude toward modern culture, acceptance of critical secular scholarship regarding Judaism's sacred texts, and commitment to traditional Jewish observance. The Conservative Movement took institutional form in the United States and Canada in the early 1900s with the creation of the United Synagogue organization. As early as its 1913 constitution, the Conservative movement called on its members "to preserve in the [prayer] service the reference to Israel's past and hopes for Israel's restoration." From 1917 on, the annual reports of the United Synagogue always featured the Zionist cause. The 1917 report states that the body "joins with the Zionists throughout the world in voicing the claim to a legally recognized and internationally secured homeland for the Jewish people in Palestine."

The Jewish Reconstructionist movement was also pro-Zionist from its early days in the 1920s. A main tenet of Reconstructionism is that Judaism is continually evolving and brings together the ideas of modern social, intellectual, and spiritual Jewish life and a respect for traditional

Celebrating Yom Hazikaron in Montreal, 2002.

(Mickey Gutstein Photo)

Judaism. Long before the rise of the National Socialists in Germany, Reconstructionists believed that the successful rise of nationalism sweeping Europe in the nineteenth and early twentieth centuries would make life for European Jews even more tenuous than it already was.

Notwithstanding the varied positions taken by different streams in Judaism at different times, religion was part of the woof and warp of Jewish national expression at the very inception of the Zionist movement and continues to be so today. Inspired by the aim of ensuring that the ideals and traditions of Judaism remain a part of the national project, religious Zionists assured that Israel would not be just another state. Instead, some major components of Jewish religious affirmation were integrated into the Israeli system from the outset, including public observance of Shabbat and religious festivals, and observance of dietary laws in most public places. Marriage and divorce laws conform to Orthodox laws. Today, a religious Zionist orientation may be found among Jews from all the main branches of Judaism—Orthodox, Conservative, Reform, and Reconstructionist.

There are several Zionist organizations in Canada with a religious Zionist orientation. For example, the first religious Zionist organization, Mizrachi of Canada, was established in 1941. Rabbi Seymour M. Zambrowski was one of the organization's founders and leaders for many years, until he moved to Israel, where he continued to play a major role in Mizrachi and in Bar Ilan University. Mizrachi is an ideological and educational movement, best encapsulated by the motto "the Jewish people in the Land of Israel living according to the Torah of Israel." Its aims include the spread of religious learning—Torah Learning—amongst its members and education toward aliyah.

Mizrachi of Canada has shown its commitment to what it terms Torah Zionism by establishing the Torah Lecture Series, sponsoring the Steinsaltz Talmud, publishing *Or HaMizrach* (an annual magazine received in over two thousand Jewish homes and libraries around the world), and establishing two yeshivot in Toronto, Or Chaim and Ulpanat Orot. Mizrachi of Canada's activities also include Israel missions and support for more than two hundred institutions in Israel, the Bnei Akiva youth movement, Camp Moshava, as well as Sabbath events, lectures, and public *shiurim* (lessons).

Evolving out of the early Mizrachi Women's chapters, Emunah Women of Canada was officially established in 1984. In Hebrew, *emunah* means "faith." Emunah's activities focus on the welfare of Israel's disadvantaged population, caring for the young, and assisting in youth education. In addition to the care and understanding Emunah provides, they also stress reverence for the Torah. Their aim is for the children in their schools to emerge proud of their heritage and secure in their identity, well on their way to becoming self-respecting and dedicated religiously observant Jews and citizens.

In Israel, Emunah is the third largest women's organization. It runs a network that consists of two hundred daycare centres, nursery schools, sleep-in facilities, vocational and academic high schools, and a community college, and provides social welfare services. The Children's Village of Neve Michael in Pardess Channa is both home and school to children who have been removed, for a variety of reasons, from underprivileged and broken homes. The children receive guidance and education to build new lives within a Torah-based value system.

Conservative Judaism's Zionist arm is Merkaz, represented in this country by Merkaz Canada. Merkaz originated in the United States as a result of concern over marginalization faced by the Conservative and Reform congregations and rabbis in Israel, where Orthodoxy has a disproportionate influence on the country's official religious life. In contrast to many Orthodox institutions, for example, there is no Israeli government funding for Conservative and Reform congregations and institutions. By creating a grassroots organization like Merkaz, the Conservative movement hoped to be able to promote and support Zionist education and programs; represent the interests of Conservative Judaism in the World Zionist Organization (WZO), the Jewish Agency for Israel (JAFI), and the Canadian Zionist Federation (CZF); and lobby on behalf of religious pluralism and recognition of Conservative Judaism in Israel. Since its founding, Merkaz Canada has worked to bring Conservative Jews closer to Zionism and Israel, increase Zionist activities, Israel programs, tourism, and aliyah within Conservative synagogues, offers matching scholarships to young people attending Conservative-sponsored trips in Israel, supports short and long-term study programs in Israel, and disseminates Zionist educational materials and programs.

ARZA, a Reform religious Zionist organization, got its start in the mid-1970s (when it was called Kadima). It was established after members of the Reform movement, who had initially been part of the World Zionist Organization, decided they would need their own political arm of the WZO if they were to have a significant voice in Zionist affairs. Reform religious Zionist organizations were soon established in countries around the world, and they came together in 1980 in a world body called Arzenu, which represents them in the World Zionist Organization. Arzenu and its constituent organizations aim to promote the cause of pluralism in the Zionist movement and to ensure the provision of equal religious rights for all Jews. They seek a more equitable distribution of the resources of the World Zionist Organization and have lobbied to make its decision-making process more transparent. More broadly, Arzenu works to stimulate Zionist interest and activities in progressive communities throughout the world.

Since the thirty-fourth World Zionist Congress in 2002, Arzenu and Merkaz have emerged as the strongest voices, offering new leadership at the international level. One result was the revamped 2004 Jerusalem Program that reflects a renewed commitment to the centrality of a Jewish, Zionist, and democratic Israel in Jewish life.

General Zionism

There are a number of Zionist organizations that are politically or ideologically unaffiliated. Some, like the Confederation of United Zionists of Canada, serve to express general support for Zionist ideals and work on behalf of Israel. Others, like the Canadian Sephardi Federation or Hadassah-WIZO (Women's International Zionist Organization)— the Zionist movement's largest women's organization—serve the interests of specific groups.

The Confederation of United Zionists is a large, Diaspora-centred coalition of classical Zionist parties represented at the World Zionist Organization. It has branches in all countries where Zionist activities are carried on, including Canada. The confederation is firm in its belief that the Zionist movement is the Jewish people's major instrument for strengthening Jewish unity and maintaining Israel's centrality in Jewish life.

Although the Confederation has no direct ties to political parties in Israel, it does believe that Diaspora Jews have the right to participate in the clarification of matters that are of concern to Jewish people everywhere. The Confederation also believes that in order to ensure that the bond between the State of Israel and Jews throughout the world remains strong, greater emphasis should be placed on Jewish education in the Diaspora. To this end, it encourages promotion of the Hebrew language and culture, the study of Jewish history, and knowledge of contemporary Israel. In the Confederation's view, the Jewish day school with an Israel-oriented program, based on the concept of the unity of the Jewish people, is one of the most effective means of

Canada's former justice minister and solicitor general Irwin Cotler, an outspoken supporter of Israel.

achieving this goal. Thus, support for the day-school movement is seen as a central component of Zionist activity.

The Canadian Sephardi Federation (CSF), located in Toronto and Montreal, is similar to other Canadian Jewish and Zionist organizations. Composed of Jews whose origins are in Algeria, Egypt, Morocco, Syria, and Tunisia, the Sephardic community concentrates its efforts on organizing trips to Israel for youth, hosting events for prominent Israeli spokesmen, and publishing materials that detail events that are relevant to the Sephardic world. The Federation was founded in 1977 by a group of Jews of North African origin and is part of the World Sephardi Federation, which has branches in fifteen countries. The Canadian branch of the Federation, which serves approximately 50,000 Sephardi Jews in Canada, is committed to preserving and promoting Sephardic religious, spiritual, cultural, political, and social patrimony and assists in the integration of new Sephardic immigrants to Israel.

Ever since it was founded in 1917 by a small group Jewish women in Toronto, Canadian Hadassah-WIZO has provided a vital link between Canada and Israel. It currently has a membership of approximately 17,000 women and 1,500 male life-associates. Hadassah-WIZO supports projects in Israel for the benefit of women, children, and senior citizens, while at the same time promoting Jewish culture and advancing the cause of women's rights in Canada.

The first project that the organization undertook in the early 1920s was the establishment of a girls' school for domestic and agricultural science in Nahalal. Today, it is Israel's foremost agricultural school for both girls and boys. In co-operation with Youth Aliyah, Canadian Hadassah-WIZO has helped to integrate hundreds of thousands of children into Israeli life, as well as house and educate them.

A crowd of 40,000 people turned out for the 1983 Hadassah-WIZO Bazaar held in the Automotive Centre of the Canadian National Exhibition in Toronto.

(*Canadian Jewish News*)

The two organizations operate Magdiel, a comprehensive high school and residential centre for the Hod Hasharon region that offers special vocational courses to local youngsters and new immigrants. They also assist in the absorption of Ethiopian immigrants to Israel and run Natanya Day Centre, which offers a two-year special education program in such fields as diamond cutting, carpentry, and clerical work.

In addition to these activities, Canadian Hadassah-WIZO supports fifteen daycare centres and kindergartens for Jewish and Arab preschoolers from culturally or economically deprived homes; youth clubs in disadvantaged neighbourhoods; three women's clubs for upgrading skills and teaching trades; the Hadassim Children and Youth Village; the Neri Bloomfield College of Design in Haifa; and the Rose Kanee Community Centre in Ramat, which provides various social services to adults, senior citizens, and youth. The organization is affiliated with the Canadian Hadassah-WIZO Research Institute in Jerusalem, the Abe and Sophie Bronfman School at Nehalim, and the Asaf Harofeh Hospital near Rehovot, which serves many chronically ill, impoverished, and malnourished patients.

Into the Twenty-First Century

Zionism's second century has brought change to Zionist organizations in Israel, in Canada, and at the international level. At the thirty-fourth Zionism Congress held in 2002 in Jerusalem, the most vocal participants were from the Reform and Conservative movements and a fresh new leadership emerged—25 per cent of the delegates were under the age of thirty—along with energized discussions of building a new vision of Zionism based on the principles of pluralism, innovation, and revitalization. Out of these debates came a revamped Jerusalem Program in 2004 as a new Zionist platform that emphasizes (or in some cases re-emphasizes) the core principles of Zionism—the unity of the Jewish people and the centrality of Israel as the historic homeland, Eretz Israel, in Jewish life; encouraging aliyah to Israel from all countries and the effective integration of all immigrants into Israeli society; strengthening the State of Israel as a Jewish, Zionist, and democratic state marked by mutual respect for the multi-faceted Jewish people and a striving for peace and justice; preserving the identity of the Jewish people through the fostering of Jewish, Hebrew, and Zionist education based on Jewish spiritual and cultural values; and protecting Jewish rights and representing national Zionist interests throughout the world.

The new Zionist platform has been integrated into the Jewish community in Canada in a variety of ways. A central vehicle for taking the Zionist message to young Jewish adults in the Diaspora has been the Hagshama Department of the World Zionist Organization that was founded in 1998 to "empower participants in an ongoing process…the expansion of the person's growing commitment from the personal to the Jewish communal to the State of Israel." Beginning in 2004, USD/Hagshama—the University Student Division, which is the North American arm of the Hagshama—began bringing its Zionist Seminars to Canadian university campuses and Jewish youth organizations such as birthright israel and Toronto Jewish Teens at Risk. These dynamic, interactive educational programs led by young Israeli *shlichim* are designed to strengthen a sense of Jewish identity and heritage among Canadian Jewish youth and encourage Zionist activity in the Jewish community in Canada.

A new organization to emerge within the Canadian Jewish community in the twenty-first century is the Canadian Council for Israel

The 2004 reunion of Second World War Jewish Veterans from across Canada held in Montreal. The attendees included Colonel Joel Wolfe (fourth from the right), one of the most senior Jewish officers in the conflict.

(Howard Kay Photograph)

and Jewish Advocacy (CIJA). Created in 2004 in an agreement among Canadian Jewish advocacy groups, federations, and community groups across Canada, CIJA brings together the advocacy work of two of the most venerable Jewish organizations in Canada—the Canadian Jewish Congress and the Canada-Israel Committee—to direct a broad range of non-partisan advocacy initiatives on behalf of the Canadian Jewish community and Israel. The architects of the new Council— UIA Federations Canada, through its president Shoel Silver, and the Israel Emergency Cabinet, through its co-chairs Steven Cummings, Gerald Schwartz, and Larry Tanenbaum—created CIJA in response to a perceived need to streamline advocacy efforts in the face of the many challenges that continue to confront both Israel and the Canadian Jewish community. The two founding co-chairs of CIJA are Brent Belzberg of Toronto and Steven Cummings of Montreal; the organization also encourages direct participation through membership in the CIJA Public Affairs Committee and supports the National Committee for Jewish Campus Life and the Canadian Friends of Israel.

Many of the Canadian Zionist organizations that developed in the twentieth century continue to thrive and serve both the Jewish community in Canada and Israel. Along with the new organizations, they strengthen the ties between the two countries, raise funds to support the State of Israel, and promote the cause of Zionism into the twenty-first century.

10

Focusing on Youth

THE ROLE OF ZIONIST YOUTH movements has changed over the years—whereas they once were at the forefront of Zionist organizational activism, they now play an important role in reaching out to Jewish youth generally. However, all Zionist youth organizations continue to be committed to the concerns of the Jewish people and the Jewish state.

Zionist youth movements first came into existence at the turn of the twentieth century. Many Jews in this period were searching for a new form of Jewish lifestyle and expression. One example of this was the kibbutz. In a happy example of the synthesis between Zionism and then current Western ideological trends, the early pioneers put a distinctive and successful Jewish twist on the popular idea of utopian commune living.

One aim of the youth groups in the early period was to encourage people to undertake aliyah, to settle in their ancient homeland in Palestine, which decades later would become the State of Israel. To prepare people to do so, they encouraged the study of Hebrew and established programs of Zionist education. The organizations' founders urged members of the community, especially the younger generation, to learn about Jewish history and Hebrew literature and strove to instil in them a strong sense of Jewish national consciousness and of the importance of establishing a national home. Their activities provided a basis for the new national identity of Jews everywhere in the Diaspora.

With the birth of the State of Israel in 1948 and the successful establishment of state and social institutions, the role of Zionist youth movements shifted. Previously, the youth movements had been faced with the critical tasks of nation building, tasks that required dedication, commitment, and self-sacrifice. These groups of young people were at the forefront of the efforts to spread the ideology of Zionism, to provide settlers for towns, villages, and collectives, and to provide men and women who would protect the *yishuv*. Their reward was the establishment of the State of Israel, the realization of their dream.

After 1948, however, the long-awaited government of the Jewish homeland undertook the responsibilities that the youth movements previously had helped to carry. The new state provided support to its citizens and acted as a beacon of hope for Jews all over the world; the state welcomed *olim* (new immigrants), who now came or fled to Israel; the state protected its citizens through its young, brave, and deeply committed citizens' army.

As Zionism became part of mainstream Jewish communal life and the establishment of the state was no longer the final goal, the youth movements had to redefine themselves and set new goals, a challenge that also affected the entire Zionist movement in Israel and throughout the Diaspora. Redefinition did not mean that the youth movements, which had often been in the vanguard of the Zionist movement, no longer had a role to play, but the role had changed and, if anything, become even more difficult.

The new role of the youth groups, like that adopted by the Zionist movement generally, was to strengthen Jewish identity among youth, to provide a basis for Jewish consciousness through education, and to strengthen the link between Israel and the Diaspora by fostering a commitment to the Jewish national home. In a very real sense, these challenges were as significant as the adventurous, pioneering challenges of the past. Books might not be as romantic as battles. Schools might not be as monumental as settlements in the malarial swamps of the Galilee or the hills of Judaea. But they were and are just as important for the survival of the Jewish people.

Activities

The various youth groups established in the early twentieth century represented a range of different political and social ideologies, and various levels of religious observance.

Betar was named after the last stronghold to be held by the Bar Kochba rebels until it was finally destroyed seventy years after the fall of Massada in 74CE. This group, which runs a summer and winter camp in Liberty, New York, has been functioning in Canada since 1931 as part of the Zionist Revisionist movement. The youth group affiliates itself with Herut, the nationalist political movement the Zionist-Revisionist Movement of Zeev Jabotinsky and Menachem Begin, the commander of the Irgun and later prime minister of Israel. Betar's program has a strong nationalist character. In Canada, it does not operate within the framework of the Canadian Zionist Federation.

Bnei Akiva (The Children of Rabbi Akiva), created in 1939, filled the void that existed for religious Zionist youth before Jewish day schools came into being. It currently runs a variety of Zionist-oriented activities, stresses educational programs with religious content, and attracts many religious children to its summer and winter camps.

The Habonim-Dror (The Builders-Freedom) movement promotes Socialist Zionism and social action, traditionally via kibbutzim and more recently through urban communes. The first Canadian branch was founded in Montreal in 1923 as an organization for men over twenty-one; the first under-eighteen lodge opened in 1946. Over the years, its activities have included debates, leadership-training groups, seminars, lectures, sports club, an orchestra, a choir, and dance groups. Today, Habonim-Dror runs seminars and educational groups.

Ideologically aligned with left-wing socialism and founded in 1913 in Galicia, Ha-Shomer Ha-Tzair is the oldest youth movement still in existence. Today its socialist origins are reflected in the collectivist nature of its activities, especially its summer camps (in Canada, Camp Shomna in Perth, Ontario). The group runs activities aimed at promoting the peace program and social justice in Israel and the world. An Aliya Kibbutz Desk is sponsored jointly with Ha Bonim—aimed at recruiting new immigrants—as is the Union of Progressive Zionist campus network.

Founded in 1917, Young Judaea is Canada's largest Zionist youth movement, active across the country from Halifax to Vancouver. Its ideology is apolitical and pluralistic. The group focuses on strengthening Jewish identity and emphasizes the centrality of Israel. One of its most illustrious graduates and founding president was Bernard Joseph—who, as Dov Yoseph, later became legal adviser to the Jewish Agency in Palestine, military governor of pre-state Jerusalem, member of the Knesset, and Israel's second minister of justice. Unlike other youth organizations that have their roots in Europe, Young Judaea has strong North American origins. Canadian Young Judaea's program include summer camps, educational activities and conferences, as well as community singsongs, Jewish festivals, social events, and athletic training.

Whether these organizations have a nationalist, socialist, religious, or secular orientation, they all share a common emphasis and focus: Jewish youth and Israel.

Canadian Zionist Youth Programs

The Israel Youth Program Centres were one of the key Zionist-oriented programs for youth in Canada in the 1980s and 1990s. Established through the initiative of Israeli *shlichim* to the Youth and Hehalutz Department of the Canadian Zionist Federation, the program focused on creating drop-in centres for Jewish youth as a way to renew enthusiasm for Zionism and Israel among the younger people.

The Israel Youth Program Centres and the Montreal Zionist Youth Council published booklets in an attempt to reach out to as many young people in the Jewish community as possible, encouraging Jewish youth to participate in programs from the various movements and to turn to the Israel Youth Program Centres for more general Israel-oriented activities. These centres, soon established in Jewish communities throughout Canada, provide summer youth programs in Israel, kibbutz visits, academic programs, and community outreach projects. In addition, the centres have Kibbutz Aliyah desks that distribute information about kibbutz programs as well as kibbutz-university programs with credits available to students for work and study on kibbutzim.

Members of Jewish youth organizations over the age of eighteen serve as group leaders and regional organizers, guided and assisted by *shlichim* brought from Israel. The *shlichim*, most of whom come from the kibbutzim and the Scout Movement, are indispensable. They work as instructors, educators, and leaders in youth clubs and have successfully reached out to Jewish Canadian youth over the years and instilled the desire to learn all about Israel and study its language, perhaps as part of preparation for personal aliyah.

Israel Summer Youth Programs, provided through the youth centres, have been operating in Canada since the 1970s. The programs, organized by the Youth and Hechalutz Department of the Canadian Zionist Federation and the World Zionist Organization, are designed to bring Canadian Jewish youth face to face with the reality of Israeli life. They serve as a bridge between Canada and Israel, while helping to create a bond among youth across Canada. The programs are intended to give Jewish youth of Canada a multi-faceted experience of life in Israel. Participants spend four weeks working on a kibbutz, followed by nineteen days of travel in the country. An alternative program, the Israel Summer Happening, features four weeks of camping and touring.

School and University-Based Programs

The Canadian Jewish community is a leader in offering quality Jewish education for elementary and high school students, then following up with effective university student organizations. Zionist youth activities are also carried on through Jewish day schools and after-school programs, which provide a general Jewish education with a special focus on Israel and Zionism. This approach reaches an overwhelming majority of the Jewish students in Canada who are eligible for such education.

Perhaps the most important form of support for Jewish and Zionist activity among young people in Canada are the Jewish student unions and Hillel organizations that exist on most university and college campuses. Supported by the Jewish federations, B'nai Brith, and other community organizations, these groups play a critical role in helping Jewish students reinforce their own commitment to Israel and advocate for the Jewish homeland in the face of anti-Israel pressures on campus.

Hillel: The Foundation for Jewish Campus Life—the largest Jewish campus organization in the world—began on the campus of the University of Illinois in 1923 and established its first affiliate outside the U.S. at Queen's University in Kingston, Ontario in 1942. The vision of the organization of student-run groups that now exists on campuses across Canada is to "inspire every Jewish student to make an enduring commitment to Jewish life"; its motto is "Wherever we stand, we stand with Israel."

In 1969, the North American Jewish Students' Network, affiliated with the World Union of Jewish Students, emerged to provide an international voice for Jewish students in the U.S. and Canada; ten years later, Network Canada was founded as a separate organization. In 2004, a new organization—the Canadian Federation of Jewish Students (CFJS), supported by the Canadian Council for Israel and Jewish Advocacy and UIA Federation Canada—was established to address the twenty-first-century issues that face Canadian Jewish students. The founding principles of the CFJS are to unite Jewish student groups across the country and advocate of their behalf; to connect them to Jewish and non-Jewish communities in Canada and Israel and around the world; and to help Canadian Jewish students build their sense of Jewish identity and their bond with Israel while at the same time valuing their Canadian ideals. In a myriad of ways, these various student organizations work to foster a strong communal identity and support for the State of Israel on college and university campuses across Canada.

11

Education

From its earliest beginnings in 1778, when Reverend David Jacob Cohen tutored the children of Montreal's Shearith Yisrael Congregation, to the extensive learning opportunities offered today, Jewish and Zionist education in Canada has undergone a variety of changes.

Zionist and Israel Education

From the beginning, Talmud Torahs, or Hebrew day schools, formed the backbone of Jewish education and were centres for Jewish community activities in Montreal, Ottawa, Toronto, Winnipeg, Edmonton, Calgary, and Vancouver. Today, a diverse mix of schools serve the Jewish community. Some schools are synagogue-sponsored, while others are independent. Some integrate Jewish and secular studies, in effect replacing the public school, and others are afternoon or Sunday schools that supplement public instruction. The language of instruction may be Hebrew, Yiddish, English, or French.

A significant number of Jewish children across the country, in both large and small communities, have participated in Jewish day schools and supplementary Jewish education programs. In 1990, for example, about 90 per cent of Jewish children in Toronto received some form of Jewish education, and a 1996 survey of the Montreal Jewish community showed that 73 per cent of adults had participated in various forms of organized Jewish education. In 2000, Morton Weinfeld wrote that "the level of formal Jewish education of Canadian Jewish children today is, on the whole, much greater than that of their Canadian-born parents or grandparents."

Few Jewish communities in the world can boast a Jewish-Hebrew educational system as extensive as that developed in Canada. The major cities of Canada (Montreal, Toronto, Hamilton, Winnipeg, and Vancouver) all have a rich tradition of Jewish educational opportunities. In 2004, in the greater Montreal area alone, there were twenty-five Jewish day schools, serving students from pre-kindergarten to high school, offering curricula ranging from secular Yiddishist to ultra-orthodox. In Metropolitan Toronto, there were twice as many schools, with a similarly impressive ideological range.

The day-school program uses textbooks developed in the United States or in Israel. In recent years, a curriculum originating in Montreal, Tal Selah, has been used more frequently. It covers language skills as well as topics and themes appropriate to Jewish education such as Jewish holidays, traditions, knowledge of Israel, and the Sabbath. The curriculum includes literature that Israeli children commonly read, which assists Canadian Jewish children in their understanding of both the life and language of Israel.

At many schools, students are encouraged to write to prominent Israelis, such as the prime minister, the president, and the mayor of Jerusalem. Israeli songs are commonly heard filtering out of the classrooms into the corridors of the schools, and the walls are usually adorned with the Israeli flag and portraits of prominent Israelis. The day schools celebrate all the Jewish holidays that fall within the school year, as well as Tu bi-Shevat, Yom Hazikaron and Yom Haatzmauth, and Yom Yerushalayim—all holidays reflecting Israel and its centrality to Jewish existence.

Jewish high schools in Canada offer a wide range of Israel-oriented programs as part of the basic curriculum for Grades 9, 10, 11, and 12. The various summer programs offer students a wide range of activities.

The summer programs in the two Montreal schools and Joseph Wolinsky Collegiate in Winnipeg offer students a variety of activities that encompass aspects of Israeli life. These courses are designed to provide students with some essential background on life in Israel to help them prepare for a visit to the country. After the students arrive in Israel, they spend time in specially designed educational programs geared to Diaspora students. After this, the students experience life on a kibbutz, do some forest preservation work in a JNF forest, go on archaeological digs, and participate in guided tours and hikes.

Special School/Community Programs

The Bible has served for millennia as the basis of Jewish identity and as the chronicle of Jewish experience. It is, therefore, most fitting that the Bible serves as a major component of Zionist education for youth.

For more than forty-five years, Jewish communities have participated in the International Bible Contest for Jewish youth, a highly popular contest for the children of Israel and the Diaspora, including Canada. Sponsored by the Department of Zionist Education of the Jewish Agency for Israel, along with local Jewish educational agencies, the contest encourages a love of Jewish text by inspiring the students to read the Bible carefully.

In Canada, the contest has two stages, regional and national. In the regional contest, hundreds of students, divided into three divisions based on age, write a test geared to their age groups. After this stage, approximately two to three hundred contestants continue on to the national stage. The national contest takes place over two days during which the children participate in oral and written work. The winners of the two older age groups go on to become Canada's representatives to the International Contest held in Israel every Independence Day.

The national contest involves cultural programs and an award ceremony and is co-sponsored by the Canadian Zionist Federation in Montreal, the Jewish Education Committee, the Winnipeg and Toronto Boards of Jewish Education, the Jewish National Fund, and the participating schools and students. It is the only educational event that gathers secular, Conservative, Reform, and Orthodox Jewish students together in an Israel-focused event.

Another activity that has increased in prominence in recent years is the March of the Living run by local Jewish communties. It is a subsidized program for Canadian youth between the ages of sixteen and eighteen that includes an in-depth preparatory seminar about the Holocaust, followed by a visit to Poland. From there, the group travels to Israel for ten days, where students can make the connection between the past and the present Jewish fight for survival.

In another initiative, the Youth and Chalutz Department of the Canadian Zionist Federation offers one-year programs for high school graduates, taught in English, at one of seven institutions of higher learning in Israel: Bar-Ilan University, Ben-Gurion University of the Negev, Haifa University, Technion-Haifa, Tel Aviv University, the Hebrew University in Jerusalem, and the Weizmann Institute of Science.

University-Based Activities

Canadians have figured prominently in the organization and ongoing functioning of all seven post-secondary institutions in Israel. The following are only some of the many notable examples.

The Canadian Technion Society was founded in 1958 by Samuel Bronfman, D. Lou Harris, Nicholas Munk, and Eugene Stearns. Its purpose is to educate Canadians about the importance of the Technion-Israel Institute of Technology in Haifa, which is dedicated to the study of science, high technology, medicine, engineering and architecture and plays an essential part in Israel's survival. Through the Society, Canadians such as Bernard Bloomfield, Peter Munk, Seymour Schulich, and David Azrieli generously continue that tradition and the Technion's Faculty of Architecture and Town Planning hosts the Morley Blankstein Academic Lectureship. The Canadian Society also encourages academic exchanges between Technion and Canadian universities, provides information to prospective Canadian students regarding courses of study at the Technion, and helps to raise funds to support the institution.

The Institute of Contemporary Jewry and the in-service teacher training program of its School of Education are located in the Faculty of Humanities of the Hebrew University in Jerusalem. Many Canadian professionals have had the opportunity to enhance their qualifications through the teacher-training program, facilitated by programs of the Canadian Zionist Federation.

Under the auspices of its Office of Academic Affairs, the Canadian Friends of Hebrew University promotes and provides financial assistance to Canadian youth who want to attend the Hebrew University's teaching programs for overseas students. In addition, there is a formal academic exchange program for both students and faculty involving the Hebrew University and the University of Toronto, McGill University, York University, Concordia University, Carleton University, University of Manitoba, University of Alberta, and University of British Columbia. Canadian Friends also serves as an intermediary between the governments of Canada and Israel. In 1978, the Program of Canadian Studies at the Hebrew University was established by the government of Canada and Ralph and Roz Halbert of Toronto to promote Canada-Israel academic exchanges, conferences, and research projects. The program has now been expanded to include the exchange of faculty between Canadian teaching hospitals and the Hebrew University's Faculty of Medicine.

Another society that has been established in Canada to support research in Israel is the Canadian Society for the Weizmann Institute, which has five faculties in the fields of physics, mathematics, chemistry, biophysics-biochemistry, and biology. The Canadian Society's goals include mobilizing support for research in Israel, arranging exchange professorships between the institute and Canadian universities, and the stimulation of interest in scientific research.

There are also chapters of Canadian Friends of Tel Aviv University, a group of Canadian Friends that has played a continuing role in the progress of the university. Its accomplishments include, among others, the Bronfman Project for Israel-Arab Research in the Shiloah Institute, the Nathan and Lily Silver Chair for Mathematical Analysis and Operator Theory, the establishment of the Annie and Marcel Adams Super Centre for the Study of the Brain, the David Azrieli School of Architecture, and the Overseas Student Program.

Canadian support and involvement is vital for the continued development of the Ben-Gurion University of the Negev, Haifa University, Bar-Ilan University, and the Bezalel Academy of Arts and Design, and another important institution is the Canada-Israel Foundation for Academic Exchanges. When it was established in 1973, it was intended to foster closer contacts between Israeli and Canadian institutions of higher learning and better understanding between Israeli and Canadian academics working in the humanities and the social sciences. What began as a modest program at Carleton University in Ottawa has grown to include every major Canadian and Israeli institution. Hundreds of senior Israeli and Canadian scholars have worked, travelled, and lectured widely under its auspices. It became the basis and forerunner for all other exchange activity.

Teacher Education

Two seminaries for the training of teachers, the Hebrew Teachers' Seminary in Montreal and the Jewish Teachers' Seminary of Canada, were established in 1946. Within three years, the two seminaries merged to form the Canadian Jewish Teachers' Seminary. While in the past there have been all too few qualified Jewish teachers, today initiatives at major Canadian post-secondary institutions, such as the Jewish Teacher Education program at York University in Toronto and the Jewish Teacher Training Program at McGill University in Montreal, have gone a long way toward addressing that need.

Where the shortfall still exists, many day schools have employed emissary teachers, *shlichim*, from Israel. The *shlichim* are trained and screened in Israel and usually work in Canadian schools for between two and five years. The teachers help to ensure the quality of Hebrew taught in Canadian schools and provide much of the impetus for advanced-level programming on Israel. Their constant rotation ensures that the schools' educational programs remain current and also encourages a change of personnel and the avoidance of burnout in some Judaica departments.

Representatives of the World Zionist Organization's two education departments—the Department for Education and Culture in the Diaspora and the Torah Education Department—also participate in Zionist and Jewish education by visiting schools on a regular basis, offering Israeli study materials, and providing timely advice to teachers.

Canadian Hebrew and Jewish studies teachers can participate in the Canadian Zionist Federation's summer institute, which allows them the opportunity to work with agencies in Israel and take part in the in-service training for teachers. These trips are well-funded by the Dr. Leon Aryeh Kronitz Memorial Scholarship Program.

CZF Educational Activities

To supervise ongoing educational activities and initiate new ones, the Canadian Zionist Federation has a national pedagogical council, which meets twice a year. It supervises the National Bible Contest, deals with educational themes that are being introduced to schools, studies teacher training programs in Israel, and maintains a policy of scholarship. The CZF and boards of education also organize a biennial teachers' conference to offer administrators, teachers, Jewish educators, and lay officers an opportunity to hear high-level speakers and meet in discussion groups on topics of mutual interest. The conference provides a setting for participants to share ideas and concerns about Jewish education in Canada—information booths set up by the World Zionist Organization, publishing houses, and the boards of Jewish education give teachers an opportunity to examine new educational materials.

From the early 1950s until the early 1980s, Keren Hatarbut (the Fund for Culture), a group made up of professionals and lay people, provided a wide range of options for those interested in learning Hebrew and Hebrew culture. The mainstay of the organization during this period was Chaim Maizel, who created Hebrew courses and programs in Montreal for twenty years and founded Camp Massad, where Jewish youth could spend the summer using Hebrew in their daily lives. Keren Hatarbut organization sponsored lectures and other adult educational events to enrich the knowledge of people on a variety of topics central to Israeli life.

Adult Education

The Canadian Zionist Federation plays a prominent role in adult education in Canada. It organizes, sponsors, and takes part in many events and activities that enable Canadians generally and Canadian Jews in particular to learn about Jewish history as well as contemporary events in Israel.

Hebrew *ulpanim* (intensive language programs) offered in a variety of community settings including schools, community centres and synagogues are just one aspect of the adult educational activities offered by Canadian Zionist Federation departments and regional offices. In addition, a couple of times a year seminars are held for the public that focus on Israel's defence, politics, and economy. The CZF contacts communities across the country to find out their needs and expectations for education. Communities are encouraged to take advantage of the scholar-in-residence program that offers a choice of speakers from Israel who discuss aspects of life in the country and the political circumstances of the Middle East that affect Israel.

The CZF sponsors annual events such as Israel Day, a fair organized annually by the Eastern Region of the federation, where people can obtain information about Zionist youth movements, volunteer organizations, and other programs and activities, and participate in a number of activities such as folk dancing, singalongs, and camel rides. The federation has information centres throughout Canada that provide videos, periodicals, books, and movies. As well, the *Canadian Zionist* newspaper reaches thousands of homes, bringing them information about Zionist activities across Canada and issues in Israel.

Other Jewish organizations such as Hadassah-WIZO provide educational opportunities in Canada as well. Hadassah-WIZO also supports schools and vocational training centres in Israel and preschool education for children of working mothers. Its members are exposed to adult education programs in conferences, seminars, and missions to Israel. Another organization working in this field is the Jewish National Fund, which is involved in direct work with teachers and students concerning Israel's agriculture, scientific development, and natural habitat. The organization has produced a number of audiovisual educational programs that are currently used in most Jewish day and afternoon schools.

In addition to the tremendous amount of material and courses generated by these community organizations, formal courses on Zionism, the Hebrew language, Israeli/Middle Eastern history, and related subjects are offered in many Canadian universities. At the same time, a very strong commitment on the part of adults to the State of Israel is manifested in the outstanding financial support given to Israeli institutions. Millions of dollars are given annually to Israeli institutes, yeshivot, schools, universities, and non-educational institutions. Two Canadians initiatives in post-secondary education in Israel are the Adams Fellowships, established in 2005 by Marcel Adams and the Israel Academy of Sciences and Humanities, which provide financial assistance to students in the exact sciences, mathematics, and the life sciences, and the Azrieli Fellows program, established in 2006, which supports graduate studies in the fields of interdisciplinary and applied sciences, education, and architecture.

Jewish Traditions and Zionism

Judaism was born and grew to maturity in the towns and countryside of ancient Israel, the birthplace of Jewish national identity. Consciously and unconsciously, the rituals and festivals of Judaism reflect those origins and the history of the Jewish people. As Jewish communities evolved in the various diasporas, such customs and practices reinforced the bonds between the community and its ancient home. This important affirmation was as true in the early diasporas of warm, Mediterranean Spain as it was later in the suffering communities in the European ghettos; it continues to be true to this very day in the Jewish communities of North America.

The very texture of prayers uttered in Canada reflects the seasons of Israel rather than the frigid zones of a country north of the forty-ninth parallel. In the time between Sukkot and Passover, when snow covers the countryside, Canadian Jews ask for rain—*mattar*. In April, when frost is still on the ground, congregations in synagogues in Montreal, Toronto, and Winnipeg prey for dew or *tal*. The words of the daily prayers build on this and in a formulaic fashion reflect the ancient yearning to return home to Zion, a yearning that is at the heart of Zionism. Phrases such as *uvneh yerushalayim irkha* (and thou shall rebuild Jerusalem your city), *chadesh yameinu kekedem* (renew our days as of old) and *shuvekha le-Zion* (return to Zion) daily reinforce the link to Israel, a link that is solemnly reaffirmed twice yearly in the phrase "Next year in Jerusalem!"

Festivals observed in day schools and afternoon schools, in places of worship and at home have consciously been used to create a bond, a sense of kinship. On some levels the link is simple and clear, as in Tu bi-Shevat, the Jewish nature festival known as the New Year for Trees, an occasion on which successive generations of children have sold "tags" for the Jewish National Fund. Similarly, the ties flourish during the religious-based national festivals such as Jerusalem Day or Israel Independence Day.

In other cases, the link is subtle and implicit, but no less powerful. Thus, Hanukkah, the celebration of an ancient victory, has modern implications that are stressed in school and during prayer. Passover, Shavuot, and Sukkot are more than agricultural holidays that mark the seasons and crops of Israel; they are symbols of national redemption that teach contemporary lessons.

Finally, the most awe-inspiring holiday of all, Yom Kippur, the Day of Atonement, becomes not only a time of personal accounting but also one of national reckoning. It is no accident that Kol Nidre night traditionally has become the night on which pledges are made for Israel. It is said that "good deeds" can help redeem the new year. Obviously, work on behalf of the Jewish home has become the best of all "good deeds."

Centres of Communal Mobilization

Communal mobilization begins with education, and synagogues and temples serve as centres for lifelong education—both formal and informal, for both youth and adults.

Education for youth in places of worship is usually provided through day schools or afternoon schools. These locales, together with community-based schools (such as those affiliated with federations) and independent schools (such as the Solomon Shechter or Lubavitch schools) form the core of formal youth education. The centrality of Israel, which forms part of the focus of Jewish worship, is also reflected in the formal synagogue and temple-based schools.

School curriculum and activities offer numerous opportunities for intellectually mobilizing the Jewish communities throughout Canada on behalf of Israel. This impetus is facilitated by the various national and international Jewish and Zionist organizations that see education as one of their primary functions.

The daily *sheur* (lesson) taught by the rabbi before prayer, the lesson on Shabbat before afternoon prayers, *minchah*, Shabbat sermons, holiday sermons, public lectures, adult education programs, seminars —all are part of perhaps the most extensive and integrated program for popular education Canada has ever known. And some of the country's larger places of worship—in Montreal, Ottawa, Toronto, Winnipeg, or Vancouver—have Institutes of Jewish Studies with course offerings and programs that rival those of neighbouring universities. And in times of need and crisis, synagogues and temples mobilize the Jewish "street," or public, in a way that no institution can. Whether the places of worship are the basis for letter-writing campaigns, emergency fundraising, or demonstrations on behalf of Russian or Syrian Jewry, they provide the underpinnings for communal mobilization on behalf of the Zionist movement.

PART III:

Canadian Zionism: Its People

The ABCs of Canadian Zionism

W HEN A LIST IS COMPILED of those who have provided crucial leadership within the Canadian Zionist family, it is immediately apparent how many thousands of people have made important contributions to Zionism, the State of Israel, the world Jewish community, and Jewish life in Canada. Their fundraising and their endless hours of labour on behalf of their people and the right of the Jewish people to a flourishing homeland have been and will continue to be tremendous.

That being said, it also becomes apparent how difficult it is—within the confines of a book that attempts to cover such a breadth of time and material—to mention all the individuals who make up the "alphabet" of Canadian Zionism. So many people have worked and continue to work with extraordinary devotion behind the scenes as well as on the front lines. This chapter, therefore, can mention only some of those who have made a difference to the lives of their fellow Jews, their fellow Canadians, and the rebirth, support, and development of the State of Israel as the realization of Zionism. The authors are well aware that the list of people included here cannot help but be incomplete. Nonetheless, in the spirit of honouring the contributions made by the leaders of Canadian Zionism—along with the untold and often unsung efforts of scores of their fellow Zionists—what follows is at least an overview of the men and women who formed the ABCs—the building blocks—of Zionism in Canada.

Marcel Adams (b. 1920)

Born Marcel Abramowicz in Romania, Marcel Adams escaped to Turkey in 1944, with the help of the Jewish Agency, and then wended

David Azrieli with Teddy Kollek, mayor of Jerusalem from 1965 to 1993 and founder of the Jerusalem Foundation.

his way to Israel, where he fought in the War of Independence. He arrived in Canada in 1951, followed shortly thereafter by his Romanian-born wife, Annie. Initially based in Quebec City, then in Montreal, he built a commercial real estate empire by developing shopping malls.

In 2005, Adams announced the establishment of a major fellowship program that offers generous annual support to ten of Israel's brightest doctoral students in the natural and exact sciences for up to four years. Endowed at $20 million, the Adams Fellowship Program is administered by the Israel Academy of Sciences and Humanities in Jerusalem.

Marcel and Annie Adamses' previous major gifts were to Tel Aviv University, creating the Adams Institute for Business Management Systems and the Adams Super Center for Brain Research.

David Azrieli (b. 1922)

Born in Makow, Poland, David Azrieli escaped to the Soviet Union in 1939, just ahead of the invading Nazis. Surviving in the USSR for almost three years, he made his way to British-mandate Palestine in late 1942, where he studied architecture at the Technion-Israel Institute of Technology, joined the Haganah, served as an officer in the Seventh Brigade during Israel's 1948 War of Independence, and participated in the liberation of Jerusalem.

In 1954, he moved to Montreal, where he earned a BA from the Thomas More Institute (Université de Montreal). David Azrieli launched a career in design, real estate development, and property management in the mid-1950s; in 2007 he completed the Azrieli Center and Towers, the largest mixed-use commercial complex in the Middle East. In 1997, he earned his Masters of Architecture from Carleton University.

David Azrieli has founded numerous Canadian and Israeli institutions in the fields of architecture and education and made endowments to universities in Canada, Israel, and the U.S. in various fields, notably in Jewish studies and Holocaust education. He has, for example, endowed a chair in architecture and town planning, a computer lab, and the library at the Technion-Israel Institute of Technology in Haifa. He has served as president of the Canadian Zionist Federation, the Canadian Technion

Society, and the Jerusalem Foundation of Canada. In 1989, he established the Azrieli Foundation to support and promote initiatives in education (Jewish and secular), architecture and design, Holocaust commemoration, scientific and medical research, and the arts; the Foundation operates the Holocaust Survivor Memoir Publishing Program, the Azrieli Institute for Educational Empowerment, and the Azrieli Fellows Program. He has received five honorary degrees, the Order of Canada, the Chevalier of the Ordre Nationale du Québec, and in 2002 was invested as a Ne'eman, or Honorary Trustee, of the City of Jerusalem.

Harry Batshaw (1902–1984)

Harry Batshaw was a prominent Montreal lawyer, educated at McGill University and the Sorbonne, who was appointed to the Superior Court Bench of Quebec in 1950, the first Jew to be appointed to a high court in Canada.

Active in a number of Jewish causes, Batshaw served as president of the Canadian Young Judaea from 1931 to 1934. He was subsequently secretary of the Baron de Hirsch Institute, co-chairman of the Canadian Council of Christians and Jews, honorary vice chairman of the Zionist Organization of Canada, and the founder and president of the Canadian Friends of the Alliance Israélite Universelle.

When the United Zionist Council established a public relations committee under Batshaw's chairmanship in 1941, the first thing he did was form a pro-Palestine committee made up of Jews and Christians friendly to the Zionist cause. In late 1944 he worked with David Rome of the Canadian Jewish Congress to garner support in Quebec for the Jewish cause. In addition to his advocacy work specifically on behalf of Jews in both Canada and Israel, Harry Batshaw was a founding director of the Canadian Human Rights Foundation and founding chairman of the International Law Association's committee on human rights. A year before his death in 1984, a foundation was established in his name to help subsidize the Karem Institute, which trained secondary school humanities teachers in Israel.

Lavy Becker was one of Canadian Jewry's most distinguished voices, continuing to make himself heard internationally well into his nineties. His career ranged from aiding survivors of the Holocaust in Europe, to playing a management role in the family's business in Montreal, to working for the Jewish community and Israel through Canadian Jewish Congress and the Montreal Jewish Federation, to helping to found three Montreal synagogues. He concluded his community career as a rabbi.

(Canadian Jewish Congress National Archives, Montreal)

Lavy Becker (1905–2004)

Lavy Becker was a rabbi and social worker in Boston, Detroit, New Haven, and New York from 1930 to 1947, who was very active in the Reconstructionist Branch of Conservative Judaism.

During the Second World War, he was a director of the United Service Organizations–Jewish Welfare Board (USO-JWB) program for servicemen in New England and served as director of the Joint Distribution Committee in the American Zone in occupied Germany. After the war, Becker was one of the founders and the first rabbi of the Reconstructionist Synagogue of Montreal, a vice-president of the Canadian Jewish Congress, director of the Vanier Institute of the Family, and chairman of the Centennial Interfaith Conference.

Lavy Becker continued to be active in Jewish community affairs well into his nineties and served as member and chair of the World Jewish Congress's Committee on Remote Jewish Communities.

Hyman Bessin (1910–1978)

Hyman Bessin was the second president of the Canadian Zionist Federation, succeeding the founding president, Samuel Chait, and holding office from 1970 to 1972.

Born in Ottawa, Bessin became president of the Ottawa Jewish Community Council and headed up the community's United Jewish Appeal. He focused on Jewish education—serving as national president of Canadian Friends of Bar Ilan University. He was also involved with the Canadian Foundation for Jewish Education and Yeshiva University. He was treasurer of the Mizrachi Organization of Canada.

Myer Bick (b. 1944)

Myer Bick played several important roles in the strengthening of Canadian ties with Israel. His first formal involvement was during the period from 1963 to 1967, when he served as national director of the Student Zionist Organization of Canada. He served as national director of the Israel Peace Corps (Sherut La'am of Canada) from 1967 through to 1970, and as national program director of the Canadian Zionist Federation and editor of the *Canadian Zionist* magazine.

In 1972, Bick transferred his communication skills to the Canada-Israel Committee, working for seven years to heighten understanding of Israel's difficult position in the Middle East. He also played an important role vis-à-vis higher education in Israel, serving as vice-chairman of the Board of Governors of Tel Aviv University, working closely with Jack Cummings—the first Canadian to chair the university's board—from 1982 to 1985.

Myer Bick also served as president of Canadian Friends of Tel Aviv University and the Canada-Israel Foundation for Academic Exchanges. In 2001, he became president and CEO of the Sir Mortimer B. Davis Jewish General Hospital in Montreal.

Bernard Bloomfield (1904–1984)

Bernard Bloomfield was born in Montreal and educated at McGill University. He made his mark in both the Zionist world, serving on the boards of numerous Israel-oriented organizations and institutions, and in the business community. He was national president for the Canadian Histadrut Campaign, the Jewish National Fund of Canada, and the Canadian Technion Society. He served as a governor of the Sir Mortimer B. Davis Jewish General Hospital, sat on the board of the hospital's Lady Davis Medical Research Institute, as well as the boards of Hebrew University, the Technion, St. Francis Xavier University, the Tel Aviv Museum, the Canadian Friends of Hebrew University, the Canada-Israel Maritime League, Jewish Immigrant Aid Services of Canada, the Canada-Israel Chamber of Commerce and Industry, and the Eldee (Lady Davis) Foundation, established by Henrietta Davis, the first wife of Imperial Tobacco founder, Sir Mortimer B. Davis. With his brother Louis, Bernard Bloomfield managed the foundation and used the proceeds to build sixteen of the more than one hundred Amal vocational high schools in Israel. His wife, Neri (see below) has also been very active in the Canadian Zionism Federation. Bloomfield received numerous awards and honours for his community service.

In addition to his community work, Bloomfield served as president of the Israel Continental Oil Company, which drilled for oil in Israel from 1954 to 1967, the New Continental Oil Company of Canada, and the Canadian Manufacturers Sales Company. He was honorary consul general of the Republic of Korea from 1969 until his death. In 1950, he wrote *Israel Diary*, an account of his first trip to Israel.

Neri Bloomfield (b. 1924)

Like her husband, Bernard, Neri Bloomfield has been prominent in numerous Zionist and Jewish organizations. Born in Bucharest, Romania, and educated in London, she immigrated to Canada in 1941, where she has been a leading fundraiser and active volunteer associated with cultural and academic institutions in Canada and Israel. She has been a member of the International Board of the Hebrew University since 1971—from which she received an honorary doctorate—and is a member of the Board of Governors of the Technion.

Within the Canadian Zionist movement, Neri Bloomfield served as the youngest national president of the Hadassah-WIZO Organization of Canada from 1972 to 1976, the first woman president of the Canadian Zionist Federation from 1984 to 1987, and the first woman president of the Jewish National Fund of Canada from 1988 to 1991. She was also a member of the Board of Directors of Bank of Hapoalim (Canada)—up to that point the only woman director in the bank's history. In 1996, she chaired the committee organizing the Canadian celebration of Jerusalem 3000. At the time of publication she is serving as president of the Lady Davis Research Institute of the Jewish General Hospital in Montreal.

Allan Bronfman (1895–1980)

Allan Bronfman, younger brother of Samuel, played an important role in helping to build the family empire and was active in many community endeavours. He became president of a Jewish orphanage in 1921, led a fundraising campaign to build a Jewish hospital in Montreal from 1927 to 1934, joined the military reserves during the Second World War, and headed up a recruiting drive in Montreal for the enlistment of Jews in the armed forces. He received the Legion of Honour from the French government in 1949 for donating tons of wheat to the hungry town of Troyes after the war.

Allan Bronfman was a founder and strong supporter of Canadian Friends of Hebrew University. He was also the only person to serve as general chairman of two Combined Jewish Appeals in Montreal.

Andrea Bronfman (1945–2006)

Andrea Brett Morrison, wife of Jewish philanthropist Charles Rosner Bronfman, grew up in family committed to the rebirth of Israel. Her father, Hyman Morrison, served as president of the United Palestine Appeal in Britain, and her American mother, Doris, also shared the Zionist dream. As children, Andrea (Andy) and her sister, Marcia (Kappy), listened as their parents discussed Israeli developments in their home with such notables as David Ben-Gurion, Golda Meir, and Shimon Peres—all of whom served as prime ministers of the Jewish state. She immigrated to Canada and in 1982 married Jewish philanthropist Charles Bronfman (see below).

Bronfman's numerous Israel and Jewish-related activities included co-founding the Group of 35, comprised of thirty-five dynamic women aged thirty-five who campaigned vigorously to pressure the Soviet Union to allow Soviet Jews to emigrate to Israel. She organized the travelling exhibition *A Coat of Many Colours: Two Centuries of Jewish Life in Canada*, which wound up at the Jewish Museum in New York after a national Canadian tour.

With her husband, Bronfman became a major force in generating programs building Jewish identity, with Israel at the centre. Their efforts culminated in co-founding of birthright israel, a program that brings young people to Israel for short term stays for free. In 2003, she founded the Association of Israel's Decorative Arts (AIDA) to introduce Israeli artists to North American galleries and collectors and make North Americans more aware of decorative arts in Israel.

Charles Bronfman (b. 1931)
Charles Bronfman, son of Samuel, made his name in his father's company, Seagram Canada, where he held positions on the executive committee as co-chairman, vice-president, president, and chairman.

Among his many Jewish community activities, Bronfman has served as honorary president of the United Israel Appeal of Canada, president of the Allied Jewish Community Services of Montreal, director of the Canadian Council of Christians and Jews, and chairman of the Charles Bronfman Foundation (CRB) and the Andrea and Charles Bronfman Philanthropies. He also served as chairman of Claridge-Israel Incorporated, Koors Industries Limited, director of both the Power Corporation of Canada and E. I. Du Pont de Nemours and Company, and was once the owner of the Montreal Expos.

Among the many programs and institutions that the CRB supports are Israel's seven universities, the alliance of Educational Programs in Israel, the Karev Program for Educational Involvement, the Israel Museum, the Israel Philharmonic Orchestra, and birthright israel, the program he co-founded with his wife, Andrea (see above), that generously supports youth who want to visit Israel.

Samuel Bronfman (1889–1971)
Samuel Bronfman, one of the most important members of the Montreal Jewish community, made a name for himself as a powerful businessman through the development of Seagram enterprises and as a leading finan-

cial supporter of Jewish causes. Late in 1938, he assumed the presidency of the Canadian Jewish Congress and from this position mobilized the upper levels of the Jewish community, the Zionist movement, and a major portion of the Jewish working class in a common cause.

His work in strengthening the Canadian Jewish community during the war was instrumental in setting the stage for greater efforts in the postwar period. In particular, Bronfman helped raise considerable sums of money during the Six Day War in 1967.

The distinguished Canadian historian Michael Marrus has written about the elder Bronfman in his biography *Mr. Sam:*

> As a Jewish leader, Sam riveted on a few fundamentals—Jewish responsibility for other Jews, for which he set the highest personal standards with his own philanthropy; a simplified notion of Jewish unity, for which he appealed in innumerable contexts; and a dignified Jewish standing in the non-Jewish world, for which he posed an example as an active contributor to his own, Canadian society…To immigrant Jews who hungered for material success he provided a model of how Jews could succeed in Canadian society while remaining intensely Jewish. To a Jewish community with an only rudimentary national existence in 1939, he brought a flair for public relations, a sense of the importance of administration, and an ambitious programme of fundraising. As in the liquor industry, he was deeply concerned with status—and he managed to give Canadian Jewry, in its public face at least, a position of authority and respect on the national plane.

Gordon Brown (1909–2001)

Also known as "Mr. Campaign," Gordon Brown made sure every one of his eighteen grandchildren and sixteen great-grandchildren visited Israel before they turned thirteen.

Born in Ukraine, Brown arrived in Montreal in 1919, aged eleven, after experiencing the 1917 Russian Revolution. He served as general chairman of the Montreal Combined Jewish Appeal in 1961 and continued to take an active part in succeeding campaigns, serving also as president of the Allied Jewish Community Service from 1967 to 1969 and as honorary president and then honourary chairman of Combined Jewish Appeal. He raised the funds to build the Gordon Brown Canada House in Jerusalem, where new immigrants spend a month while seeking a job and a home in Israel. He retired from his business in 1970 and

went to work full-time for the Jewish community, and
particularly Israel. In all, he made 125 trips to Israel
and lived there for extended periods. He was a Fellow
of Hebrew University of Jerusalem. He was named to
the Order of Canada in 1996.

The Toronto Negev Dinner
in 1985 honours Donald Carr
(right) and his extraordinary
wife, Judy Carr, who organized the rescue of hundreds of
Syrian Jews. Her dramatic
story is told by the Canadian
historian Harold Troper in his
book *The Rescuer*. The presentation was by Dr. A. A.
Epstein.

(*Canadian Jewish News*   Graphic Artists
photo)

Donald Carr (b. 1928)

Born in London, England, Donald Carr has held important posts in the Jewish community and in the Canadian
legal and business communities. He served in executive
positions in numerous organizations and businesses,
including vice chairman and director of the Bank Leumi Le-Israel, president and director of the *Canadian Jewish News*, vice chairman of the
Canadian Jewish Congress Ontario Region, honorary counsel for both
the Canadian Friends of Haifa University and the United Israel Appeal
of Canada, and president of the United Jewish Welfare Fund of Toronto
and the Community Hebrew Academy of Toronto.

Carr, a former senior partner in the Toronto law firm Goodman
Carr, has also held the directorship of such companies as McDonald's
of Canada, Edper Enterprises, and the Oshawa Group.

Samuel Chait (1904–1982)

Born in London, England, Montreal lawyer Samuel Chait, Q.C., was
a major figure in Canadian Jewish leadership. His first efforts on
behalf of Zionism were at McGill University where he served on the
executive of the Maccabean Circle, the organization preceding the
Hillel Foundation on campuses.

He was founding president of the Canadian Zionist Federation,
the organization that succeeded the Zionist Organization of Canada.
The new organization turned fundraising for Israel over to the federations and instead focused on education. Chait occupied the
presidency from 1967—the year of Israel's pivotal Six Day War—to
1970, when he turned the gavel over to Ottawa's Hy Bessin. Chait
oversaw the period of transition between the ZOC and the CZF.

Rabbi Zvi Hirsch Cohen (1862–1950)

Born in Lithuania, Rabbi Zvi Hirsch Cohen received his rabbinical
ordination in Vilna and Volozhin. In 1889 he came to Montreal,
where he became one of the most important pioneer Zionist leaders at
the local, regional, and international levels. He organized the Central

Rabbi Zvi Hirsch Cohen, president of the Montreal Council of Orthodox Rabbis, raised hundreds of thousands of dollars to aid Jews in distress.

War Sufferers Relief Society during the First World War, raising hundreds of thousands of dollars to aid Jews in distress, in both Europe and Palestine. Author of many learned articles on religion, Rabbi Cohen was dean of the Canadian Rabbinate and president of the Montreal Council of Orthodox Rabbis; in this capacity he opened the first session of Canadian Jewish Congress with a prayer in 1919. He was treasurer on the first executive of the Jewish Immigrant Aid Society, established in Montreal in 1920; founded the Jewish Community Council of Montreal (Va'ad Ha'ir) and Talmud Torah School; was active in the Mizrachi organization of Orthodox Zionists and the Ukrainian War Orphans Society; and served on the executive of the Federation of Jewish Philanthropies.

Lazarus Cohen (1844–1914)

Lazarus Cohen played a significant role in the early days of the Canadian Zionist movement. In 1892, he was a founder and served as the treasurer for the Society Hovevei Zion of Montreal, Canada's first Zionist organization. In the following year, Cohen led a delegation to New York to investigate the possibility of assisting Jewish settlement in Palestine. His persistence in this endeavour met with success and a sum of over 24,000 francs was sent to Hovevei Zion headquarters in Paris to purchase land in Palestine and support Jewish settlement there. In 1891, Lazarus Cohen also served as president of Congregation Shaar Hashomayim in Montreal.

Lyon Cohen (1868–1937)

In 1897, Lyon Cohen, the son of Lazarus (see above), co-founded Canada's first Anglo-Jewish newspaper, the *Jewish Times*, with S. W. Jacobs. Cohen also served as founding president of the Canadian Jewish Congress in 1919. He later served as president, and in other executive capacities of the Federation of Zionist Societies of Canada, the Jewish Colonization Association, the Baron de Hirsch Institute, Jewish Immigrant Aid Services, the United Talmud Torahs of Montreal, the Shaar Hashomayim Congregation, and the Montefiore Club.

A well-known industrialist and businessman, Lyon Cohen was the president of the Freedman Company, one of Canada's largest wholesale clothing manufacturers.

Maxwell Cohen (1910–1998)

Maxwell Cohen was a professor of law at McGill University, a judge, and Canada's first Jewish Dean of Law. He served as Canada's representative at the World Court and on many commissions of inquiry, including the Minister of Justice's Special Committee on Hate Propaganda.

Cohen served as Canadian chairman for the International Joint Commission. He also chaired both the Public Relations Committee of the Zionist Organization of Canada and the Foreign Affairs Committee of the Canadian Jewish Congress. He was an honorary legal adviser for Canada-Israel Securities.

Maxwell Cohen received numerous awards, including the Humanitarian Award of the Council of Christians and Jews (1969), the John Read Gold Medal of the Canada Council on International Law (1979), the Columbia University Wolfgang Friedmann Memorial Award (1981), a Distinguished Service Award of the Manitoba Bar Association (1984), and the President's Award of the Canadian Bar Association (1986). His writings included articles in international

Maxwell Cohen in Montreal in 1969 with some of his students. The dean of McGill Law School was a brilliant spokesman for Israel.

(McGill University Archives)

journals, pamphlets, and books on subjects as diverse as public international law, the law of outer space, the Canadian Constitution and federalism, labour law, and legal education, as well as nuclear, environmental, and Arctic concerns.

Irwin Cotler (b. 1940)

A law professor at McGill University, Irwin Cotler, has been an eloquent voice for Israel, World Jewry, and international human rights. A member of Parliament since 1999, Cotler served as justice minister and as the Attorney General of Canada from 2003 to 2006.

Cotler has served as counsel to many prisoners of conscience, including Natan Sharansky, who was imprisoned by the Soviet Union in the 1970s and 1980s for his Jewish activism. Appointed to the Order of Canada in 1991, *Maclean's* magazine has called him the "counsel for the oppressed."

For more than thirty years, he has lectured in both Israel and Arab countries, encouraging dialogue between Israel and the Palestinian Arabs. He negotiated an agreement among the justice ministers of Egypt, Jordan, Israel, and the Palestinian Authority to take part in the first Joint Justice Forum. In 2003, he negotiated the freedom of the Arab democracy activist Saad Ibrahim, imprisoned by the Egyptian government.

Cotler frequently addresses the dangerous new perils facing Israel and the Jewish people in the early twenty-first century. At a 2007 conference in Jerusalem, Cotler told the audience, "Not since the Nazi menace rose to annihilate European Jewry in 1938 have the Jewish people faced the threat that confronts them today." He then called for the indictment of Iranian president Mahmoud Ahmadinejad for incitement to genocide. Also in 2007, the Canadian Zionist Federation awarded him the Jerusalem Prize.

Jack Cummings (1922–1995)

Jack Cummings played a strong leadership role both in the Montreal Jewish community and on behalf of Israel. While he generously supported Ben-Gurion University and the Canadian Society for the Weizmann Institute of Science, Cummings was particularly committed to Israel's largest institution of higher learning—Tel Aviv University. He was the only Canadian to serve as chairman of TAU's International Board, holding that position for six years. At the time of his death, he was honorary chairman of the university's International

Board of Governors. The Cummings family created the Cummings Center for Russian and Eastern European Studies at TAU in 1971.

Jack Cummings was a co-founder of the *Canadian Jewish News* and founding chairman of the newspaper's Montreal editorial board.

Maxwell Cummings (1898–2001)

Maxwell Cummings was born in Saint John, New Brunswick, and during his 103 years made exceptional contributions to the Jewish people in Canada, internationally, and in Israel. Cummings moved with his family to Montreal in 1911, and at age twelve went into the shoe business with his older brother, Nathan. While Nathan moved to the United States and became a major figure in American industry, Maxwell remained in Montreal and went into real estate, developing Canada's first open-air pedestrian mall, the Norgate Shopping Centre in St. Laurent, Quebec. He was a pioneer in the construction of low-cost housing.

In 1973 Maxwell Cummings built Montreal's first dedicated Federation CJA building—Cummings House, now called Cummings Square. He also gave generously to the Jewish National Fund, most of Israel's major universities, to three Montreal universities—Université de Montreal, McGill University, and Concordia University—the Montreal Museum of Fine Arts, and numerous other organizations. Evidence of his support for Israeli institutions shows in the many prestigious entities that bear his name: the Maxwell Cummings Family Chair for Mediterranean History and the Maxwell and Queenie Cummings Plaza and Auditorium at Ben-Gurion University, and the Maxwell Cummings Family Chair for Mediterranean Culture and History and the Maxwell Cummings Professor of Modern European History at Tel Aviv University.

Maxwell Cummings was made a member of the Order of Canada and Grand Officier de l'Ordre national du Québec in 1978.

Clarence de Sola (1858–1920)

Clarence de Sola, son of renowned rabbi Abraham de Sola of Shearith Israel synagogue in Montreal and the first Jewish professor to teach Hebrew at McGill University, was a founder and the first president of the Federation of Zionist Societies of Canada from 1899 to 1919. During his leadership, Zionism began to spread quickly across Canada, reaching beyond Montreal, Toronto, Winnipeg, and Vancouver. He proudly held the federation up as a model for Zionists in other countries to follow.

De Sola ensured that Zionist activity centred on three priorities: fundraising, education, and improving relations between Jews and gentiles. He made the federation the first national representative organization, and his presidency was a period of general goodwill toward the Zionist cause.

De Sola's work outside the Zionist movement included serving as the Belgian consul in Montreal from 1904 to 1919. As a businessman, he was president and director of several transatlantic steamship companies.

Betty Dubiner (1913–1995)

Betty Dubiner, a pioneer in the fields of social welfare and charity, was one of the founders of the Soldiers Welfare Society and the Ilanshil Polio Organization, now known as ILAN—Israel Foundation for Handicapped Children. It serves the emotional and educational needs of about 15,000 children with neuro-muscular disabilities.

Dubiner made an enormous contribution to the State of Israel by setting up the first voluntary welfare organization administered along North American lines. It was also the first welfare organization founded outside the framework of facilities provided by the government of Israel. She also organized the first summer camps for handicapped children, initiated a voluntary program for polio immunization, organized the first March of Dimes campaign in Israel, and founded the ILAN Sport Centre for the Disabled. With her husband, Sam (see below), Betty was active in Canada in Betar and supported the Irgun through the Canadian League for a Free Palestine. The couple made aliyah in 1950.

Sam Dubiner (1914–1994)

Sam Dubiner was extremely active as a businessman in Israel after he and his wife, Betty (see above), moved to Israel in 1950. In 1949, he had built the first approved enterprise by a foreign investor in Israel— a factory that began producing precision tools and dies in B'nei-Brak. Dubiner subsequently opened numerous other industries, such as Zinkal, Jerusalem Pencils, Jerusalem Ball Point Pens, Amgo Containers, and the Kalit Wire Factory. In these enterprises, he introduced many innovations that were widely adopted and improved industrial productivity in the State of Israel. He was a founder of the Foreign Investors Association, which co-operated with the Israeli government to improve conditions, change laws, and create new laws to encourage foreign investment in Israel. In addition, he organized the Citrus Growers Association.

Before making aliyah, Sam and Betty Dubiner had been active in the Canadian League for a Free Palestine. In the late 1950s and early 1960s, Dubiner began to collect, research, and write books, as well as produce films on the discovery of Amlash art in a small village in northwestern Iran. The Dubiners' contribution to the arts in Israel is extensive.

Benjamin Dunkelman (1913–1997)

Ben Dunkelman fought for Canada in the Second World War in the Queen's Own Rifles regiment and was awarded the Distinguished Service Order in June 1945. Following the war, he became a public relations officer for the Zionist Organization of Canada and chairman of the Haganah Committee of Canada.

During the War of Independence, Dunkelman assisted in recruiting and fundraising for the Israeli forces. He fought heroically in key engagements, including Operation Nachshon and Operation Maccabi, and was commander of the Seventh Brigade. After the war, he was involved in the training and reorganization of the Israel armed forces and the creation of a model code of military law.

Ben Dunkelman eventually returned to his family's business in Toronto, but chaired the second Israel Bonds Campaign and made regular trips back to Israel. He is the author of *Dual Allegiance: An Autobiography*, published in 1976.

Joseph N. Frank (1906–1983)

Born in Manchester, England, Joe Frank was four years old when his family immigrated to Montreal. His earliest leadership Zionist role was as national president of Young Judaea in 1936; he had become a Young Judaean at age twelve. In 1940, he became national president of the Zionist Order of Habonim, and in 1942 he chaired the United Palestine Appeal in Montreal.

Joe Frank was president of the Zionist Organization of Canada from 1962 to 1964, and prior to that had served thirteen years as national treasurer. He also served as national treasurer of the Jewish National Fund for eleven years, from 1955 to 1966, and was honoured at the Negev Dinner in Montreal in 1963.

Frank supported higher education in Israel, was a founder of Bar Ilan University, a governor of both the Hebrew University and the

Following in his parents' footsteps, Lawrence Freiman served as national president of the Zionist Organization of Canada from 1958 to 1960.

(Canadian Jewish Congress National Archives, Montreal)

Weizmann Institute of Science, and a founder of the Canadian Society for the Weizmann Institute.

Archibald Jacob (A. J.) Freiman
(1880–1944)

Archibald Freiman was born Aharon Yaacov in Lithuania and came to Canada with his family at age thirteen. He and his wife, Lillian (see below), became important Zionist leaders in Canada between the First and Second World War. Prior to serving as chairman of the Federation of Zionist Organizations of Canada from 1919 to 1944, Freiman was the head of the Million Dollar Campaign for the Relief of Jewry in Europe.

In the autumn of 1924, he founded the Canadian Keren Hayesod Campaign that revolutionized the concept of Zionist fundraising in Canada. This campaign assisted in the construction of an infrastructure in Palestine for the *chalutzim*. Through the Jewish National Fund, Freiman encouraged Canadian Jews to raise enough money—US$1 million—to buy land for a Canadian *moshav*. One of the resulting 1927 settlements was named Moshav Bitan Aharon—after Archibald—and another was named Moshav Havatzelet Hasharon—for Lillian.

Freiman was also the founder and president of A. J. Freiman Ltd., an Ottawa department store.

Lawrence Freiman (1909–1986)

Lawrence Freiman, son of Archibald and Lillian Freiman (see above and below), became president of his father's company, and served as president of the Zionist Organization of Canada from 1958 to 1960. Among his initiatives as ZOC president, Freiman and Sam Bronfman led the first National Canadian Leadership Mission to Israel in 1960 in answer to an invitation from Israeli prime minister David Ben-Gurion. The trip provided an opportunity for a select group of leaders of the Canadian Jewish community to be briefed by prominent Israelis on social and economic planning in Israel.

Freiman was active in the Jewish community of Ottawa, where he served as president of the Jewish Community Council. He also served in 1967, the year of Canada's centenary, as chairman of the committee that established Ottawa's National Arts Centre.

Freiman was named to the Order of Canada in 1967.

Lillian Freiman (1885–1940)

Lillian Freiman was a community leader and executive member of the Women's International Zionist Organization and president of Canadian Hadassah-WIZO from 1919 to 1940. Under her leadership, many new Hadassah chapters opened across Canada.

Lillian Freiman worked tirelessly on behalf of Jewish children who became orphans as a result of the First World War. As a result of these efforts, she became known as "Mama Freiman." In the 1930s, as Jews throughout Europe faced increasing threats of persecution, she led the call for Canadian Jews to open their homes to the Jews of Europe, especially the children.

In 1934, her charitable work was honoured when she was named an officer of the Order of the British Empire. With her husband, Archibald (see above), she was a major figure in Canadian Zionism in the inter-war years.

Michael Garber (1892–1977)

Early in his career, Michael Garber wrote a weekly column in the *Canadian Jewish Chronicle* under the pseudonym "Calumnist." He went on to become a barrister and solicitor and a prominent Montreal Jewish community leader.

Garber served as president of the Zionist Organization of Canada from 1956 to 1958 and the Canadian Jewish Congress from 1962 to 1968. During the period from 1955 to 1959, he was a city alderman for Westmount, Quebec.

Philip G. Givens (1922–1995)

Mayor of Toronto from 1963 to 1966, member of Parliament from 1968 to 1971, and two-term member of the Ontario Legislature from 1971 to 1977, Philip Givens campaigned vigorously for Zionist causes. He served as president of the newly constituted Canadian Zionist Federation in

Michael Garber (right) with Nahum Goldmann (left) and Samuel Bronfman. Garber became involved in Canadian Zionist activities in 1919 and, during a half century of community involvement, worked in tandem with the legendary Ottawa Zionist leader A. J. Freiman. He also served as president of Canadian Jewish Congress in the early 1960s.

(Canadian Jewish Congress National Archives, Montreal)

1967, as president of the Toronto Zionist Council, president of a B'nai Brith Lodge, and a leader in the fundraising activities of United Israel Appeal and Israel Bonds. A strong advocate of support for the Jewish National Fund, he visited Israel several times. During the Six Day War in 1967, he headed the Coordinating Committee for Emergency Aid to Israel. At his funeral, the coffin was draped in both the flag of Canada and the flag of Israel.

Marc Gold (b. 1951)

Marc Gold was born in Montreal and educated at McGill University, University of British Columbia, and Harvard Law School. A former law professor and associate dean at Osgoode Hall Law School in Toronto, he is vice-president of Maxwell Cummings & Sons Holdings Limited and an adjunct professor in the Faculty of Law at McGill University.

Among his many community activities in support of Israel, Marc Gold was chair of the Canada-Israel Committee, the first vice-president of Federation CJA, a member of the executive committee of United Israel Appeals Federations Canada, and a member of the board of governors of the Jewish Agency for Israel. He is also a member of the Conseil de l'Université, Université de Montréal; a member of the Conseil de Direction, Centre de recherche en droit public, Université de Montréal; a director of the Montreal Symphony Orchestra; and a member of the executive committee of la Fondation de la Tolérance.

Yoine Goldstein (b. 1934)

Senator Yoine Goldstein is one of Canada's most distinguished lawyers and a leading figure in the Montreal Jewish community. He served as president of Montreal's Federation/CJA from 1995 to 1997, associate chairman of the Appeal from 1977 to 1985, and has been vice-president of the Jewish National Fund since 1988. He was past president of the Montreal Jewish Community Foundation and has been a member of the Board of Governors of the Jewish Agency since 1995 and of the American Joint Distribution Committee since 1999.

Goldstein was a co-founder of Canadian

Edward Elisha Gelber (1903–1971), member of a prominent Toronto Zionist family, was national president of the Zionist Organization of Canada from 1952 to 1956, and made aliyah to Israel shortly thereafter. He served as chairman of the Administrative Board of Hebrew University and chairman of the Jerusalem Conservatory of Music. Here he is addressing a meeting in Vancouver in 1955.

(Canadian Jewish Congress National Archives, Montreal)

Friends of Tel Aviv University. His wife, Elaine, served as president of Federation CJA's Women's division and has lent her considerable skills in communications to a variety of Jewish projects.

Max Goody (1917–2008)

Born in Wadena, Saskatchewan, Max Goody's parents were immigrants from Russia. The family moved first to Winnipeg, and later, when Max was in his late teens, to Toronto, so that the children could get a good Jewish education. During the war he served in the Royal Canadian Air Force as a wireless operator and, after the war, established his business, Budget Household Products. Goody was a two-term president of the Canadian Zionist Federation, a founding member and twice president of Beth David B'nai Israel Beth Am Synagogue, and a longtime member of the fraternal Zionist Ajalon Lodge. Goody was a key Canadian advocate for the State of Israel at the time of its creation in 1948. He made many trips to Israel and raised funds for the nascent Jewish state, and helped develop Zionism in Canada.

Alexander Harkavy (1865–1939)

Alexander Harkavy was an accomplished scholar and Hebrew teacher in Montreal. He was one of the first scholars to devote himself to the formal study of Yiddish, which at the time was seen by Jewish intellectuals as mere jargon. Harkavy demonstrated that Yiddish is equal to all other languages in its elements and characteristics. In order to assist Jewish immigrants to Canada, he prepared dictionaries and other learning instruments to familiarize them with North American culture and opened a library for immigrants in Montreal.

Professor Harkavy also started his own Yiddish paper, *Die Zeit*, marking the birth of the Canadian Yiddish press. He published his views on a variety of subjects—for example, the Russian language—in the Montreal English-language press and in European Hebrew periodicals. He compiled the *Yiddish-English Dictionary*, a very useful reference work for Jewish Canadians.

In 1887, Harkavy formed the Hovevi Zion Society in Montreal and within three weeks had enlisted a considerable membership. In so doing, he and his colleagues paved the way for the Zionist movement, which formally began in Canada eleven years later.

Saul Hayes (1906–1980)

In the late 1930s, Saul Hayes served as executive director of the United Jewish Relief Agencies, which helped raise funds for Jewish refugees overseas. During the Second World War, under the direction of Hayes and Sam Bronfman, Canadian Jewry spoke for the first time with a national voice. In his book *Samuel Bronfman: The Life and Times of Seagram's Mr. Sam*, historian Michael Marrus noted that "The amount of help [Hayes and Bronfman] provided to their European brethren was unprecedented, as was their effort, albeit with little success, to pry loose some favours from the mandarins in Ottawa."

Hayes, along with Bronfman and Samuel Zacks, attended the United Nations Conference in San Francisco in 1945, which included a large gathering of Jewish non-governmental delegates representing organizations from around the world concerned with how the new United Nations would deal with the former League of Nations mandates, particularly the Palestine mandate.

After the Second World War, Saul Hayes, Bronfman, and Montreal lawyer Harry Batshaw formed the new leadership for the Canadian Jewish community. Hayes went on to become the community's senior civil servant as executive vice-president of the Canadian Jewish Congress. It was from that platform that he became the professional voice of Canadian Jewry and an eloquent spokesman for Zionism and the Jewish homeland.

Julius Hayman (1907–2000)

Julius Hayman served as national president of the Zionist Organization of Canada, but his greatest contribution to Zionism came through the pages of his magazine, *The Jewish Standard*. He edited the publication for a remarkable sixty-three years (1937–2000).

Born in Winnipeg, Hayman studied law at the University of Manitoba, but went into journalism rather than practising his profession. The *Standard*'s pages consistently reflected his passionate support for Zionism (and still do with his son Michael at the helm).

In his tribute to Julius Hayman, Toronto journalist Gershon B. Newman wrote in the *Jewish Standard*, "Hayman performed the feat of being a member of the Zionist and Jewish Establishment and being, at the same time, a dissenter and giving expression to non-comformity."

Speaking in 1965 to the Jewish People's Order in Toronto, Hayman declared, "Zionism is that movement in Jewish life which believes that this Jewish life can best be preserved and enriched through its tie with Israel."

A. M. Klein (1909–1972)

A. M. (Abraham Moses) Klein, whom many consider to be one of Canada's greatest twentieth-century poets, wrote poems that expressed a longing for redemption of the Jewish soul lost in a sea of modernity. His work generally fell into three categories: the law, poetry, and editing.

During his time at McGill University in the late 1920s, Klein was one of the leading figures in Canadian Young Judaea. He subsequently went on to obtain a law degree at the University of Montreal and then divided his time between the practice of law and writing. Over the years, he served as the editor of the *Judaean*, *Canadian Zionist*, and the *Canadian Jewish Chronicle*, and was a personal public relations consultant and writer for Samuel Bronfman. He published four books of poetry and a novel, *The Second Scroll*. Much of his creative writing centred on Jewish themes, using traditional stories, symbolism, and both historical and contemporary issues. In his 1951 article "A Work of Splendour" for *The Nation*, Harvey Swados wrote that Klein's *Second Scroll* was "the most profoundly creative summation of the Jewish condition by a Jewish man of letters since the European Catastrophe."

Murray Koffler (b. 1924) and Marvelle Koffler (b. 1929)

Born in Toronto and educated at the University of Toronto, pharmacist and businessman Murray Koffler developed the Shoppers Drug Mart chain. He built on his experience in Canada by introducing a similar chain of stores, known as Super-Pharm, in Israel. Koffler has also been prominent in encouraging Canadian investment in Israel, serving on the Canada-Israel Chamber of Commerce.

Marvelle and Murray Koffler in 1969. He introduced advanced marketing techniques into Israel with his Super-Pharm chain.

(*Canadian Jewish News*—Robert Stamenov photo)

In addition to his business pursuits, Koffler is known as a community leader and philanthropist. He has received the B'nai Brith Distinguished Citizen's Award; the Canadian Council of Christians and Jews Humanitarian Award; and, with his wife, Dr. Marvelle Koffler, the Israel Cancer Research Fund Humanitarian Award. He has served on the board of governors of the Canadian Council of Christians and Jews, as well as on the boards of Mount Sinai Hospital, the United Jewish Welfare Fund, and the Jerusalem Foundation, and is a past chairman of the United Jewish Appeal. In 1979 Murray Koffler was the Toronto Negev Dinner honoree.

Both Murray and Marvelle Koffler are major supporters of the Weizmann Institute of Science in Israel. Both sit on the Institute's board of governors, and Murray Koffler is chair of the international board of directors. He is also chairman emeritus of the Canadian Society for the Weizmann Institute. Another of his contributions to the Weizmann Institute is his funding of the Koffler Accelerator—a sophisticated twin-tower instrument for nuclear research.

Murray Koffler was named to the Order of Canada in 1977 and in 1996 was promoted to an Officer. He was also named to the Order of Ontario in 1992 and received a honorary doctorate from the Weizmann Institute of Science in 1976.

Henry Koschitzky (b. 1933) **and Julia Koschitzky** (b. 1944)
Born in Poland, Henry Koschizky, was taken with his parents to Siberia, where they spent much of the Second World War. After immigrating to Canada with his family, he became a successful industrialist and turned to promoting Jewish continuity with a special emphasis on Israel.

Henry and his wife, Julia, have been active for more than two decades in the work of Keren Hayesod in Toronto. He was chairman of Jerusalem's Lev Ha'ir Project Renewal Commttee for over fifteen years, transforming one of the city's most run-down neighbourhoods.

The longtime Zionist leader Dr. Leon Kronitz was an advocate for strengthening Jewish education.

(Canadian Jewish Congress National Archives, Montreal)

Julia Koschitzky has served as world chairman of the Keren Hayesod Board of Trustees, and both Henry and Julia have worked for more than twenty years for the United Israel Appeal and the United Jewish Appeal in Toronto.

Julia has chaired the Board of Israel Now, and in 2008 became president of the Jerusalem Foundation as well as being a member of the Council for Israel and Jewish Advocacy and the board of the *Canadian Jewish News*. She also served on the Board of Trustees of the York University Foundation and as chair of the Advisory Committee for the York Centre for Jewish Studies.

Leon Kronitz (1917–1985)
Leon Kronitz, a European-trained educator, was principal of Herzliah High School in Montreal

from 1945 to 1948 and the Solomon Schechter Academy there from 1955 to 1972. He was also a three-term national president of the Labour Zionist Organization of Canada, as well as founder and chairman of the editorial board of the organization's publication *Viewpoints*. In addition to these accomplishments, he was one of the founders of the Canadian Zionist Federation, its first deputy president, and editor of the *Canadian Zionist*. In 1972 the chairman of the World Zionist Organization invited him to serve as the WZO's executive vice-president, a position he held until his death. He served as national executive director of Keren Hatarbut–Hebrew Culture Organization of Canada and as director of Camp Massad of Canada from 1948 to 1955.

Abraham Lieff (1903–2007)

Abraham Leiff's lifelong love affair with Israel began when he was nineteen years old and handled publicity for a Keren Hayesod Campaign in Ottawa. Judge Leiff, who died at the age of 104, made support for Israel a central component of his long and distinguished life. "It was, I believe, the first Keren Hayesod Campaign run by A. J. Freiman, whose gift of $5,000 represented one-third of the sum raised," he said in a 2007 interview with writer Joe King.

Justice Abraham Isaac Leiff

(Canadian Jewish Congress National Archives, Montreal)

Abaham Leiff was born in Antopot (then in White Russia, now in Poland) and was one year old when his parents brought him to Canada in 1904. He put himself through law school wielding a sledgehammer in a scrap yard, teaching Sunday school, selling newspapers, working as a bellhop in a hotel, performing in a play, and playing the banjo in a band—although when times were too tough, he had to pawn the banjo. He once delivered a telegram to Sir Wilfrid Laurier.

Called to the bar in 1926, Lieff blended the practice of law with service to the community. He became a magistrate in Carleton County and in 1963 was named a justice of the Superior Court of Ontario.

He visited Israel half a dozen times and was passionate in his support for the Jewish state. "I'm pleased that today Jews can be in every big law firm, hospital, university—and all of this happened after the State of Israel was born."

Judge Leiff's Zionist activities ranged from membership in Young Judaea (where he met his future wife) to fundraising for the Jewish National Fund. He was most active in Ottawa, but later, when living in Toronto, he journeyed across the country and into the United States speaking on behalf of the JNF.

David Monson (b. 1917)

Born in Ottawa, Rabbi Dr. David Monson went overseas at age twenty-two as a Jewish chaplain in the Canadian armed forces. His convoy was attacked by German submarines, setting two tankers ablaze. The chaplains held a joint service on deck—"Christians knelt, Jews stood."

Rabbi Monson was national president of the Zionist Organization of Canada, and his activities in Israel have included strong support for the Shaare Zedek Medical Center in Jerusalem. He first visited the medical centre, then a small hospital, during the Six Day War. It has since, thanks in part to his efforts, become a state-of-the-art facility. He has also helped establish Or Yehuda, a community centre for underprivileged Iraqi and Romanian children in Israel.

W. Gunther Plaut (b. 1912)

Rabbi W. Gunther Plaut was born in Munster, Germany, and received a law degree in 1933 and a doctorate in international law from the University of Berlin. Prevented from practising law by the Nazis, he continued his studies at the Hochshule für die Wissenchaft des Judentums. In 1935 he was able to leave Germany when he received a scholarship from the Hebrew Union College in Cincinnati. He was ordained in 1939. During the Second World War, he served for three years as chaplain in the U.S. army in Europe and was decorated with the Bronze Star. He was present at the first American-liberated concentration camp, the first rabbi to bring a Sefer Torah back to Germany, and conducted the first religious service in the gutted shell of the Cologne Synagogue in March 1945.

After the war, Rabbi Plaut led a congregation in St. Paul, Minnesota until in 1948 he was called to Holy Blossom Temple in Toronto, where he remained first as senior rabbi and then as senior scholar. Rabbi Plaut served as national president of the Canadian Jewish Congress from 1977 to 1980. He was president of the World Federalists of Canada from 1966 to 1968, national co-chair of the Canada-Israel Committee from 1975 to 1977, vice-chair of the

Ontario Human Rights Commission from 1978 to 1985, president of the Central Conference of American Rabbis from 1983 to 1985, and vice-president of the Governing Board of the World Union for Progressive Judaism. He wrote numerous books and articles of both religious commentary and explorations of Judaism.

Rabbi Plaut was the 1975 Toronto Negev Dinner honouree and was appointed an Officer of the Order of Canada in 1977.

Heather Reisman (b. 1948)

Born in Montreal and educated at McGill University, Heather Reisman, with her husband Gerry Schwartz, chair and CEO of Onex Corporation (see below), has an impressive history in business, philanthropy, and support for Israel. Before launching Canadian bookstore chain Indigo Books & Music in 1996, she was president of Cott Corporation, and is a former governor of McGill University and the Toronto Stock Exchange. She sits on a number of corporate boards, is a director and officer of Mount Sinai Hospital, and a member of the steering committee of the Bilderberg Group, an elite international conference.

Reisman and Schwartz have lent their support to Jewish and Israeli charities as varied as sponsoring a chair in the Tel Aviv University School of Business and sponsoring basketball for the 17th World Maccabiah Games. Reisman also donated the Peace Library to the Shimon Peres Peace Center and, with Gerry Schwartz, provides financial support for exchange programs between pediatric specialists at Toronto's Hospital for Sick Children and Israeli pediatric fellows and between business students at the University of Manitoba and Tel Aviv University. They have established Heseg, a foundation that gives full university scholarships and financial support to "lone soldiers"—Israeli soldiers who have no family in Israel—after they leave the army.

Heather Reisman has received several awards for her business acumen, and honorary doctorates from Tel Aviv University and Ryerson University in Toronto.

Moshe Ronen (b. 1959)

Toronto-based lawyer, international business advisor and a prominent community leader who was raised in Toronto, Moshe Ronen received his BA from York University and his law degree from the University of Windsor. By age twenty, he was a well-known human rights activist. He was the youngest national president of the Canadian Jewish

Congress and serves as chair of the organization's board of governors. He is vice-president of the World Jewish Congress, as well as national chair of the Canada-Israel Committee and head of its special missions committee. He is also an honorary director of Magen David Adom, Israel's emergency medical, health, blood, and disaster services. In 1996 Ronen was recognized by the Jewish National Fund with its prestigious Jerusalem of Gold Award for his outstanding communal service and two years later, the government of Ontario recognized him with a Volunteer Service Award. Mr. Ronen is a member of the board of directors of two leading schools, the North York General Hospital, and several other major charities and institutions.

Moshe Ronen's business activities include serving as a director of First Capital Realty Corporation, and a member of the Advisory Board of Skylink Aviation Group of Companies Inc., which specializes in emergency relief operations for the United Nations and many governments.

Gerry Schwartz and Heather Reisman (on the far left of the back row) with some of the Israeli soldiers they have assisted with scholarship funds, 2004.

(Canadian Jewish News)

Kurt Rothschild (b. 1920)

Kurt Rothschild was born in Cologne, Germany and, as a youngster, was sent to England to study. He was interned in 1940, along with thousands of other German and Austrian Jews considered to be "enemy aliens" and sent to detention camps in Canada. Largely through the

intervention of the Canadian Jewish Congress, he was released (as were many students), and studied engineering at Queen's University in Kingston, Ontario. He ultimately settled in Toronto and established a large national contracting firm, the State Group

Rothschild has devoted much of his time and financial resources to efforts on behalf of the Jewish community, especially in Israel. He sold his company in 1987 and devoted himself full time to working for the community. In addition to his presidency of the Canadian Zionist Federation (1990–2004), he has served as chairman of the board and co-president of Mercaz Olami-World Mizrachi and was an active board member on behalf of Bar-Ilan University, Shaare Zedek Medical Center, the Jewish Federation of Toronto, and the United Israel Appeal.

Gerald Schwartz (b. 1941)

Born in Winnipeg, businessman Gerald Schwartz was educated at the University of Manitoba and Harvard University. He and his wife, Heather Reisman, founder and CEO of Indigo Books & Music (see above), are strong supporters of higher education and social welfare programs in both Canada and Israel. Before creating Onex Corporation, Schwartz was a co-founder of what is now CanWest Global Communications. He is vice chairman of Mount Sinai Hospital and holds positions on a number of corporate and non-profit boards such as the Bank of Nova Scotia, Indigo, the Simon Wiesenthal Center, and the Canadian Council of Christians and Jews.

In 2002, Gerald Schwartz co-founded the Israel Emergency Cabinet to combat rising anti-Israel sentiment in Canada, particularly on Canadian campuses; out of this initiative emerged the Canadian Council for Israel and Jewish Advocacy. With Heather Reisman, he established the Schwartz-Reisman SickKids Exchange Program with Israel to support exchanges between pediatric specialists at Toronto's Hospital for Sick Children and their counterparts in Israel, and the University of Waterloo-Haifa International Experience Program to support exchanges between computer science students at the two institutions. Among many others that followed, Schwartz and Reisman's first public donation in Israel was their 2004 gift to Yad Sarah, Israel's largest voluntary home-care support organization. In 2005, they established Heseg to provide full university scholarships and financial support to former "lone soldiers" who have no family in Israel.

Gerald Schwartz was made an Officer of the Order of Canada in

2006, has been inducted into the Canadian Business Hall of Fame, and received honorary doctorates from Tel Aviv University and St. Francis Xavier University in Nova Scotia.

Sydney Simon Shulemson, (1915–2007)
Sydney Shulemson, DSO, DFC, a decorated hero of the Second World War, attended a clandestine meeting in New York in 1947 to help plan the defence of the coming State of Israel. While others discussed providing the new Jewish state with experienced fighting men and weapons, Montreal pilot and squadron leader Shulemson argued the neccessity of forming an air force. As the Canadian military historian Stéphane Guevremont writes, "His advice was critical in the formation of the Israel Air Force."

Back in Montreal, Shulemson became deeply involved in the Canadian effort to provide Israel with arms and fighting men—focusing particularly on recruiting pilots and obtaining urgently needed aircraft. It was Shulemson who went to the Montreal suburb of Verdun to meet with Canada's greatest Second World War flying ace, George "Buzz" Beurling. Beurling readily agreed to join the Israeli Air Force, without compensation, even though Arab countries were offering him large sums to fly for them.

Sydney Shulemson was the most decorated Jewish warrior of the Second World War.

Norman Stern (b. 1935)
Norman Stern succeeded Kurt Rothschild as president of the Canadian Zionist Federation in 2004. In addition to his presidency of the CZF, he also served as president of Mercaz Canada, the Zionist wing of the Conservative movement, until 2007 and treasurer of Canadian Friends of Boys' Town, Jerusalem. Stern has been a member of the board of governors of the Jewish Agency for Israel and chaired a division of the Toronto United Jewish Appeal for three years. From 1974 to 1978, he served as president of Canadian Friends of Bar Ilan University.

Nathan Silver (1915–1997)
Nathan Silver was born in Warsaw and came to Canada in 1934. During the Second World War he served as a gunner in an artillery division of the Canadian army. After the war, he became a prominent Toronto builder and developer, the founder of Metrontario Group.

Married to Lily Ann Cooper, the Silvers' homes in Toronto and Jerusalem were meeting places for politicians, communal leaders, business associates and friends. They were personal friends of the late Israeli prime minister Menachem Begin and his wife, Aliza. Nathan Silver was national chairman of the Zionist-Revisionist Organization of Canada, a member of the world executive of the Zionist-Revisionist Movement, and an executive member of the United Zionist Council of Canada.

Father John Walsh (b. 1942)

One of Canada's most fervent and outspoken Christian Zionists is Father John Walsh, Montreal-born pastor of St. John Brebeuf Parish in LaSalle, Quebec. Father John, whose flock included former Canadian prime minister Paul Martin Jr., has enormous influence in Montreal through his open-line radio program. A pivotal moment in the priest's views on Israel came in 1967, immediately after the Six Day War, when he embarked on a year's study at the Hebrew University in Jerusalem. "It changed my life," he said. "It opened me to the Christian-Jewish dialogue in which I have been involved for more than thirty years." Father John's understanding of the role of the Jewish state for Jews around the world permeates the priest's life— through his broadcasts and his involvement in Jewish community activities in Quebec.

Father John Walsh was awarded the Jerusalem Prize in 2000 by the Consul General of Israel in Montreal; the Canadian Zionist Federation, Eastern Region; the World Zionist Organization; and the Canada-Israel Committee, Eastern Region. In 2001 the Quebec Region of the Canadian Jewish Congress presented him with the Ezekiel Hart Award, given to an individual outside the Jewish community who has made an outstanding contribution to intercultural relations "for his tireless commitment and dedication to improving intercultural relations in Quebec."

Joe Wilder (b. 1907)

In 1967, when he was a young lawyer, Joe Wilder temporarily put his practice on the backburner and canvassed for Israel. The Six Day War had just concluded and Wilder believed that following its victory, Israel needed financial assistance as well as moral and political support. Along with other like-minded individuals in Winnipeg, Wilder went door to door in Jewish and non-Jewish neighbourhoods to do

The efforts of Ray D. Wolfe, a Toronto businessman, on behalf of Zionism included his leadership as chairman of the *Canadian Jewish News*.

(Canadian Jewish Congress National Archives, Montreal)

what he could to create goodwill for the Jewish state. Those efforts eventually led to creation of an organization that evolved into the Canada-Israel Committee (CIC). Since then, Wilder has held a variety of Jewish organizational positions, most recently as chair of the CIC.

Julius Joel Wolfe (b. 1917)

Born in Montreal, Lieutenant-Colonel Julius Joel Wolfe enlisted in the Canadian Army in October 1941 as a sapper (engineer). He served in Africa and Italy—during his nine months of service in Italy he was attached to the Jewish Brigade—and by war's end had been promoted to captain. After the war, he spent time in Israel assisting in the organization of the Israeli Engineering Corps. Returning to Montreal, he continued to serve in the military, ultimately becoming commanding officer of 3rd (Militia) Engineer Regiment from 1963 to 1966.

Joel Wolfe was president, and later honorary president, of the Eastern Region of the Canadian Zionist Federation, and the first national commander and founding member of the Jewish War Veterans of Canada.

He was awarded the Order of Canada in 2001.

Ray D. Wolfe (1921–1990)

Ray Wolfe, with his wife, Rose (see below), participated in diverse activities on behalf of the State of Israel, as well as social and cultural causes, both Jewish and non-Jewish, in Canada and throughout the world. He was a founder of both the Canada-Israel Committee and the Canada-Israel Chamber of Commerce, and served as the president of the United Jewish Welfare Fund.

In the field of education, Wolfe established the Ray D. Wolfe Centre for the Study of Psychological Stress at Haifa University. He was also involved with the State of Israel Bonds, the United Jewish Appeal, various yeshivot, and other educational institutions. Before his death in 1990, he helped establish a post-doctoral fellowship in Jewish studies at the University of Toronto.

Wolfe's business expertise was welcomed by Israel and the Zionist community. Following the Six Day War, he served as a member of an economic advisory board of the Israeli government. In Canada, his company in Toronto purchased Oshawa Wholesale, acquired the Ontario franchise for IGA stores, and purchased Towers department stores and Kent Drugs. Ray Wolfe was awarded the Order of Canada in 1981.

Rose Wolfe (b. 1938)

Rose Wolfe, with her husband, Ray (see above), has a record of varied and extensive service to the Jewish community in Canada. She served as vice-president of the Canadian Jewish Congress, Ontario Region, and, as a member of the executive committee of the national Canadian Jewish Congress. She was a member of the executive committee, board of directors, and advisory committee of the *Canadian Jewish News* and a life member of the executive committee and board of directors of the Jewish Family and Child Service. Her involvement in the welfare of Jewish children began after the Second World War, when, as a social worker in 1941, she helped find Canadian homes for Jewish Orphans from the Nazi concentration camps.

Rose Wolfe was chancellor of the University of Toronto from 1991 to 1997 and in 2000 helped raise funds to create the Chancellor Rose and Ray Wolfe Chair in Holocaust Studies at the university. She also served as president of the Toronto Jewish Congress, director of Mount Sinai Hospital, and a member of both the board of trustees for the McMichael Canadian Art Collection in Kleinburg, Ontario, and the Lester B. Pearson College of the Pacific in Victoria, British Columbia.

She was awarded the Order of Canada in 1990.

Hirsh Wolofsky (1876–1949)

Hirsh Wolofsky's Eagle Publishing Company put out the most widely read English-language Jewish weekly in Canada, the *Canadian Jewish Chronicle*. He was also founder of the Yiddish publication *Keneder Adler*.

An immigrant from Poland, Wolofsky used his Yiddish newspaper to help ease newcomers into Canadian society and to strengthen the bond among Jews in Canada.

Prominent Montrealer H. M. Caiserman wrote of Wolofsky's contribution: "From its first day, the *Jewish Daily Eagle* [*Keneder Adler* means Canadian Eagle] has been the spokesman of the community."

A committed Zionist, Wolofsky visited Israel several times and wrote frequently about flourishing Jewish life there.

Hirsh Wolofsky

(Canadian Jewish Congress National Archives, Montreal)

Dov Yosef (1899–1980)

Dov Yosef was born Bernard Joseph in Montreal and educated at McGill University, Université Laval, and the University of London, where he qualified as an attorney. A lifelong Zionist and key figure in the formation of the new State of Israel, while still in his teens Yosef helped organize and became the first president of Canadian Young Judaea. He then helped organize the Canadian Jewish Legion and immigrated to Palestine under their auspices in 1918. Dov Yosef remained in Palestine under the British Mandate and became legal adviser to the Jewish Agency in Jerusalem. When the Second World War began, he helped recruit volunteers for Jewish units in the British Army and, during the War of Independence, was appointed military governor of Jerusalem.

After the war, Dov Yosef represented David Ben-Gurion's Mapai, the forerunner of the Labour Party, in the Knesset from 1949 to 1965, holding a variety of portfolios. He was initially appointed minister of rationing and supply in the first government—a key position during the austerity period—and then became Israel's second minister of justice. His other portfolios included agriculture, transportation, trade and industry, development, and health.

Sidney Zack (b. 1917)

Born in Regina, Sidney Zack's family settled briefly in the Prairie provinces before moving to Vancouver in 1923. He married the former Gertrude Fouks in 1941, joined his father-in-law's business, Puritan Canners, during the war, and became very successful, branching into a variety of business interests. Sidney Zack was active in the Jewish community and an ardent Zionist. He was chairman of the UJA drive in 1963, national vice-president of the UIA of Canada during the 1960s, a member of the board of directors of the UIA of Canada, chairman of the Pacific Region and regional president of the Zionist Organization of Canada, and national vice-president of the Pacific region of the Canadian Jewish Congress in 1987. With his wife, he was the 1967 Jewish National Fund Negev Dinner honoree and is an honorary life member of the Canadian Jewish Appeal/Jewish Federation of Greater Vancouver.

Ayala Zacks-Abramov (b. 1912)

Ayala Zacks and her husband, Sam (see below), contributed immensely to the world of art in Canada and Israel. Her extensive collection of European art includes masterpieces by Soutine, Chagall,

Rouault, Picasso, Braque, Léger, Renoir, Degas, Gauguin, Matisse, Klee, Giacometti, Moore, and others.

Following Sam's death in 1971, Ayala married Israeli lawyer and politician Zalman Abramov in 1976 and in 1982 moved to Israel, where she continued her interest in art philanthrophy. She established a History of Art Fund for guest professors at the Hebrew University in Jerusalem. She also created the Ayala Zacks-Abramov Pavilion at the Israel Museum, which celebrates both historical and contemporary Israeli art. She and her second husband endowed S. Zalman and Ayala Abramov Library on the Jerusalem campus of the Hebrew Union College–Jewish Institute of Religion in 1988.

A longtime supporter of the Weizmann Institute of Science, Zacks-Abramov was awarded an honorary degree in 1985. To honour her support of the arts in Canada, she was named an Officer of the Order of Canada in 1972.

Samuel J. Zacks (1904–1970)

Sam Zacks served as president of the Zionist Organization of Canada from 1943 to 1949. He was chairman of the Canadian Jewish Congress Refugee Committee and helped to raise funds for 3,000 German Jewish internees to settle in Canada during the Second World War, as well as for Jewish refugees during Israel's War of Independence.

With Sam Bronfman and Saul Hayes, Zacks attended the 1945 United Nations Conference in San Francisco, where they were part of a large gathering of Jewish delegates from non-governmental organizations around the world.

Throughout the Second World War and immediately after, Sam Zacks actively lobbied Canadian government officials to recognize a national Jewish homeland in Palestine.

He was co-founder of the Canada-Israel Association and Canada-Israel Securities, and was a member of the "Sonneborn Institute," a fictious enterprise created in New York to acquire arms arms for Israel. He was also vice-president of both the American Committee of the Weizmann Institute and the Canadian Friends of Hebrew University.

Samuel J. Zacks of Toronto broadened the reach of Zionism in Canada by organizing the Canadian-Palestine Committee headed by Sir Ellsworth Flavelle.

(Canadian Jewish Congress National Archives, Montreal)

With his wife, Ayala (see above), he pursued a passionate interest in the arts and amassed an impressive collection of modern European art.

Rabbi Tsemach (Seymour) Zambrowsky (1911–2002)

Born in Warsaw, Poland, Rabbi Tsemach (Seymour) Zambrowsky moved to the United States shortly before the outbreak of the Second World War. He was educated at the Orthodox Rabbinical Seminary of America in Cleveland and was ordained in 1934. In 1948 he and his wife, Belle, moved to Montreal, where he became very involved in Zionist activities. He was national chairman of the Mizrachi Hapoel Himzrachi of Canada for many years, as well as vice-president of the United Zionist Council, national chairman of both the Religious Welfare Committee and the Canadian Jewish Congress, vice-president of the Jewish National Fund Canada, and honorary president of the Canadian friends of Bar-Ilan University. In the 1980s he made aliyah and continued his involvement in Zionist activities through Mizrachi. He served on the board of governors of the Israel Bonds Fundraising Cabinet, Mosad Harav Kook (Jerusalem)—one of the largest and oldest publishers of scholarly religious books in Israel—and the Mizrachi Bank of Israel.

Yizkor

THROUGH A TROUBLED, and even endangered, existence of some thirty-four centuries, Israel has never lacked courageous people to defend its existence. From Canada, a young nation aged less than a century and a half, have come countless hundreds of individuals determined to make their contribution to the well-being of a reborn Jewish homeland.

The yeshiva student Zvi Halevi Freiman of Hamilton was one of seven young men killed in the 1929 Hebron massacre.... In 1938, Eliezer Krongold of Toronto was killed in an ambush on the road to Ein Hashofet.... In the 1973 Yom Kippur War, paratrooper Eli Wedel, Hillel Sanders Israeli, and Meier Weiss from Toronto were all killed in action.... A year later, David Bar from Ottawa was mortally wounded in an incident on the Golan Heights.... Shmuel Aaron Mermelstein, a student from Montreal, was killed in a 1980 terrorist attack.... Five years later, Anita Griffel of Montreal was killed in a terrorist attack.... In 1989, Dr. Shelley Wolochow Halpenny of Vancouver, in Israel to plan a volunteer dental program for disadvantaged areas, was killed in a terrorist attack on the number 405 Tel-Aviv-to-Jerusalem bus, along with another Canadian, Fern Shawna Rykiss.... A year later, when a terrorist bomb exploded in a group of young people, among the dead was Marnie Kimelman of Toronto.... In 1992, Haim Bar-Natan of Montreal was mortally wounded on a mission into Lebanon.... Jason Friedberg of Montreal was abducted by terrorists in 1993 and his body found along the Jerusalem–Tel Aviv highway.... Gal Grossman was killed in 1996 while serving with the border police.... Livney Atara and Baruch Maekus of Toronto died in terrorist attacks in 2002.... Terrorists killed

Shalom Har-Melech in 2003 (and seriously wounded his wife, who gave birth to a baby in the seventh month).... Daniel Ya'akov Mandel of Toronto died in a battle with terrorists in Shchem, in 2003.... Forty-one-year-old Yechezkel (Chezi) Goldberg of Toronto was killed in a terrorist attack on Jerusalem's number 19 bus in 2004.... Helicopter pilot Thom Farkas was killed in the second Lebanon war when his aircraft crashed....

Recommended Reading

Bercuson, David J. *The Secret Army*. Lester and Orpen Dennys, 1983.

Brown, Michael Gary. *Jew or Juif? Jews, French Canadians and Anglo-Canadians, 1759–1914*. Jewish Publication Society, 1987.

Dunkelman, Ben. *Dual Allegiance: An Autobiography*. Macmillan of Canada, 1976.

Encyclopedia Judaica. 1982.

Fenson, Melvin *Canadian Jews in Israel: New Encyclopedia of Zionism and Israel*. Edited by Geoffrey Wigoder. Fairleigh Dickinson University Press, 1994.

Figler, Bernard. *Lillian and Archie Freiman: Biographies*. Northern Print and Lithographing, 1962.

Figler, Bernard. "History of the Zionist Ideal in Canada," in Eli Gottesman, ed. *Canadian Jewish Reference Book and Directory 1963*. Central Rabbinical Seminary of Canada, 1963.

Goldman, Leon. "History of Zionism in Canada," in Arthur D. Hart, ed., *The Jew in Canada*. Jewish Publications, 1926.

King, Joe. *From the Ghetto to the Main. The Story of the Jews of Montreal*. Montreal Jewish Publication Society, 2000.

King, Joe. *Baron Byng to Bagels: Tales of Jewish Montreal*. Montreal Jewish Publication Society, 2006.

Lambert, Richard S. *For the Time Is at Hand*. London, 1947.

Laqueur, Walter. *A History of Zionism*. Schocken Books, 1989.

Levy, Daniel S. *Two Gun Cohen: A Biography*. St. Martin's Press, 1997.

Lipsitz, Edmond Y. *Canadian Jewry Today: Who's Who in Canadian Jewry*. J.E.S.L. Products, 1989.

Lipsitz, Edmond Y. *Who's Who in Canadian Jewry at Year 2000 and Beyond*. J.E.S.L. Products, 2000.

Marrus, Michael R. *Mr. Sam: The Llife and Times of Samuel Bronfman*. Viking, 1991.

Newman, Peter C. *The Bronfman Dynasty*. McClelland and Stewart, 1978.

Rosenberg, Stuart E. *The Jewish Community in Canada* (2 vols.). McClelland and Stewart, 1970.

Sack, B. G. *History of the Jews in Canada*. Harvest House, 1965.

Slater, Leonard. *The Pledge*. Simon and Schuster, 1970.

Tulchinsky, Gerald. *Taking Root: The Origins of the Canadian Jewish Community*. Lester Publishing, 1992.

Tulchinsky, Gerald. *Branching Out: The Transformation of the Canadian Jewish Community*. Stoddart, 1998.

Wigoder, Geoffrey. *New Encyclopedia of Zionism and Israel*. Fairleigh Dickinson University Press, 1994; and Macmillan of Canada, 1976.

Index